D1071086

Big City Boss

in Depression and War: Mayor Edward J. Kelly of Chicago

Roger Biles

Northern Illinois University Press • DeKalb, 1984

Library of Congress Cataloging in Publication Data

Biles, Roger, 1950–
    Big city boss in depression and war.

    Revision of thesis (Ph.D.)—University of Illinois
    Bibliography: p.
    Includes index.
    1. Kelly, Edward J. (Edward Joseph), 1876–1950.
2. Chicago (Ill.)—Politics and government—To 1950.
3. Chicago (Ill.)—Mayors—Biography.   I. Title.
F548.5.K44B54   1983   977.3'11042'0924 [B]   83–19391
ISBN 0–87580–098–X

FOR MY Mother and Father

Contents

Acknowledgments

MANY PEOPLE generously contributed to the making of this book, and I am pleased to acknowledge their efforts. First, Professor Melvin G. Holli suggested that I make Ed Kelly the subject of my doctoral dissertation and subsequently guided me in the research and writing that followed. Professors Peter d'A. Jones, Perry Duis, and Richard Fried also read the manuscript at the dissertation stage and encouraged me to expand the study for publication. I am also grateful to Arthur Mann and John Allswang, whose critical suggestions significantly contributed to the preparation of my final draft. While all of these scholars contributed in some way to this effort, I bear sole responsibility for any shortcomings the book may have.

Among the many libraries whose facilities I used, the most helpful were the Franklin D. Roosevelt Library, the National Archives, and the Chicago Historical Society. As for the latter, a special note of thanks is due Archie Motley, whose seemingly boundless grasp of the source materials proved invaluable. Memphis State University's College of Arts and Sciences and Department of History provided financial assistance to have the manuscript reproduced by a word processor. That work was capably and diligently done by the staff of the University's Word Processing Center. Janis Bolster and Leslie Wildrick provided much useful editorial assistance. I would especially like to thank Mary Livingston, Director of Northern Illinois University Press, for her enthusiastic support of this book. Her interest in making this study appealing to a large audience, as well as to a scholarly one, has spurred me into making a stronger commitment to the "general reader."

Finally, my wife Mary Claire's saintly patience during the life of this project deserves special mention. She now knows more about Ed Kelly and Chicago politics than anyone should have to. Her contribution has been the greatest of all.

Introduction

 THE BIG city boss and the political machine he commanded were uniquely American phenomena that developed in the chaotic metropolises of the post–Civil War era. The American city, its runaway growth fueled by rural migrants and transplanted Europeans, was buffeted by a series of revolutions—transportation, industrial, agricultural, and communications—which resulted in sudden and dramatic change. Residents of these rapidly expanding cities sought the services necessary for a safe and comfortable existence: streets, sewers, clean water, police and fire protection, public transportation, and other utilities. Unfortunately, the cities outgrew the capabilities of municipal governments, which failed to respond quickly enough, or with sufficient resources, to meet the demands of the newcomers.

Traditionally, the governing of cities fell to the gentry, who out of a sense of noblesse oblige voluntarily donated part of their time to perform avowedly apolitical tasks. Confronted with such herculean new challenges, these "respectables" resigned themselves to failure and retreated into their middle- and upper-class isolation. Rushing in to fill this newly created power vacuum was the full-time professional politician. Unlike the gentry, the new politician learned his craft in the saloon, pool hall, or neighborhood club. Depending upon political success for his very livelihood, this aggressive vote getter made no pretense of disinterested public service. He appealed to his constituents as their champion, a man able to deliver jobs, services, and favors—in short, a man able to cut through the mazes of the confounding urban environment.

Contributing to the confusion of city life was the obsolescence of formal governmental structure. Translating decision making into forthright action seemed a lost art as the lines of authority disappeared in a bureaucratic jumble of commissions, councils, and governments. Diffusion of authority, overlapping jurisdictions, and anachronistic city charters based upon antebellum conditions bred inefficiency, duplication, inertia, and mountains of red tape. And, of course, one result was an increasingly impersonal and remote government. The political machine, an extralegal entity, could circumvent many of these obstacles; at a time when formal governmental structure militated against effective problem solving, the machine cut corners and took liberties. This pragmatism offended many among the better element, reformers and the like, but pleased countless others frustrated by an unresponsive system.

Foremost among the ranks of the befuddled urbanites were the immigrants. Whereas many reformers assumed a blatantly nativistic stance, the boss welcomed all comers, whose votes represented grist for their electoral mills. In return for their support on election day, the immigrants received many benefits: the machine would help them find jobs and places to live; teach them the language, customs, and mores of the new society; provide them with temporary assistance in times of scarcity; grant them recognition by placing representatives of their group on the party's slate of candidates; and even remember them with the proverbial Christmas turkey. Usually naive about democratic institutions and impervious to complex issues like monetary reform and tariff revision, most immigrants responded to the machine's attention to their immediate socioeconomic needs. It is little wonder, then, that frustrated reformers railed against the "perfidious" marriage of the bosses and the city's polyglot masses.

The financial community constituted a second major supporter of the political machine. Also frustrated by the inefficiency of municipal officialdom, businessmen responded to the machine's ability to expedite financial transactions. Many entrepreneurs desired special considerations enabling them to procure franchises for public works and the operation of public utilities, and an administration unfettered by moral restraint frequently suited their purposes admirably. In return for its financial and political support, the business community could expect preferred treatment from a beholden boss.

Just as "legitimate" business entered into a mutually satisfactory relationship with the machine, so did "illegitimate" business. By looking the other way and not enforcing the laws against prostitution, gambling, and illegal liquor, the boss could count upon remuneration from the favored vice lords. At the same time, the machine's stance in favor of personal liberties appealed to many of the European immigrant groups accustomed to such freedoms. Although the machine frequently denied any association with the city's seamier elements, the link between the two was manifest.

Because of this association with organized crime, along with such noted failings of political machines as graft, waste, and inefficiency, the boss was long pilloried as a self-seeking, power-hungry enemy of democracy whose rule of cities hailed from expediency rather than altruism. More recent scholarship, attempting a balanced assessment, has emphasized the role of the machine in humanizing and personalizing politics, socializing the newcomer, and, most important, bringing some order to an otherwise chaotic situation. Both critics and defenders recognize the sizable imprint the boss and his machine left upon American cities at a crucial stage in their development. This was certainly no less the case in Chicago than elsewhere.[1]

In the Windy City, where the rough-and-tumble game of politics has long been the city's leading spectator sport and its players, the politicians, a genuine rogue's gallery, few men have succeeded in holding the scepter of power for long. The most conspicuous exception, of course, was Mayor Richard J. Daley, whose twenty-one-year reign overshadows all others. Second in longevity was the fourteen-year rule of Mayor Edward J. Kelly, who, with Pat Nash, controlled the most powerful—and probably the most infamous—political machine in the nation. Along with his contemporaries, men like Jersey City's Frank Hague, Kansas City's Tom Pendergast, Boston's James Michael Curley, Memphis's Ed Crump, and the Bronx's Ed Flynn, Kelly represented the last of a vanishing breed: the autocratic big city boss who controlled not only the affairs of his urban domain but, to a considerable degree, those of his state and the nation as well.

A household name throughout the United States in his day, Ed Kelly has been largely forgotten in the aftermath of the Daley years. Known chiefly as the first of the mayors hailing from the Southwest Side neighborhood of Bridgeport—Martin H. Kennelly, Daley, and Michael Bilandic following in succession—Kelly has been dismissed as a custodian for the political machine assembled by Anton Cermak and perfected by Daley. Furthermore, when mentioned at all, Kelly has been conveniently labeled a corrupt ward boss satisfied with presiding over the distribution of spoils.

Shortly after Kelly's death, Illinois governor Adlai E. Stevenson praised the "strong, adroit and tireless" mayor, exclaiming, "Here was a leader!" Since that time, however, few students of Chicago political history have concurred in Stevenson's assessment. In his description of Richard Daley's rise to prominence in the Democratic party in the thirties and forties, Mike Royko wrote that "Kelly was running both the party and city government, and doing badly at both jobs." In his biography of Daley, Len O'Connor dismissed Kelly as a "venal man" who "did little with Chicago, except let things run away from him." Harold F. Gosnell, appraising the Chicago polity in 1937, was equally contemptuous of "Boss" Kelly, pointing out that "jobs and spoils were the currency of Chicago politics in 1936 as well as in 1928, and not issues which concerned the functions of municipal government in times of great economic stresses and strains." In his treatment of Kelly's nemesis, Henry Horner, Thomas Littlewood contended that "Kelly and Nash were not ideological New Dealers" and that the mayor ruled in an "arbitrary and blatantly disdainful" manner. In short, Kelly has been readily pigeonholed as the stereotype of the big city political boss.[2]

For several reasons, Ed Kelly deserves closer scrutiny from historians. As mayor of Chicago during the depression, he had to face the mammoth problems of unemployment, financial ruin, and poverty that plagued the United States in the thirties. His strategies for combating these problems, to a great extent molded by Franklin D. Roosevelt's New Deal, revealed the interplay between local and federal government during that decade. As mayor throughout the United States' involvement in the Second World War, Kelly's brand of leadership was put to a different kind of test. And during his brief tenure as mayor in the postwar years of 1945–46, Kelly had to face the problems of restructuring his city for a peacetime existence totally unlike either the economic despair or the boom period that preceded it. Therefore, one aspect of an analysis of Kelly must be based upon his performance as Chicago mayor during these fourteen critical years.

A second focus must be the Kelly-Nash machine. The leadership of the two Irishmen, following on the heels of the Bohemian Cermak's brief rule, raised several questions about the operation of the Democratic machine: Did the elevation of two Irishmen to the head of the organization constitute an ethnic rebellion against the "house for all peoples" constructed by Cermak? What were the roles and responsibilities of Kelly and Nash, and to what degree was theirs a partnership of equals? Was the Kelly-Nash leadership merely "minding the store" in the thirties and forties, or did it build significantly on the foundation bequeathed by Cermak? And finally, how did the machine affect the political, social, and economic development of Chicago?

The traditional view of Chicago during the Kelly years envisions a wide-open city in which gambling and organized crime flourished. Moreover, Kelly became known as a bludgeoning purveyor of political power, a ruthless autocrat who ruled the city with the same single-mindedness he brought to the domination of Cook County's Democratic party. To a great extent, these impressions accurately reflected the boisterous Chicago of that era, and the Bridgeport mayor, a self-made man of humble origins in the Stockyards district, cultivated that image with his roughhewn oratory and straightforward political style. But, within the limits of political constraints, Kelly exhibited some unexpectedly humanistic traits as well: a concern for the underprivileged; a belief in the New Deal and its philosophical underpinnings; and perhaps most surprising, considering his background and the attitudes of his peers, a commitment to black Americans. To illuminate these lesser-known traits, and to establish the importance of the Kelly administration in the history of American cities, a healthy dose of revisionism is in order.

1　From Axman to City Hall

IN 1865 fifteen-year old Stephen Kelly came to Chicago from Galway, Ireland. He settled in the Southwest Side neighborhood of Bridgeport, on Archer Avenue—Finley Peter Dunne's Mr. Dooley called it "Archey Road" and said that it "stretches back for many miles from the heart of an ugly city to the cabbage gardens that gave the maker of the Chicago seal his opportunity to call the city 'urbs in horto.'" Mr. Dooley described the predominantly Irish area:

> Bridgeport was surrounded by industry—the stockyards were nearby, the steel mills were just to the south; the South Branch of the Chicago River and the Illinois and Michigan Canal ran by, and a McCormick Harvesting Machine Plant was not far away from the black road (Blue Island Avenue). . . . Other factories made fertilizer, or soap, or glue. All of these unclean places dumped effluent into the Chicago River and poured it into the air. Some days the miasma was so foul and the visibility so poor that the street lamps had to be lit at noon.[1]

In this maelstrom of industrial activity, employment was readily available, and young Kelly immediately found work as a teamster. He married a young German girl, Helen Lang, in 1873 and joined the city's fire department the next year. When that job proved unsatisfactory, Kelly worked at several others before entering the police department in 1884. By that time, the Kellys had started a family that would eventually include nine children. The oldest, Edward Joseph, born May 1, 1876, was already working to help support the family.[2]

Ed Kelly had his first job, as a newsboy, while attending the city's public grammar schools. At the age of twelve, when he was in the fifth grade, he dropped out of school to work full time. He was a cash boy at Marshall Field's, ran messages for a law office, washed windows, and earned four dollars a week carrying long sticks of beer buckets to men during lunch breaks at the Armour cannery. At sixteen he worked as a "number grabber" for the Santa Fe Railroad; that is, he copied down the numbers that were printed on the sides of freight cars as they passed him in the switchyards. Then, at age eighteen, he found a job with the Chicago Sanitary District, in whose employ he would remain for almost forty years.[3]

Kelly started at the Sanitary District as an axman chopping down trees on canal banks. At night he took classes in engineering at the Chicago Atheneum, and in 1889 he became a rodman for the surveying crews, that is, the person who held the rod that the instrument man sighted to determine elevation. It was the lowest job on the engineering crew, but young Kelly was establishing a reputation as a hard worker and slowly moving up the ranks.[4]

While he was proving himself at the Sanitary District, Kelly was dabbling in other activities. At his father's urging, he went into the undertaking business; he and a friend, John Doran, opened a funeral parlor at 2500 West 38th Street. His interest quickly waned, however, and soon his parents, who had moved in over the funeral parlor, were managing it. Doran, the brother-in-law of an alderman, had met Kelly at the Brighton Park Athletic Club, a popular youth gang headquartered at 36th and Western. Kelly had helped found it, and he was elected its president. The club, with about two hundred members, sponsored baseball, boxing, wrestling, and swimming for the neighborhood youth but, more important, fostered political involvement. Even before reaching voting age, Kelly had cast his lot with local Democratic politicians and had impressed them by successfully handling eight precincts in one election.[5]

But Kelly's well-known political activities proved to be a mixed blessing, for the road to success in the Sanitary District, like that in other city departments, was strewn with political obstacles. After his promotion to surveyor, he served for three years with the War Department on the Great Lakes–to–Atlantic Canal. He then returned to the Sanitary District but was fired within a week, replaced by someone with better political connections. He recaptured his position only when South Side Democratic leader Tom Carey championed his cause. In 1905 he ran for trustee of the Sanitary District but lost in a Republican landslide.[6]

Kelly found his job repeatedly threatened because of his constant campaigning on work sites; his biggest scare came when he tangled with one of his superiors, an equally avid Republican. While working on the North Shore Channel, Kelly later recalled, his life was made miserable by the "slave-driving of a straw boss"—the son-in-law of a local Republican chief. The hot-tempered Kelly finally erupted, flattening his antagonist with a single punch. When called on the carpet by Sanitary District president Robert R. McCormick, a staunch

Republican whose *Chicago Tribune* served as the party organ for the entire Midwest, Kelly expected to be fired. But Kelly's bravado impressed McCormick, who said, "I'm glad we've got someone around here who has guts enough to hit a politician in the nose." He not only kept Kelly on the job but gave him a raise of fifty dollars a month.[7] This act initiated a lifelong friendship between the roughhewn Irishman and the aristocratic scion, two men who seemingly had little in common.

In the meantime, Kelly had in 1910 married Mary Roche, the daughter of Edmund H. Roche, a prosperous grain merchant from New York. Two years later the Kellys had their first child, Edward Joseph, Jr. Mary Kelly died during a flu epidemic in 1918, and Ed Kelly remarried in 1922, this time to Margaret Noll Kirk, whose first husband had died the previous year. In 1926 Edward Joseph, Jr., then a student at Culver Military Academy in Indiana, died of a mastoid tumor. Ed and Margaret Kelly later adopted three children—Stephen, Joseph, and Patricia.[8]

During these years Kelly's career was steadily progressing. He received numerous promotions, culminating in the decision of Robert Isham Randolph, the District's chief engineer, to name Kelly his assistant. When Randolph retired in 1920, Kelly took his place. At forty-four years of age, having started at the bottom and possessing no formal training in engineering, Kelly had reached the pinnacle of his profession.[9] But the 1920s proved a turbulent decade for the Sanitary District, and as one of its leaders, Ed Kelly found himself at the vortex of the storm.

First came the claim that Kelly lacked the qualifications to be chief engineer. Some observers contended that he was a figurehead and had received the appointment solely because of his political connections and friendship with Colonel McCormick. Elmer Lynn Williams, a Chicago muckraking journalist and persistent Kelly critic, even suggested that the Sanitary District covertly paid several leading engineers (L. K. Sherman, Cornelius Lynde, and the recently retired Robert Isham Randolph) as consultants to do the chief engineer's work.[10] But the issue of Kelly's lack of expertise paled in comparison with the startling revelations that gross malfeasance, waste, and graft pervaded the Sanitary District in the so-called Whoopee Era.

In 1928 first assistant state's attorney John E. Northrup concluded his investigation of the Sanitary District by returning indictments against Kelly, former president Timothy J. Crowe, six trustees, and five other employees for defrauding the district of $5 million. Despite Kelly's immediate claim that the indictments were "baseless and wickedly false," the evidence that Northrup produced at the ensuing trial seemed devastating. Over seven hundred witnesses appeared, many unwillingly, and the resulting testimony revealed what one observer called "hideous corruption in a public office created by the legislature . . . to provide for the sanitation and guard the health of the community."[11]

Among the disclosures was the report of Major General Harry Taylor, retired chief engineer of the U.S. Army, which revealed that Kelly awarded a Calumet sewage plant construction contract to one of his neighbors for $4.75 million; Taylor estimated that figure to be about $2 million in excess of fair cost. At the same time, the Sanitary District paid $1.08 per cubic foot for dredging, while the U.S government allotted $0.44 for identical work in the same river. The district payed $0.24 per pound for reinforced steel when the going rate stood at $0.08 per pound. Officials estimated Sanitary District "payroll padding" at 75 percent; indeed, two thousand of the four thousand employees were dropped when the scandal broke, with another thousand singled out to go in the immediate future.[12]

Perhaps the most spectacular example of inflated costs was the building of McCormick Boulevard, a 4.5 mile road along the North Side canal. Named for one-time District head Robert R. Mc-Cormick, the boulevard cost $2,519,493, a price that earned it the sobriquet "the world's most expensive road." The lights for the road cost $727,000, though experts estimated that $75,000 would have been a fair price. And in order to add a bridle path of cinders paralleling the road, at a net cost of $1,062,439, the Sanitary District sold its cinders to an independent contractor and then bought them back at a greatly inflated price.[13]

When Kelly, whose job as chief engineer entailed approving all work contracts, consistently awarded jobs to the same firms, many people began to question the supposedly competitive bidding system. Contractors submitted their bids in envelopes provided by the Sanitary District, a system that allowed bids to be opened, put in fresh envelopes, and resealed with no signs of tampering. These suspicions were confirmed with the submission of bids for construction work on approaches to a South Crawford Avenue bridge: The Underground Construction Company admitted to submitting a bid for $343,315, while another firm bid $266,275. But when the envelopes were opened several hours after their submission, the Underground Construction bid read $264,950.[14]

Further testimony disclosed that Sanitary District officials accumulated sizable fortunes as a result of payoffs, bribes, and other gratuities. It became widely known that a well-greased palm was essential to doing business with the department. Some trustees received gifts of twenty-five cases of liquor a month from favored contractors, one of whom testified that he delivered liquor valued at

$3,000 to $4,000 a month to an official. And the recipients of those perquisites maintained conspicuous levels of consumption despite their modest salaries: Several trustees admitted financing lengthy European vacations with illegally solicited contributions. Former president Crowe achieved much notoriety by motoring around Chicago in an $8,700 car, while Ed Kelly's cost a "modest" $5,400. Flashy life-styles and shameless spending by Sanitary District chiefs added fuel to the fire ignited by the evidence presented at the trial, and Chicagoans eagerly waited to see what punishment would befall the "whoopee boys."[15]

The saga of the legal proceedings against the indicted Sanitary District officials was not readily concluded, however. When Northrup initially brought the case before the criminal court in 1928, Judge Joseph B. Davis, a cohort of former Democratic party boss George Brennan, quashed the indictments. Northrup had to reassemble a case frantically in order to beat the statute of limitations, and a new grand jury was impaneled. It chose to re-indict everyone except Kelly—interestingly, the foreman of the new jury was an official in a firm that sold material to the Sanitary District through its purchasing agent, Kelly—and the trial dragged on for months. Thus, although much of the evidence proved damaging to the chief engineer, Kelly escaped personal liability. By the time sentences were returned, on February 5, 1932, two of the defendants had died. The grand jury found Crowe guilty and sentenced him to one to five years in the state penitentiary; two trustees received similar sentences. (Though some of those found guilty served some time in prison, Crowe died before he was due to begin his sentence.) In the end, despite some sullying of his reputation, Kelly managed to escape the Whoopee Era scandals relatively unscathed. The grand jury's decision not to re-indict him left Kelly free to remain at the shell-shocked Sanitary District and to further his career in his alternate capacity as president of the South Park Board.[16]

Prior to the establishment of a citywide park district during Kelly's mayoralty, several separate governing bodies, complete with taxing powers, administered the affairs of Chicago's parks. The largest and wealthiest were the South Park, Lincoln Park, and West Park boards. In 1922 judges of the circuit court of Cook County had unanimously appointed Kelly a South Park commissioner. Two years later, when incumbent South Park president John Borden Payne rejected a popular movement to rehabilitate the Columbian Exposition Fine Arts Building and preserve it as an arts center, Kelly led the forces of opposition. Thanks to the backing of such civic groups as the Chicago Club, Kelly defeated Payne in the board's presidential election that year. With the help of a bond issue passed by the voters and that year. With the help of a bond issue passed by the voters and generous financial contributions by Julius Rosenwald, Kelly fulfilled his promise to refurbish what is now the Museum of Science and Industry. This would prove only the first of many spectacular achievements of Kelly's ten-year reign as the South Park Board's chief executive.[17]

Kelly initiated the task of filling in the lake front, secured a publicly owned six-mile strip of shore land from Jackson Park to the center of the city, and directed the transformation of Grant Park from a "tin can dumping ground" to a beautiful adjunct to the downtown area. As a result of these efforts, Kelly came to be called the "father of the lake front." During his presidency, private citizens donated the Shedd Aquarium and the Adler Planetarium, along with the Buckingham Memorial Fountain, to the newly developing civic center in Grant Park. Kelly also supervised the construction of Soldier Field, which he quickly established as a national showplace by using it as a venue for such activities as the Army-Navy football game and the Dempsey-Tunney heavyweight championship bout. And although some citizens complained about the inflated costs of construction— Soldier Field cost $8.5 million to build, while the larger Los Angeles Memorial Coliseum, built at the same time, cost only $1.7 million— the citizenry seemed to accept Chicago's age-old practice of paying a little more for public services to accommodate graft-prone administrators and politicians.[18]

As chief engineer of the Sanitary District and head of the South Park Board, Ed Kelly became a well-known public figure by the late twenties, but Chicagoans did not perceive him as one of the city's political kingpins. Kelly did not, after all, hold any elective office in city or county government, nor did his name appear in the daily newspapers as an insider in the Democratic party. Independent of his influence, however, the party was undergoing some fundamental transformations, changes that would ultimately elevate him to the pinnacle of power in the city.

In the first two decades of the twentieth century, a vigorous two-party system existed in Chicago politics, with the Democrats and Republicans alternating control of city hall. By the late twenties, however, the Democrats were able to parlay their traditional opposition to movements like Prohibition, Sabbatarianism, and other attempts at limiting personal liberties into a growing support from the city's many ethnic groups. By 1930, members of white ethnic groups— that is, the foreign-born and second-generation immigrants—made up 64.3 percent of the city's population. (The U.S. Census reported that only 27.9 percent of Chicagoans were native Americans; see Table 1.) With the exception of the Italians, who remained faithful to the Republican party throughout the decade, most of the other major ethnic

Table 1.   Ethnic Groups in Chicago, 1930 (Chicago Population = 3,376,438)

Group	Number of Foreign Born	Number in Second Generation[a]	Percentage of Total City Population
Czechoslovakians	48,814	73,725	3.6
Danes	12,502	16,193	0.8
Germans	111,366	266,609	11.2
Hungarians	15,337	15,090	0.9
Italians	73,960	107,901	5.4
Lithuanians	31,430	32,488	1.9
Norwegians	21,740	30,968	1.6
Poles	149,622	251,694	11.9
Russians	78,462	91,274	5.0
Swedes	65,735	75,178	4.2
Yugoslavians	16,183	16,108	1.0
Jews	325,000[b]	—	9.6
Native Americans[c]	943,301	—	27.9
Blacks	233,903[d]	—	6.9
White ethnics	842,057	1,332,373	64.3

Source: John M. Allswang, *A House for All Peoples: Ethnic Politics in Chicago, 1890–
    1936* (Lexington: University Press of Kentucky, 1971), p. 19.
[a]Includes native-born of foreign or mixed parentage.
[b]Includes all Jews, regardless of country of origin.
[c]Includes native-born whites of native-born white parentage.
[d]Includes all blacks.

groups—the Czechs, Poles, Germans, and Jews—increasingly came to support Democratic candidates and platforms.[19]

Despite the influx of great numbers of voters from other ethnic groups, the Irish clung to their traditional perch atop the city's Democratic party hierarchy. Relying upon their well-honed political skills and a unity lacking among the other ethnic groups, the Irish installed one of their own as party chief—first Roger Sullivan and then George Brennan. When the latter died in 1928, however, no Irish leader emerged to replace him, and the mantle of leadership fell instead to a Czech, Anton Cermak. The fact that the Czechs were less numerous in Chicago's melting pot than the Poles, Jews, or Germans actually worked to Cermak's advantage, for these other groups had no desire to replace Irish hegemony with control by another large faction. Cermak acted as a broker and successfully coaxed the various ethnic groups, including the resentful Irish, into a powerful political coalition.[20]

Already the head of the party, Cermak consolidated his power by adding the political clout attendant on the mayoralty. This dual control was vital, since the mayor's office in Chicago is legally weak in relation to the statutory powers granted the fifty-man city council. Previous mayors had never been able to combine both positions, and they had therefore suffered at the hands of the council. What gave Cermak his mastery over the city's legislative body was his status as individual leader of the party, able to command the allegiance of the Democratic aldermen; indeed, both the Kelly-Nash and Daley machines of later years would be based on the same manner of control.

The strength of Cermak's nascent coalition and the importance of ethnic politics were evidenced by his campaign for the mayoralty against the incumbent Republican, Big Bill Thompson, in 1931. Thompson erred egregiously in conducting a viciously nativistic campaign; his references to Cermak as "Pushcart Tony" and "Tony Baloney" served only to alienate the thousands of ethnic voters who saw the Czech as their champion. In the end, only blacks and Italians gave the majority of their votes to the Republican, and then in smaller numbers than before. Cermak's election seemingly boded ill for the Irish generally and for Kelly in particular, since the new chief executive would surely open the party hierarchy to broader representation. But in seeking to effect a rapprochement with the deposed Irish contingent of the party, Cermak chose Pat Nash to be Cook County Democratic chairman, and the choice of Nash proved fortuitous for Kelly's rise to political power.[21]

Patrick A. Nash, 28th Ward committeeman, was one of the elder statesmen of Chicago's Democratic party. His father, Thomas, emigrated to the United States from Ireland in 1850 and to Chicago four years later. He first settled in "the patch," a Near North Side area populated by poor Irish immigrants, and then moved to the area of Grand and Ashland, right next door to Democratic leader Roger Sullivan. Thomas Nash worked as a laborer for the city, helping to build the first water tunnels under the streets. Long before dying at the age of 101 in 1928, he founded a sewer contracting business, which he bequeathed to his sons. Patrick A. Nash ("P.A.," as he came to be called by intimates) was born in 1863 and worked for the family business from his adolescent years until his death. But thanks to the influence of his next-door neighbor, he also took an active interest in the local Democratic party.[22]

Nash ran for public office only twice—he won a position on the County Board of Review in 1918 and lost his bid for reelection in 1924—but he served behind the scenes as a major force in Democratic affairs. Known for loyalty and honesty, Nash frequently served in the role of mediator in intraparty disputes; he became known as "the great harmonizer." When Cermak assumed the mayoralty, Nash's age (sixty-eight) and avowed lack of ambition, coupled with his widespread popularity with both Irish and non-Irish alike within the party, made him the perfect choice as second-in-command of the Democrats. He adopted a very low-key role in party affairs, spending most of his time at a summer home in Paw Paw, Michigan, wintering in Florida, and raising thoroughbreds on his Kentucky farm; he returned only a few weeks before election time to affix his approval to the slates chosen by Cermak and to campaign for the ticket. All in all, it was a totally satisfying relationship for the hard-driving Cermak and the less ambitious Nash.[23]

While Nash may have been content to let Cermak enjoy carte blanche authority, many Irish Democrats chafed at having to follow his leadership. According to Cermak's biographer, Alex Gottfried, Ed Kelly should be included in the ranks of the malcontents. His attitude toward Cermak was tinged with condescension and thinly veiled contempt. Clearly, Kelly held no personal allegiance to the Cermak regime. But while others among the Irish, men like Mike Igoe and John S. Clark, openly voiced their dissatisfaction and threatened rebellion, Kelly consistently remained silent. Close ties with Nash and fear that he might fail to be reelected to the South Park Board—unlike some of the other dissidents, Kelly had neither a ward organization nor an electoral home base—kept Kelly loyal.[24] Whether he would have joined an Irish-led rebellion against Cermak when his mayoral term expired in 1935 became a moot question with the premature termination of that administration.

In February 1933 Cermak traveled to Miami to confer with President-elect Franklin D. Roosevelt about the distribution of federal patronage. Cermak felt uneasy about his chances for federal largess, because he had steadfastly refused to support Roosevelt at the recent Democratic National Convention in Chicago. As Kelly recalled, "His mind was made up to be with Smith win or lose because it was helpful in Chicago and because he was wet." Because of Cermak's prolonged commitment to New York's Al Smith, Illinois was tardy in endorsing Roosevelt and thus missed an opportunity to jump on the FDR bandwagon when the tide turned on the convention's critical fourth ballot. So Cermak made the pilgrimage to Miami's Bayfront Park to curry Roosevelt's favor, and there the fanatical assassin Giuseppe Zangara's attempt on the life of the president-elect went awry and critically wounded the Chicago mayor.[25]

Kelly, vacationing in Cuba with several Chicago politicians, heard the news of the incident while at a Havana racetrack. He put aside his fears of flying and took his first plane ride, arriving at Cermak's bedside in Miami within hours of the shooting. Kelly remained with Cermak until the mayor's death nineteen days later on March 6, accompanied the body back to Chicago, and then served as a pallbearer at the funeral.[26] But before the martyred mayor's corpse had been lowered into the grave—indeed, as soon as the question of his ability to recover arose—the battle for succession was under way.

As early as February 24, party leaders conferred well into the night at Democratic party headquarters in the Morrison Hotel to determine what would happen if Cermak died. It quickly became apparent that several men had their sights set on city hall. Among the Irish, three principal candidates emerged: city council finance committee chairman John S. Clark from the affluent 3rd Ward on the West Side; 19th Ward alderman John Duffy from the Far South Side neighborhood of Beverly; and county commissioner Dan Ryan, son of the deceased county board president of the same name.[27]

The most powerful of the non-Irish was Jacob Arvey, alderman of the sprawling West Side 24th Ward. For Arvey, a Russian Jew, to succeed Cermak, a Bohemian, while so many Irishmen saw the death of the mayor as an opportunity to restore the party leadership to its traditional place among the sons of Erin, would have been difficult under any circumstances; that the governor of Illinois, Henry Horner, happened to be Jewish increased the difficulty significantly. Arvey explained: "There was some suggestion that I would be the successor. Nash thought, and I agreed with him and other Jews (Henry Horner had just been elected governor after a bitter primary fight with Mike Igoe) that to have a governor of Illinois Jewish, and a mayor of Chicago Jewish, at that time would have been rubbing it in to the Irish."[28]

Meanwhile, the Chicago newspapers engaged in vigorous speculation about the identity of the anointed successor. At first the press favored Clark, the forty-two-year-old alderman and finance committee chairman. Clark had precedent on his side: when Mayor Carter Harrison had been assassinated in 1893, finance committee chairman George B. Swift had assumed the position of mayor pro tempore. He also enjoyed the support of a great number of the West Side Irish, including influential alderman James Bowler, who was acting as Clark's "campaign manager." But, the pundits noted, Clark had accumulated his share of enemies in the city council over the years, largely because of his inflexibility and fiery temper. (He once threw a copy of the hefty city council *Journal of Proceedings* at Mayor Thompson, and he argued frequently with Mayor Cermak in council meetings.) As the days passed, other names appeared in the political columns of the dailies: Colonel A. A. Sprague, wealthy former commissioner of public works; corporation counsel William H. Sexton; and Oscar Nelson, a Republican alderman who enjoyed good relations with the Democrats. And one name appeared repeatedly—Patrick A. Nash. Although his age could be a drawback, the papers opined, Nash seemed to be the only candidate who might be able to command enough loyalty from the various groups within the Democratic party to avoid a destructive internecine struggle.[29]

On March 8, two days after Cermak's funeral, the Democrats met in the Morrison Hotel to plan for the party's future. County clerk Robert M. Sweitzer moved that Nash's position as titular head of the party be affirmed, and the motion passed unanimously; later that week the party chose Nash to succeed Cermak as its national committeeman. But while willing to grant Nash the title of party leader, some of the Democrats continued to have designs on the mayoralty—especially Alderman Clark.[30]

Of the fifty members of the Chicago City Council, thirty-one were Democrats, eighteen were Republicans, and one was an independent. Clark felt assured of twenty-eight votes, ten Democrat and eighteen Republican, two more than the total necessary for election if the city council chose the new mayor. The council had called a special meeting for 10:00 A.M., March 10 to hear the opinion of corporation counsel Sexton on the legal points involved in choosing Cermak's replacement. Clark was confident that he could win a council election if it were held soon, but feared that much delay would give Nash time to whittle away at his twenty-eight votes. So he planned, under an obscure statute which said that three aldermen could convene the council by serving notice on the city clerk, to call an impromptu meeting for 5:00 P.M. that same day and force a roll call vote.

At the 10:00 A.M. meeting Sexton argued that the council had no authority to elect a temporary mayor and that it could legally only call for a special election. Under the existing laws, the earliest possible date for a citywide election would be June 19—a full three months away. While Sexton's opinion cast serious doubts on the efficacy of Clark's scheme, the finance chairman continued his plans for the special meeting later that day: If Sexton was right and the council vote would bear no legal sanction, Clark would still benefit by achieving a position in which he could exercise three months of leadership as the most powerful alderman. And if Sexton's opinion proved wrong, as the courts might determine, the council election would stand, and Clark would be the new mayor.

In preparation for the second council meeting, Nash called a party caucus of the fifty Democratic ward committeemen for 2:30 P.M. in the Morrison Hotel. But he also scheduled an earlier meeting of several of the party's most influential leaders, *sans* Clark, in his private apartment on the top floor of the Morrison. At this meeting, several party leaders questioned Clark's suitability for the mayoralty. Was he too independent? Too lacking in party loyalty? One committeeman recalled that when Cermak had demanded Clark's resignation as finance chairman, Clark had threatened to take the floor of the city council and, naming names, talk about payoffs in city hall. Another committeeman charged that Clark entered into personal deals with individual Republican politicians, often to the detriment of other Democrats. Soon a consensus developed that Clark's independence precluded his selection. After the mention of several other possible candidates, Nash pointed out that such decisions should not be made hurriedly. Why not, he suggested, pick an alderman, one who refused election for any length of time, to serve until the law was definitively interpreted or changed? Nash suggested Francis J. Corr, the rather nondescript 17th Ward alderman. The group then broke up and headed downstairs to the larger party gathering.[31]

In the meeting of the fifty ward committeemen, Nash quickly effected his plan. "On Sunday you elected me leader of the party in Cook County," he said. "As a leader, I recommend Alderman Jimmy Quinn for temporary chairman of tonight's meeting. I recommend for acting mayor, Alderman Francis J. Corr of the Seventeenth Ward. Now let's see if the new leadership can cooperate. Meeting's adjourned." Nash banged his gavel and abruptly left the room. The meeting over, the committeemen stood to leave as Clark shouted in vain to be heard.[32]

The 5:00 P.M. council meeting opened with an acrimonious debate over the selection of a chairman. The gallery, as well as the councilmen, recognized that the vote between Nash's candidate, Jimmy Quinn, and Clark's man, James Bowler, would serve as a barometer of the strength of the warring factions. An argument ensued about how the votes should be cast. Clark wanted secret ballots, but Arvey, speaking for the Nash forces, said: "Let the three million people in Chicago know how we vote. There's nothing to hide." The Nash men had apparently succeeded in changing some votes and wished to make certain how everyone balloted. The final tally bore this assumption out: Of Clark's twenty-eight "sure" votes, twelve defected. Quinn became acting chairman by a vote of thirty-four to sixteen. Clark and Bowler railed on for hours, charging payoffs, but the battle was lost. At 9:40 that night city clerk Peter J. Brady swore in Francis J. Corr as acting mayor.[33]

On the same day in Springfield Benjamin Adamowski, Illinois Senate minority leader, introduced an amendment allowing the Chicago City Council to choose the new mayor from without as well as from within the council. (The current law, Section Two of the "act to provide for the incorporation of cities and villages," provided only for the selection of a temporary mayor from the ranks of the city council.) Democrats in Springfield, hesitant to challenge Nash after his recent victory over the Clark forces, worked for passage of the bill in the General Assembly. Calling for an end to a chaotic situation in the midst of the depression, the press urged prompt action as well. And the public seemed to respond to Nash's contention that the move made sense for financial reasons as well: "I am not opposed to primaries," he said. "But I'm for economy too. The $500,000 or so that a primary and election would cost could better go to paying the salaries of school teachers and policemen." On March 30 the Illinois House passed the bill by an enormous 120 to 22 margin—the Senate had already approved it by a two-thirds majority—and Governor Horner cooperated by signing it into law. Thus the stage was set for Nash to handpick the new mayor. But owing to his inscrutable silence, no one seemed to know whom old P.A. had in mind.[34]

In early April the city council chose five aldermen—Jacob Arvey, Berthold Cronson, Thomas Doyle, Thomas P. Keane, and James Quinn—to recommend a new mayor. After deliberating for several days in Hot Springs, Arkansas, they sent a telegram to Chicago suggesting Nash. (Cronson, the lone Republican, did not sign it.) Nash replied that he felt reluctant to accept the offer because of his age. Rumors circulated that Nash desired the job, but Tom Courtney, the powerful state's attorney for Cook County, had convinced a Democratic caucus that Nash was too old. Another report suggested that Nash wanted to accept the position and delegate much of the work to a younger man, Arvey, but that Arvey's enemies—chiefly, Courtney—rejected that plan as well. Yet another theory proposed that Nash tried unsuccessfully to convince the Democrats to pick his son.[35]

In the midst of all the speculation, however, certain clues suggested that Nash had already chosen the man he wanted: From the outset Nash insisted that the Illinois statute be amended to allow the selection of a new mayor from outside the city council; if Nash himself had designs on the office, or if his choice occupied a seat in the council, why would he force the bill through the legislature? Moreover, on March 18, almost three weeks before he eventually announced his choice, Nash said this about the type of man needed to replace Cermak: "He should be a Democrat. He should be a man outside of politics, but wholly familiar with politics."[36] Despite these clues, the eventual selection of the mayor proved to be a genuine surprise to most Chicagoans.

On April 10 Nash called a meeting of top party leaders to announce his choice. The list of invitees included Arvey; Courtney; municipal court bailiff Al Horan; Nash's nephew Ed Hughes, Illinois secretary of state; and Ed Kelly.[37] Nash's man was Kelly. Courtney phoned Governor Horner in Springfield to see if he objected. Ben Adamowski, who was with Horner when the call came through, recalled the governor's surprise at the selection. He said: "You want Ed? Does Pat Nash know? I have no objection, if that's what you guys in Chicago want."[38]

On April 14 the city council ratified Nash's decision. The

session began with Corr tendering his resignation, effective immediately. Alderman Arvey presented a statement, signed by thirty-seven aldermen, including John S. Clark, that recommended Edward J. Kelly be chosen the new mayor of Chicago. Arvey then nominated Kelly, and Aldermen Cronson, Orlikoski, and Maron seconded. No other nominations followed. The balloting began, and forty-seven aldermen voted for Kelly. (Aldermen Lindell, Moreland, and Nelson, though present, did not vote.) At 4:15 that afternoon, city clerk Brady administered the oath of office to Chicago's new mayor.[39]

In the aftermath of Nash's fait accompli, much bitterness surfaced, with charges and countercharges between the combatants of both parties. Alderman Bowler called Nash "an insipid old man" and Kelly "a thief." Both Bowler and Clark were "very abusive," according to Kelly. Knowing of Kelly's long-standing personal relationship with Colonel McCormick, many people suspected the *Chicago Tribune* of duplicity. One leading Republican contended that McCormick found out about Nash's plan to install Kelly in the mayor's office and, relishing the idea of a "friendly" Democrat in city hall, applied pressure in Springfield to get the enabling legislation passed. Some Democrats, like Abraham Lincoln Marovitz, suspected McCormick's involvement but had no proof. At the very least, most agreed, McCormick offered no resistance.[40] Undoubtedly, the knowledge that Kelly's selection would prove amenable to the man who provided the financial and ideological foundation for the state's Republican party made the chief engineer of the Sanitary District a more attractive candidate.

The choice of Kelly, though generally considered a surprise at the time, certainly makes sense in retrospect. Pat Nash had the opportunity to secure the mayoralty for himself, but at age seventy he expressed reservations: "If I were ten years younger, I would think about it, but it would be too much of a burden now. A younger man is needed."[41] Kelly had long been a friend and confidant, and as chief engineer of the Sanitary District, he had awarded millions of dollars in sewer contracts to the Nash Brothers concerns. He was Irish, a prime consideration, and from his vantage point at the periphery of Chicago politics, he had accumulated few enemies. All told, Kelly appeared the ideal candidate, and it seems likely that Nash had him in mind from the start. But if Pat Nash thought that his good friend Ed Kelly would be a "paper" mayor, easily manipulated by the party hierarchy that Nash controlled, he seriously underestimated the city's new chief executive.

A popular story relates that when Nash suggested Kelly as a possible successor, the dying Cermak replied: "Ed Kelly would make a good mayor; but if you once get him in, you'll have a hell of a time getting him out." Apprised of that conversation, Kelly supposedly responded, "What in hell would I want that job for?"[42] Indeed, Kelly consistently maintained that he resisted the initial appeals of the party to become mayor. "But I don't want the damned job," Kelly said he told Nash. "There must be somebody else." At last he relented, he later said, but only on his own terms: "All right, Pat, I'll take it. But I want you to understand this: That I am the mayor and nobody else. I will be the boss of city hall. I'll never be a figurehead."[43]

Whether or not Kelly was truly reluctant to become mayor, his version of this conversation does assume significance as a harbinger of things to come: For the next fourteen years, Ed Kelly would indeed be "the boss of city hall"—sometimes with the aid and counsel of Pat Nash and sometimes without. And his aggressive leadership would pilot Chicago through the turbulent waters of depression and global war, while building and maintaining the most powerful political machine of its time in urban America.

2 "Out of the Red, Into the Black"

CHICAGO IN 1933, when Ed Kelly assumed control of its government, teetered on the edge of collapse. The Great Depression wreaked havoc on U.S. cities generally, but the Windy City was particularly hard hit. The economic cataclysm of 1929–31 devastated Chicago, and the city veritably ceased to function. The signs of suffering and want were everywhere. As the nation's transportation hub, Chicago attracted thousands of transients to its already sizable stable of indigents and unemployed; throngs of uprooted men and women descended upon the city hoping for work and lodging, but they found only breadlines and cardboard shacks. By 1930 a shantytown had appeared at the very edge of the Loop on Randolph Street. Its residents named it "Hooverville" and its streets "Prosperity Road," "Hard Times Avenue," and "Easy Street." The relief agencies strained to meet the demand for shelter—they used asylums, poorhouses, and veterans homes to house the needy—but like all departments of city government, they were ill prepared to deal with such large-scale misery.[1]

To a great extent, the labyrinthine complexity of Chicago government militated against effective governance even in the best of times. Instead of one central authority in Cook County, there existed literally dozens, the most important of which were the City of Chicago, Cook County, the Board of Education, the Metropolitan Sanitary District, and several park boards. Each of these units possessed independent taxing and financial powers and a degree of autonomy ill suited to the effective dispensing of palliatives. Further exacerbating operation of the archaic system was a hostile state legislature that jealously guarded the city's purse strings. By imposing hundreds of regulations pertaining to the minutiae of appropriations, rigidly defining the use of corporate funds, and scrupulously limiting debt and tax limits, the General Assembly carefully circumscribed the financial powers of the ailing metropolis.

Thus hamstrung, the city increasingly failed to respond to demands thrust upon it by a depression that worsened with each year. By May 1932, Chicago's unemployment rolls included 700,000 people, fully 40 percent of its work force. Some 130,000 families received $2,612,000 in relief funds, whereas two years earlier only 13,000 families had collected $167,000. The city's relief expenditures grew from less than $11 million in 1931 to approximately $35 million in 1932. But it was not enough. The dearth of public funds led to the tapping of private resources—and Chicago raised $11 million for unemployment relief from private donations. Targeted to last from October 1, 1931 to October 1, 1932, these funds were completely dissipated by February 1, 1932. The failure of philanthropy to make a significant contribution merely heightened the dilemma, for owing to a sordid history of fiscal mismanagement, Chicago entered the depression on the verge of bankruptcy.[2]

At the root of Chicago's immediate financial problems stood the collapse of its real estate tax system. The quadrennial assessment of real estate in 1927 proved so inequitable that the Illinois State Tax Commission ordered a complete reassessment of taxable property in Chicago. While the tax commission was undeniably justified in condemning the rampant favoritism in valuations, the reassessment proved calamitous. The process took longer than anticipated—it was not concluded until the end of 1929—and all tax collections were suspended for the duration. During the time of suspended tax levies, each governmental unit of the city continued to spend money on an increasing scale from the proceeds of the sale of tax anticipation warrants. Further, property valuations in Chicago were lowered during the reassessment, so that there was less taxable income for the city when collection resumed. (The final figures for 1928 showed a reduction of over $400 million from those of 1927.) This fatal combination of intensified government spending and fewer available tax dollars served to create a runaway deficit at the beginning of the depression.[3]

Adding further to the muddled situation, a large number of property owners conducted a tax strike. Beginning in 1929 the Association of Real Estate Taxpayers, an ad hoc body composed primarily of large property holders, sued to have the act under which the tax commission ordered the revaluation declared unconstitutional. These property holders, faced with depreciating values and fearing increased valuations, hoped to postpone paying the taxes until an economic upturn ensued. They won their initial battles in lower courts but eventually lost when the Illinois Supreme Court reversed the decision in April 1932. In the meantime, however, the tax strike proved extremely effective; in June of 1930 there remained a tax payment backlog of 20 percent for 1928, 40 percent for 1929, and 50 percent for 1930. The coffers of the city remained empty.[4]

The failure of the city to produce revenue meant not only

that it could offer little in the way of welfare assistance, but that it could not even afford to pay its municipal employees. Schoolteachers, policemen, firemen, and other city workers went unpaid for months at a time. By the end of 1932, the city owed its employees $40 million in back wages. Hardest hit were the teachers. In Anton Cermak's first year as mayor, Chicago's schoolteachers received only three months' pay; by the end of his shortened term in office, the Board of Education had dropped 8.5 months behind in their salary payments. For a brief period, the school board issued scrip to the teachers, but the circuit court ruled the practice illegal: Payless paydays followed in succession. While teachers continued to work without pay, the city discharged many of its policemen and firemen. When the city's banks announced in 1929 that they would accept no more tax anticipation warrants, Chicago was flat broke.[5]

Meanwhile, Mayor Cermak labored on several fronts to combat the debilitating effects of the depression. His austerity program succeeded in reducing the cost of government: The 1932 corporate budget of $50,287,717 stood 20 percent below the 1931 budget, which, in turn, represented a saving of $11,069,203 over the previous year's expenditures under Mayor Thompson. The 1933 budget being prepared at the time of Cermak's death called for yet another significant pruning of government spending. Throughout 1932 the mayor conducted a personal telephone campaign against tax strikers owing more than $20,000, threatening to divulge their names to the desperate unpaid civic employees. Cermak also made countless appeals to philanthropic interests to buy the city's tax anticipation warrants in order to provide an immediate source of revenue. On February 6, 1932, after much lobbying by Cermak and other mayors, the Illinois Emergency Relief Commission (IERC) was created, and the state appropriated an emergency relief fund. But from the moment of its creation, state officials recognized that the amount of money the IERC could disperse was limited.[6] So, despite these efforts, the city's financial health worsened, and the beleaguered Cermak turned to the only source capable of providing massive doses of relief funds, the federal government.

On June 21, 1932, Cermak appeared before the U.S. House of Representatives Banking and Currency Committee and predicted violence in the streets of Chicago after August 1, when state funds would be exhausted. The federal government had a basic choice, he argued, between sending relief and sending troops. "It would be cheaper," he said, "for Congress to provide a loan of $152,000,000 to the City of Chicago, than to pay for the services of Federal troops at a future date." Other mayors had also spoken alarmingly of the desperate situations in their cities. And earlier that month a delegation of Chicago's leading industrialists, bankers, and civic leaders had appealed to President Hoover for federal relief assistance.[7] The chorus of pleas mounted until Congress, with President Hoover's blessing, passed the Emergency Relief and Reconstruction Bill.[8]

On July 21, 1932, President Hoover signed the bill, Title I of which provided $300 million to the Reconstruction Finance Corporation (RFC) for loans to the states. An Illinois delegation met with the RFC even before Hoover signed the bill into law. Consequently, Illinois received its first loan, amounting to $3 million, within a week of the bill's enactment. Less than a month later the RFC awarded a loan of $6 million with the stipulation that Illinois raise matching funds of its own. The Illiniois General Assembly refused to comply, so when federal money ran out in September, Cermak asked the RFC for a loan of $9,050,000. It granted $5 million. Other monthly loans followed until March 1933 when, only eight months after the program's inception, Illinois had received the statutory maximum of $45 million in loans. Thus, in the last days of Cermak's mayoralty, the temporary relief provided by the economic source of last resort had dried up, and Chicagoans faced a grim future with fear and uncertainty at unprecedented heights.[9]

When Kelly took office, the tax delinquency lists filled 260 newspaper pages. Fourteen thousand schoolteachers, not having received paychecks for months, stormed the banks and picketed in the downtown financial district. The police used tear gas to dispel the crowds and arrested scores of picketers. Undaunted, the teachers broke up public meetings and heckled the city council and school board. As many as twenty thousand high school students struck in a single day to demonstrate sympathy for their beleaguered teachers. The city's unpaid workers, aware that the financial community refused to advance anything on tax anticipation warrants signed by temporary mayor Corr, clamored for immediate action from the new mayor. Kelly did not disappoint them.[10]

In early April bankers had bought $1.7 million in tax warrants, subject to future sanction by a new mayor. In his first official act, Kelly signed the agreements and dispatched paychecks to the city's teachers, although these checks compensated for the city's indebtedness only through June 1932. The city also sent checks to the other municipal pay-rollers, most of whom had not been paid in five months. Next the mayor organized the Chicago Recovery Administration, patterned after the National Recovery Administration, as a nonpartisan coalition of business, social, and government leaders to study civic problems and make recommendations. He named Newton C. Farr of the Civic Federation as chairman. And to ensure the availability of more funds, Kelly set out to tackle the thorny problem of collecting delinquent taxes.[11]

Kelly led an entourage of Chicago politicians to the state capital to lobby for legislation that would enable cities to command payment of taxes. In his peroration before the Illinois Senate, the mayor told the legislators that he appeared before them "as mayor of the city of Chicago begging of you in behalf of starving people to rush this legislation." He related that Chicago's banks would approve more loans as soon as the state legislature passed the Skarda bill, which authorized the county treasurer to collect rents and income tax on delinquent income-producing properties. A second bill, the Graham act, required property owners to deposit 75 percent of their tax bills prior to filing objections about the rates. The passage of both of these laws constituted a triumph for Kelly, whose personal appearances in Springfield signaled his determination to commit the prestige of his office to the securing of the legislation. As a result, the city encountered considerably less opposition to the collection of taxes and succeeded in securing sizable amounts of taxes left unpaid since 1928.[12]

Recognizing the need for sustained economy, Kelly set out to trim the city's budget further. In 1933 he reduced the corporate fund tax levy to $40 million from the previous year's $44 million and lowered the corporate budget from the 1932 total of $50,293,000 to $47,883,000. He focused specifically on Chicago's white elephant, the foundering public school system. All agreed that the Board of Education's budget had to be trimmed, but questions centered on where the cuts should be made. When the board announced an economy drive to save several million dollars annually, twenty-five thousand concerned Chicagoans attended a "Save Our Schools" rally at Chicago Stadium on July 21. University of Chicago vice-president Robert M. Hutchins cited graft as the reason for high noneducational costs in the school system's budget. Other speakers urged Kelly to trim the proposed economy program, but to no avail. Endorsing the board's plan, Kelly said:

> I'm against closing the schools, but I believe the school board should cut expenses to the amount equivalent to what they would have by closing. Neither am I in favor of cutting salaries. The trustees have satisfied me they can reduce the budget sufficiently to offset closing of the schools. They have agreed to cut at least eight million dollars and possibly eleven million dollars.[13]

The subsequent program was severe in its elimination of both programs and personnel. It included the abolition of printing, physical education, and household arts classes in elementary schools, as well as printing and vocational guidance in the high schools. Physical education was curtailed, though not totally eliminated, in the high schools. Crane Junior College, the city's only two-year college, was closed. The program also increased teaching loads by 40 percent, shortened the school year by one month, reduced all teachers' salaries 23.5 percent, and closed all special schools and special departments. In September, 455 junior high school teachers, 300 kindergarten teachers, and 637 elementary school teachers lost their jobs; 146 jobless elementary school principals were placed on waiting lists or assigned to high school teaching positions.[14]

Responding to an uproar from the city's educational community, Mayor Kelly defended the extraordinary action in a time of crisis as necessary for the financial health of the community. He further deemed the action the only alternative to closing the schools altogether, and judging by the short life of the controversy, most people agreed. The question of providing quality education paled before the more urgent crises the city faced. Chicago's lack of funds, more crucial each day with the lengthening roll of relief petitioners, continued to be the first priority. So Kelly looked to other sources, first to Springfield and then to Washington, for additional assistance.[15]

The situation in Illinois proved difficult. The state's highest court held an income tax unconstitutional. Governor Horner had promised to lower personal property taxes, a move that left only a sales tax, a regressive measure unpopular with liberals, as a means of raising revenue. Horner's bill, providing for a 3 percent tax on retail sales, save farm products and motor fuel, narrowly passed both houses of the legislature. Unfortunately, the Illinois Supreme Court ruled the law unconstitutional, citing its lack of uniformity in application. A new bill, without exemptions and calling for only a 2 percent levy, won grudging acceptance in the General Assembly. When Horner signed the new bill, however, he also fulfilled his earlier pledge by suspending the state property tax. This loss of an estimated $30 million per year for the state simply offset the additional funds generated by the sales tax.[16]

Horner was establishing a precedent that a conservative legislature, ever hesitant to raise taxes for relief appropriations, would consistently endorse: The state would not jeopardize its balanced budget in order to supplement welfare funding. The cities, buoyed by as much federal largess as they could attract, would be largely left to fend for themselves. Accordingly, the mayor turned to Washington.

Kelly proposed to the RFC an arrangement by which the Chicago Board of Education would offer a first lien on some of its real estate holdings, owned by the schools but not used for educational purposes, as security for more loans. (Kelly offered as security the entire downtown block bounded by State, Monroe, Madison, and Dearborn streets, in addition to the land containing Municipal Airport.) After the state supreme court upheld the constitutionality of the transaction, the RFC gave the city $25,447,240. Kelly responded by mailing teachers checks for fourteen months' wages yet unpaid.[17]

In May 1933 the U.S. Congress approved the creation of the Federal Emergency Relief Administration (FERA), with social worker Harry Hopkins as the director. The new organization was empowered to provide nonrecoverable grants to the states with the following stipulation: One-half of the total grant would be made on a matching basis of one dollar from the federal government for every three dollars from the state; the other half would be issued without restriction. Before the end of the month Hopkins began awarding grants to the states, singling out Illinois as one of the first recipients. This action gave Chicago some much needed, if temporary, relief, but Hopkins quickly asserted that continued federal assistance depended upon the state's willingness to augment grants.[18]

In September 1933 Hopkins announced that FERA funds would be terminated if Illinois did not take immediate action to raise money for the winter months. Hopkins remained adamant and the next month sent Horner a telegram affirming that he still expected the state to provide funds "on the basis agreed upon with you and your committee. There has been no change in Federal policy in this respect." With Kelly and the Chicago Democrats lobbying tirelessly for Horner's proposal to meet this demand for state funds, the General Assembly authorized in November a bond issue of $30 million to fulfill the state's obligation through January 1935. It refused, however, to approve a Horner-Kelly proposal to raise the sales tax to 3 percent. The fight continued to be a bitter one, with modest victories accompanied by disheartening setbacks.[19]

In the first few months of his administration, then, Ed Kelly had scored a number of triumphs. His successes included meeting municipal payrolls, wiping out a significant portion of the city debt, establishing good relations with the legislature in Springfield, and keeping the schools open. He enjoyed a good rapport with the Democratic governor; and with the new Roosevelt administration more inclined than the previous Republican one to commit federal monies to help the cities, he benefited from the availability of additional resources. If Kelly had not totally vanquished the depression, conditions had improved to the extent that the riots and confrontations of prior months were not being repeated. Indeed, only the sensational disclosure of a scandal from the mayor's past sullied his otherwise impressive record of accomplishment.

In August of 1933 the Hearst papers in Chicago, the *Herald and Examiner* and the *American,* began a series of articles which charged that a key figure in the Kelly government had been found guilty of income tax evasion. After several days of conjecturing, the *Herald and Examiner*'s August 12 issue contained an exchange with Kelly to the question "Are you the prominent politician referred to in Washington dispatches as having made a $110,000 settlement with the government for income taxes on unreported income of about $450,000 or more in a little more than two years?" Kelly responded: "Now, this is off the record. I am not going to answer one way or another because any answer I might make would put me on the spot and I am not going to be put on the spot. The *Herald and Examiner* tried to reach me last night and couldn't. This is part of their school board campaign and fight against me." The newspaper then asked if Kelly intended to launch an investigation to determine the identity of the public official. Kelly said he had no such plan, nor did he care who the party in question might be.[20]

On August 16 the Chicago press revealed that Kelly was indeed the "high ranking public official" cited by the Internal Revenue Service. According to the *American*'s Charles E. Blake, the investigation of the Sanitary District Whoopee Era scandal by the state's attorney's office had uncovered several unexplained deposits and withdrawals made by Kelly in secret bank accounts. One assistant state's attorney turned the information over to the federal government, noting that Kelly also maintained covert financial connections with banks in Milwaukee, Gary, New York, and Newark.

The subsequent federal investigation showed that Kelly had paid income taxes amounting to $7,475 in 1927, $443 in 1928, and $15,530 in 1929, while his total income for those three years surpassed $450,000. The IRS ruled that Kelly owed additional taxes for 1927–29 amounting to $70,927, plus penalties of $35,463. Although the IRS investigation never identified the source of Kelly's extra income for those years, it concluded that "though it is suspected that this income was graft, the suspicions are not susceptible of proof." By paying a "compromise settlement" of $106,390, Kelly avoided prosecution.[21]

Kelly promptly responded to the disclosure of his settlement by claiming that the unreported income came from the repayment of campaign contributions. He had assumed that his loans to George Brennan for the 1926 election could be repaid without tax liability. When the *Herald and Examiner* quickly pointed out that the courts had held the reimbursement of campaign contributions tax exempt, Kelly admitted the error and promised to make public his sources of income for the entire decade of the twenties.[22]

On August 19 Kelly revealed his income from the years 1919 to 1929 in the *Chicago Tribune*. While listing his salary for the decade as $151,152.92, he admitted to a net income of $724,368.99. The difference hailed from dividends, rent, interest, and the sale of real estate and securities; Kelly refused to discuss these transactions specifically, arguing that only his salary had anything to do with his public office and duties. He further refused to discuss the $450,000 cited by the U.S. Treasury Department for 1927–29, saying: "The so-called items of unreported alleged income are not included in the above figures. I did not believe then and do not believe now that such items were taxable income within the law and I was so advised." Kelly's "full disclosure" shed little light on the question and only caused his critics to call even louder for the real figures.[23]

Kelly's tight-lipped response was assailed all the more because of the recent precedent set in the Seabury investigation involving Mayor Jimmy Walker of New York City. President Franklin D. Roosevelt, then governor of New York, had said:

> As a matter of general sound policy I am very certain that there is a requirement that where a public official is under inquiry or investigation, especially an elected public official, and it appears that his scale of living or the total of his bank deposits far exceeds the public salary which he is known to receive, he, the elected official, owes a positive duty to the community to give a reasonable, a credible explanation of the sources of the deposits or the source which enables him to maintain a source of living beyond the amount of his salary.[24]

When the Hearst newspapers, citing Roosevelt's statement, kept the heat on Kelly to make his financial history available for public scrutiny, the mayor lashed back on a radio broadcast. Speaking over station WENR on August 30, Kelly replied to the "vicious campaign of abuse, vilification and slander" that "is being conducted against me by the Hearst publications of Chicago." He alleged that the campaign against him represented merely part of a larger effort to discredit the Democratic party, that Hearst used the Kelly furor as a means of getting at Governor Horner and even President Roosevelt. While adroitly failing to mention the subject of the controversy, his unreported income, Kelly defied the demand of the Hearst editors that he resign. "I don't come from stock that resigns under fire," he concluded. "I am not that kind; as a distinguished American said, I sometimes die, never resign."[25]

On behalf of the Hearst publication, the *American's* Charles E. Blake wrote to President Roosevelt and asked him to force Mayor Kelly to make public the source of his secret income or to permit the publication of the appropriate government records. Roosevelt turned the matter over to Attorney General Homer S. Cummings, who replied that, first, the compromise settlement of May 7, 1932, between Kelly and the Treasury Department foreclosed any question of criminal prosecution and, second, the mayor's source of income could legally be divulged only if required in court proceedings, needed by heirs or executors, or requested in writing by the governor of Illinois. In a tentative draft of a letter to Blake, the president reported the attorney general's opinion and concluded that he was "without authority to comply."[26]

Meanwhile, new developments kept the story on page 1 of the Chicago dailies. First, the news broke that the federal government had also found other leading Chicago Democrats negligent in reporting their income. Pat Nash, 24th Ward alderman Jake Arvey, state tax commissioner Barnet Hodes, and former 24th Ward alderman Moe Rosenberg had been charged, but only Rosenberg was indicted. The others, like Kelly, paid back taxes and penalties; the government charged Nash the highest figure, $108,000.[27]

Second, Senator Burton K. Wheeler of Montana sent a telegram to Secretary of the Interior Harold Ickes, a native Chicagoan and head of the Public Works Administration, which Ickes released to the press:

> F. J. McCarthy, managing editor, *Chicago American*, represents to me that money from the public works department is about to be turned over to people in the city of Chicago whose records are such that it would constitute a public scandal. If what McCarthy tells me is correct, I feel that a thorough investigation should be made before any moneys were turned over to these people and sure you would concur in this view.[28]

By suggesting that the corrupt Kelly-Nash machine would jeopardize Chicago's ability to receive federal funds, the Hearst papers used the Wheeler telegram to intensify their campaign to force Kelly out of office. Fueled by their opposition to the Kelly retrenchment plan for the schools, the close connections between the mayor and Colonel McCormick of the rival *Tribune,* and the fear that the new Kelly-Nash combine would achieve hegemony over the local Democratic party, the *American* and *Herald and Examiner* kept up the attack throughout the summer and fall of 1933. But after his initial denials and counterattacks, Kelly gradually adopted a policy of silence and rode out the storm.[29] Finally the Hearst papers ceased their harassment and turned their attention to the more immediate concerns of Chicago's citizenry: the spectacular success of the Century of Progress Exposition and the repeal of Prohibition.

Mayor Kelly, second from right behind the rail, joins hordes of happy Chicagoans to toast the end of Prohibition. (Chicago Historical Society, *ICHi-17456.*)

When Kelly first became mayor he quipped, "Maybe it isn't so healthy being World's Fair Mayor of Chicago. Two of them have been shot you know." A demonstration by a thousand unpaid teachers halted the opening ceremonies of the 1933 Century of Progress Exposition, over which Mayor Kelly presided. Despite this faltering start and Kelly's misgivings, the fair proved to be a major success, luring vast numbers of people to the city and generating millions of dollars in revenue for Chicago merchants. It also provided considerable political capital for Mayor Kelly, who took every opportunity to cut a ribbon opening a new exhibit, honor an ethnic group, or welcome a visiting dignitary to Chicago's showplace.[30]

To assure that the fair offered suitable family fare, Kelly insisted upon adherence to certain standards of dress and conduct on the midway. Once, when visiting the fair's Oriental Village, the mayor turned "bashful pink" at seeing women dancers scantily clad in "purely hypothetical costumes." He ordered that the "nudity be denuded" and instructed all managers to make their performers put on clothes. Sally Rand, the dancer-sensation of the fair, reluctantly complied but appeared thereafter in a transparent gauze costume. The disgruntled production manager of Oriental Village doubted that the mayor was a "reliable weather vane when it came to art and morality."[31]

The fair became so successful that Mayor Kelly ordered it continued for a second year. When it finally shut down on October 31, 1934, the Century of Progress Exposition closed as an unqualified success. Daily attendance had averaged over one hundred thousand and the grand total of people entering the gates surpassed thirty-nine million. It repaid all debts, returned a 6 percent interest to bondholders, and accumulated a cash surplus of $160,000. In the depths of the depression, people prized their diversions, and Mayor Kelly astutely recognized the importance of escapism.[32]

In the same vein, the repeal of Prohibition met with tremendous popular approval. The ratification of the Twenty-first Amendment raised several questions for state and local government officials, however—the primary one concerning who should license and regulate the sale of liquor. Repeal had been effected, Governor Horner maintained, chiefly because Congress deemed liquor regulation a function of the states. Consequently, the states must assume control as the appropriate governing bodies. Kelly, on the other hand, argued that local governments were best suited for the role of regulation. Citing the importance of the principle of home rule, Kelly argued that local governments—some added that he really meant the local Democratic machine—would benefit from the increased source of revenue the power of licensure represented. With the Chicago legislative contingent voting as an obstructionist bloc, the General Assembly failed to pass regulatory legislation. On December 5, 1933, repeal went into effect in Illinois without any sort of controls.[33]

As time passed with no compromise in sight, rancor surfaced between the two principals. Horner said: "I'm growing tired of having the administration obstructed by personal and private interest in matters affecting the welfare of the entire state. I want to warn these obstructionists that soon the people of the state will be aroused and will protest against this sort of tactics." Kelly countered by saying, "I don't know whether it's the governor or the downstate drys around him who are tying to kick Chicago all over the lot," adding that Horner's plan would signal a return to the "snooping era of Prohibition."[34]

Both men interspersed their criticisms of the other with assurances that all was still well between them. "Governor Horner and I may not agree in all matters," announced Kelly, "but that is no reason for believing that we shall not continue as friends." Horner agreed: "We have always been good friends and we are just as good friends now as we ever were. Certainly two friends have the right to a difference of opinion." It proved to be a prolonged difference of opinion. Both Kelly and Horner used their influence in the state legislature to defeat compromise bills, as each demanded total surrender to his position. After several months of haggling, a compromise liquor control bill survived its way into law in May 1934. It mandated the sharing of regulatory powers by the cities with a state agency, but the heavy representation of Chicago interests on the state board indicated a victory for Kelly and home rule.[35] Most significantly, the battle for liquor control served as a harbinger of future conflict between the two most powerful politicians in Illinois.

While such peripheral issues as Prohibition repeal intruded into the mayor's agenda, the primary concern of Chicago's chief executive continued to be relief. In response to a critical situation in the fall of 1933, Roosevelt authorized FERA administrator Harry Hopkins to set up the Civil Works Administration (CWA). Unlike the FERA, which was a joint venture by local and federal authorities, the CWA would be totally funded and operated by the federal government. CWA workers would not receive relief but would earn a wage for services rendered on public works projects. From the outset of the program, which employed as many as thirty thousand men in Cook County at one time, CWA administrators and onlookers alike recognized that the opportunities for aggrandizement by local politicians were manifest—especially in light of a recent scandal involving another federal agency.[36]

The *American* revealed that the two highest ranking officials of the Chicago office of the Home Owners Loan Corporation (HOLC) also held key positions in the local Democratic party organization. The two men had, in fact, been sponsored by Pat Nash and approved by Roosevelt. The *American* also charged that the HOLC awarded favors to companies with political connections. Roosevelt acted quickly, replacing the bureau chief with a past president of the Chicago Real Estate Board who had no connections with local politics.[37] Nonetheless, Chicago pundits predicted a field day for the graft-prone pols in the new CWA.

In November 1933 Howard O. Hunter, Hopkins's liaison officer in the Midwest, met with Kelly and Chicago relief officials to discuss CWA projects. Hunter was acutely aware of the potential for trouble, as his report of the November meeting indicates. "We are going to need to watch these boys pretty closely," he observed. "Mayor Kelly is personally being very cooperative, but he has an awfully weak bunch of people around him." Reflecting the administration's fear of a hostile press, he added: "The Chicago papers, especially the *Tribune,* are watching us pretty closely and I am inclined to think the *Tribune* is all ready to take a strong crack at us on the first slip we make."[38]

The *Chicago Daily News* struck the first blow. In January 1934 it reported graft in the purchase of materials for a Chicago Sanitary District project. A CWA investigation confirmed the allegations. Hunter referred to the practice as "the old Cook County system of figuring a little profit for some of the boys." The politicians "can not get it through their heads that this Civil Works business is not spending local money. It is generally taken for granted that when they are spending local money there will be a reasonable amount of petty graft, and they can not change their local rules." The *American* alleged that men were given CWA jobs through political manipulation and that some individuals collected several CWA paychecks at one time.[39]

The biggest scandal involving the CWA in Chicago revolved around claims that political influence and kickbacks were necessary to receive truck-leasing contracts. The newspapers interviewed scores of truck owners, who told some eye-opening stories: Dozens of enterprising, politically-connected workers leased trucks from the owners for five to eight dollars per day and sublet them to the CWA for twelve to fifteen dollars per day. Often precinct captains commandeered trucks and substituted for regular drivers. A Chicagoan testified before a local court that he had been forced to contribute two dollars per day to the Cook County Democratic organization or lose his contract. The U.S. district attorney found petty extortion commonplace in the CWA's truck leasing. Hopkins responded by ordering a truck audit, establishing a new truck assignment center, and appointing a new Civil Works administrator for Cook County. His prompt action probably forestalled a bigger scandal; though the papers played up the story for several days, they also applauded the CWA's quick, effective housecleaning.[40]

One of the recurring problems that CWA administrators had with the Kelly-Nash group in Chicago dealt with the use of federal funds for unapproved projects. Kelly repeatedly insisted on using CWA and FERA funds for various odd jobs around the city. Frank Chase of the Chicago CWA office had to prohibit the mayor from using CWA workers for snow removal, an enterprise ruled unacceptable as a public works project. Later Kelly had to be restrained from using federally paid workers to perform other municipal services, like garbage collection.[41]

Despite the willingness of Kelly and the Chicago Democrats to use CWA resources as widely as possible, it seems unlikely that a disproportionate amount of fraud existed in the program's administration. Undoubtedly the city's newspapers contributed heavily to the impression of extensive fraud—either by casting the CWA as a well-intentioned program corrupted by the heinous local political machine or by portraying the Civil Works effort as another costly New Deal failure.[42] The overall record, however, suggests that graft and waste were kept within reasonable limits.

The primary reason for this success was the CWA officials' determination to keep a tight rein on local politicians and to respond promptly to incidents of malfeasance. Howard Hunter told Harry Hopkins that "there have been quite a number of instances in the Illinois project, especially in Cook County, where we have had to sit up nights watching potential chiseling." Harold Ickes added: "In Chicago it became necessary, as it did in several cities and states, to not only place an engineer in each state CWA office, but to use army engineers as CWA state administrators who, apparently, were relatively free from political pressures." Paramount was the determination of Harry Hopkins to run a circumspect operation. His nonpartisan appointments and willingness to take action on matters of misconduct, as noted in the truck-leasing cases, served notice that federal guidelines would be honored. In short, local politicians did attempt to gain every advantage, and a certain amount of corruption certainly went undetected, but not on a grand scale.[43]

In the spring of 1934 the federal government dismantled the CWA, which had been created as an ad hoc emergency agency to shepherd the nation through the winter, and the FERA resumed the relief burden again.[44] If few Chicago politicians had become rich through the CWA in the winter of 1933–34, Mayor Kelly's administration had certainly profited from the relief provided by Civil Works employment. Since an improved economic climate reflected positively on the mayor's stewardship, cooperation with Washington became a political, as well as an economic, necessity. In that context, Kelly sought to cement his ties with the Washington Democrats, and the best method was to demonstrate the strength of the Chicago Democratic organization at the polling place.

For Chicago political machines, success meant not only winning local elections but also influencing state politics. Like all overwhelmingly rural states dominated by one large metropolitan region, Illinois had long been a political battleground, pitting Cook County against the 101 other counties collectively known as "downstate." In part, the animosity between the two factions was cultural; downstaters looked askance at the city's cosmopolitanism, its polyglot population, and its wickedness, while Chicagoans scorned the bucolic ways of the state's "hicks," "rubes," and "hayseeds." To offset the city's great wealth and population, which roughly equaled that of the balance of the state, the General Assembly repeatedly refused to reapportion legislative districts to grant Chicago adequate representation. (From 1900 to 1933 the legislature authorized no reapportionments.) Since downstate Illinois had long been ensconced as a bastion of the Republican party, the fledgling Democratic machine in Chicago faced an uphill struggle to achieve parity.

The April 1934 primary election represented the first opportunity for the new Kelly-Nash machine to flex its muscles. It assumed great significance for several reasons: First, the total party vote in each congressional district would determine the composition of the party's central committee, and a strong showing would establish the Chicago machine as the controlling faction in Illinois. Second, control of the party in Chicago depended upon the ability of the Kelly-Nash combine to produce at the polls. And third, a convincing win for Kelly-Nash candidates in the party primary would convince Roosevelt that the machine could deliver for him in 1936 and that he should not support another candidate in the 1935 mayoral contest.[45]

On the eve of the 1934 primary, party chief Nash cracked the whip to spur party workers to a greater effort in the up-coming election. At a special meeting he reminded precinct captains that if they did not produce sizable pluralities for the party ticket, they would be in jeopardy of losing their city jobs. The strategy of the Chicago Democrats became clear immediately: Capitalize on the pop-ularity of the national Democratic administration. Nash said, "We'll tie this ticket to the tail of the Roosevelt kite and soar on to victory." The plan worked perfectly, as the members of the regular Democratic slate won handily.[46]

In the general election later that year, the Chicago Dem-ocrats repeated their success. With the slogan "Forward with Roose-velt and Recovery," the Kelly-Nash candidates swept local elections. But perhaps more significantly, the huge Democratic pluralities turned in by Cook County served to offset the heavily Republican downstate vote in the election for congressman-at-large, in which Mike Igoe narrowly defeated McCormick protégé Wayland "Curly" Brooks.[47]

Harold Ickes, who called the Kelly-Nash machine the "rottenest crowd in any section of the United States today," com-plained that Democratic national chairman James Farley had actively supported the Kelly-Nash forces. He also objected to some of the tac-tics employed by the Chicago Democrats. Frank Knox, Republican publisher of the *Daily News,* told Ickes that the machine had sent out a vast number of cards (one hundred thousand of which were used) identifying the bearer as an illiterate who desired to mark a straight Democratic ticket. Relief recipients received the cards through the mail and were encouraged to use them or forfeit their income. Ap-prised of this practice, Howard Hunter investigated and concluded: "There is nothing whatever to indicate that any official or employee of the Relief Commission had anything to do with this. I do not know how anyone could stop ward politicians from distributing anything they desire to." Apparently, the machine pols, who had no power to back up their threats of relief termination, hoped to bluff their way to additional votes.[48]

Despite the Kelly-Nash 1934 electoral successes, Roosevelt apparently shared Ickes's misgivings about supporting Kelly for mayor. Informed that Big Bill Thompson had lined up a majority of the Republican county committeemen behind his mayoral candidacy, Roosevelt said, "That would be a fine choice, wouldn't it, Thompson or Kelly?" On December 22, 1934, Roosevelt instructed James Farley to "take the necessary steps to stop Kelly's nomination." Farley checked with his Chicago sources and reported to Roosevelt their conviction that Kelly had the nomination locked up. Farley told the president that, considering the strength of the Chicago machine, it would be a mistake for the administration to oppose Kelly. FDR reluctantly agreed, but he also informed Ickes that if reformer Charles Merriam contested Kelly's nomination, he could expect at least covert support from Washington.[49]

On January 1, 1935, the Democratic Central Committee of Chicago mailed petitions to the city clerk signed by six hundred thousand persons entering Ed Kelly in the upcoming mayoral primary. The law required only 3,732 signatures, but the machine was determined to make a show of strength. The next day Kelly, accompanied by Nash, Horner, and county board president Clayton F. Smith, bowed to the will of the thousands of petitioners and assented to run for mayor.[50] His decision certainly came as no surprise, but a real air of suspense surrounded the identity of the Republican candidate.

Contrary to the Roosevelt administration's intelligence reports, Thompson did not have the Republican nomination assured. In fact, Big Bill decided not to file for candidacy at all. The Republicans who did file nominating petitions included Emil Wetten, an attorney; Sol H. Goldberg, a businessman; Mortimer B. Flynn, a coal dealer and Thompson protégé; and women's activist Mrs. John Wesley Grace. Wetten eventually won the nomination without much of a fight, for none of the lackluster group seemed to covet the nomination fiercely. The *Tribune* commented: "The spirit of contest has been entirely lacking. This is recognized as the most peaceful, the most one-sided campaign since Chicago, in 1911, began naming its mayoralty candidates through primaries. . . . It's all Kelly, so why talk about anything else?"[51]

Mortimer Flynn, the runner-up to Wetten by about thirty-two thousand votes in the Republican primary, charged that many GOP committeemen had made deals with Kelly men to support Wetten, a virtual unknown and weak candidate. Newton Jenkins, who ran that year for mayor as a third-party candidate, echoed the charge. The Republican *Tribune* refused to endorse Wetten, claiming that "the Republican nomination went by default to a man who was actually chosen by the Democrats on the basis of a bipartisan deal." One newspaperman estimated that half or more of the Republican committeemen were openly for Kelly. James F. "Spike" Hennessey, a Kelly speech writer, agreed that the Republicans' decision to run Wetten came from the Democrats; he added that several times during the campaign Wetten threatened to withdraw but was dissuaded by "Kelly-Nash" Republicans.[52]

The lackluster campaign conducted by Wetten certainly lent credibility to these charges. Consistently bedridden with a lingering illness, Wetten made few public appearances. Contributing to his low-key campaign was a serious shortage of money; the local Republican party contributed a paltry $50,000 and left Wetten to raise additional money by himself. The *Tribune* reported that the beleaguered candidate so sorely lacked funds that he paid for the printing of five thousand pamphlets out of his own pocket and then requested that Republican committeemen pay him for copies to distribute in their wards. Wetten operated without a campaign manager, and frequently his headquarters went unmanned for days at a time. To an audience of worried Republicans, Wetten explained why his inactivity would not matter in the upcoming election: "This city election is a comparatively simple matter. The issues are well known and understood. The voters either want Kelly re-elected or they want somebody else."[53]

Against such inept opposition, the Democrats felt assured of victory. They conducted a quiet campaign with few mass meetings and no parades. Kelly conducted a "front porch" campaign from the mayor's office; he received representatives of various civic groups tendering their endorsements and seldom ventured forth to give speeches. To the extent that he campaigned at all, Kelly did so on his record of reclaiming financial solvency for the city and on the boast that, as a Democrat, he had connections in Washington that benefited Chicago. He announced a $20 million plan for the construction of a permanent fair at the site of the Century of Progress Exposition. This project, to be funded largely by a federal work relief plan that Kelly assured Chicagoans would pass Congress, would provide employment for twenty to thirty thousand people. The week before the election he released plans for a "pay dirt" public works program that would employ as many as one hundred thousand jobless workers and that, because it was funded by federal agencies, would not require any increase in taxes. When the bill authorizing this massive building and reclamation project passed Congress, Kelly promised, "I'll be sitting in President Roosevelt's office. We will go after all the government money we can get."[54]

The ground swell of support for Kelly was overwhelming. Republicans in the city council joined with their Democratic counterparts on the eve of the election to lavish praise on the incumbent mayor. Alderman Oscar Nelson, the Republican floor leader, said: "In my twelve years as member of this body, I have never found a mayor who presided more impartially than Mr. Kelly." Alderman Robert R. Jackson, speaking for the predominantly black 3rd Ward, said: "The people of our race feel a deep sense of gratitude to the mayor for his activities in their behalf. I believe that the second and third wards will accord him the largest majority given a candidate for mayor in twenty years."[55]

Kelly received the support of most of the city's leading civic groups, all of its newspapers (led by the Republican *Tribune*), and many of its independent voters, including future governor Adlai E. Stevenson. The young lawyer, not yet active in politics, spoke for many nonpartisans when he wrote Kelly: "This is the first political endorsement I have ever written. . . . Under most trying circumstances, you have somehow managed to restore Chicago's safety, self-respect and solvency."[56] With such diverse support and meager opposition, the election itself held no drama—the only thing in question was the margin of victory.

On April 2 the voters elected Ed Kelly by the greatest margin in Chicago's history. He received 799,060 votes to Emil Wetten's 167,106 and carried all fifty wards. Kelly commented, "The figures, of course, are more eloquent than anything I can say" and had his vote total put on the license plates of his Cadillac. Wetten conceded, "There isn't much to say except that the result confirms what has been repeatedly published—that the Republican party is completely disintegrated. In fact, there is no local Republican party." Nash said simply, "We licked the hell out of those _____'s!"[57]

The charges of vote fraud surfaced immediately, with estimates on the number of stolen votes varying from two hundred thousand to three hundred thousand. Observers reported ballot box stuffing, chain voting, intimidation, vote buying, and all of the other varieties of chicanery practiced by political machines. While these charges were undoubtedly valid, the Kelly-Nash organization employed such methods to embellish the final result, not to assure it. The total dominance of the Democrats was based upon their superior party organization, a bankrupt opposition, the sucessful administration of the incumbent mayor, and the popularity of the national Democratic government. In the weeks prior to the election, Kelly maintained that the progress of recent months was due to the good relations between his government and the Democrats in Washington and that the continued link with "Roosevelt prosperity" depended upon the city's having a Democrat in city hall.[58]

Kelly's awesome plurality apparently fulfilled the Chicago Democrats' expectations: The day after the election, Harry Hopkins invited the mayor to Washington to discuss more public works projects for Chicago. Before the visit, Howard Hunter told Hopkins that Kelly "got elected by such a big majority that everyone feels he should get more consideration in Washington." Concerned that the Illinois lawmakers would prove difficult to work with, Hopkins asked if Kelly could "deliver the goods with the legislature for us." Hunter asserted that Kelly now stood as the most powerful politician in the state and would be a useful ally. Hopkins promised to "go right after Kelly" during the upcoming meeting.[59]

Kelly lobbied for two pet projects in Washington, a permanent fair and a lakefront airport. Both were controversial plans, staunchly resisted by local reformers who feared the despoliation of the lakefront, and both had been opposed by the mayor's old nemesis, Harold Ickes. Kelly felt that his recent electoral triumph had improved his bargaining position; before leaving for Washington he told the *Herald and Examiner* that the airport was "in the bag." While Kelly may have overestimated the success of his trip—Hopkins promised only to argue the case for the proposed projects with the president— the meeting proved fruitful for both men. Kelly said that if Hopkins "is to be the man who will have charge of government grants, I am sure that Chicago will not get the worst of it." Hopkins got Kelly's pledge to use his influence in Springfield to force the state to increase its financial contribution for relief. Upon returning from Washington, the mayor pledged to help force Horner's tax bill, which would raise the sales tax from 2 percent to 3 percent, through the general assembly.[60]

The ongoing relief crisis in Illinois had reached another impasse when Hopkins warned that the failure of the state legislature to appropriate more money for relief would force him to terminate federal assistance. When the Republican-dominated legislature refused to cooperate by the proposed May 1, 1935, deadline, Hopkins cut off all federal monies to Illinois. During the mayoral campaign, Kelly had resisted any attempt to raise taxes in the state, saying, "I do not favor saddling Chicago's taxpayers with additional burdens." But after his conference with Hopkins, the mayor reversed his stand and began to work for the tax hike. While Kelly was willing to accept any bill authorizing a tax increase, Horner had committed himself to a particular bill that would provide relief immediately upon passage. (Another bill favored by many legislators called for a July 1 starting date.) The emergency bill required a two-thirds majority, however, and Horner insisted on keeping the bill bottled up in the legislature rather than allowing a simple majority to pass the alternate measure.[61]

Hopkins, unsympathetic to the impact on Horner's political prestige, lost patience with the intricate machinations in Springfield and indicated that he would be willing to accept any tax bill. Apprised by Hunter that Horner "can't swing the crowd at all," Hopkins concluded that the administration's hopes rested with the Chicago mayor. "Somebody has got to talk turkey to Kelly," he told Hunter. After checking with the mayor, Hunter assured his boss that the Chicago Democrats would push the July 1 bill. When Horner's bill failed for the fifth time, the governor consented to accept passage without the emergency provision. With Kelly's backing, the bill passed both houses on May 23.[62]

The effect of this episode on Kelly's relations with Washington was salutary. He impressed Hopkins as the most savvy politician in Illinois, the one to deal with if things needed to be done. Both Hunter and Hopkins expressed their disenchantment with Horner, whom they considered to have bungled the whole affair and to have left the state legislature in a "shambles." Clearly, in the summer of 1935, dissatisfaction with Horner contrasted with the rising star of Chicago's mayor.[63]

At this point, glowing praise from many quarters reflected Ed Kelly's status as one of the nation's most-heralded mayors. Political columnist Arthur Krock said: "Chicago still has relief problems, slums, poverty and great groups of the unemployed. But the difference between present conditions and those in 1932 is the difference between black and white." Douglas Sutherland, director of the Chicago Civic Federation and Bureau of Public Efficiency and Economy, offered: "Mayor Kelly is giving Chicago better government than it has had in many years. He has made several strong appointments and is a man of good judgement and great strength." The *New York Times,* pondering the 1935 election results, concluded: "Why did the people of Chicago give him an unparalleled vote of confidence? Because he turned one of the worst-governed cities into one of the best-governed . . . . The floating debt has been greatly reduced and in consequence the cost of borrowed money has declined to something like a normal rate of interest. Even more dramatic has been the wiping out of the arrears in wage and salary payments of city and school employees. These are memorable achievements. . . . He is a good model of mayors and even offices of loftier title to follow."[64]

His successes at rolling back the tides of fiscal calamity, his great electoral triumph in 1935, and his rapproachement with the Roosevelt administration—at the expense of Governor Horner—established Kelly as the most powerful Democrat in Illinois. With some nagging personal scandals behind and with the local political machine functioning smoothly under the dual tutelage of Kelly and Nash, the future seemed very bright indeed. In fact, these were the halcyon times for the Kelly-Nash rule; never again would Kelly enjoy the personal popularity or the unquestioned power he possessed in 1935. In the next few years he would launch some ill-advised sorties against other Illinois Democrats with calamitous results, the myth of Kelly-Nash invulnerability being the chief casualty.

3 Hegemony Denied

 IN THE stunning afterglow of the 1935 election, the Kelly-Nash machine seemed invincible. With FERA, CWA, Works Progress Administration (WPA), state, and local positions at their disposal, Kelly and Nash controlled some thirty to forty thousand patronage jobs. It was estimated that the machine commanded five hundred thousand or more sure votes in any given election. This immense power can be explained partially by the patronage rolls and partially by illegal electioneering methods. The latter factor can be overemphasized, however. While vote stealing and ballot stuffing undoubtedly occurred, little evidence exists to indicate that the Illinois Democrats did any more of this sort of thing than their Republican counterparts. In fact, many Chicago Democrats resorted to stealing votes in order to negate the falsified returns from Republican downstate counties. With the Kelly-Nash machine scoring such one-sided triumphs, the impact of the questionable votes seems marginal. Despite a certain amount of hyperbole, Kelly struck a resonant chord when he said, "A good organization doesn't steal votes. It doesn't steal elections. If it's a good organization, it doesn't have to."[1]

The Kelly-Nash organization did not have to. The sound substructure, inherited from Anton Cermak, became even better under the guidance of the Irish co-bosses. They established clear-cut standards of performance, whereby party workers advanced or were demoted according to successes or failures within their own fiefdoms. Given a certain latitude and hope for advancement within the hierarchy, the party faithful, from ward committeemen down to precinct workers, had a reason to work hard. This system of incentives, tempered with stern discipline, was very instrumental in keeping together an uneasy alliance among disparate factions.[2]

When Kelly became mayor, he and party chairman Pat Nash sought peace among the party leaders. Since a number of people had harbored designs on the seat of power won by Kelly, the prospects for amicable relations seemed dubious—especially in light of the persistent ethnic rivalries. But Kelly and Nash took immediate steps to forestall any potential difficulties by granting membership into the party's new inner circle to spokesmen for the different factions.

The Jews had long been politically independent in Chicago, voting for Republican Bill Thompson for mayor in 1927 but then for Democrat Al Smith in the 1928 presidential contest. In 1931 they overwhelmingly threw their support to Cermak, who received the endorsement of all the leading Jewish politicians: Adolph Sabath, Henry Horner, Jacob Arvey, Moe Rosenberg, and Benjamin Lindheimer. In 1932 they supported the Democratic ticket in its entirety, including their own Horner for governor, and seemingly abandoned any connection with Chicago Republicanism. Kelly and Nash chose Arvey, chief of the large 24th Ward, to be chairman of the prestigious city council finance committee. Kelly later named Barnet Hodes, Arvey's law partner and a highly respected member of the Jewish community, corporation counsel for the city.[3]

Unlike the Jews, the Poles of Chicago had been loyal Democrats for decades. They had, of course, solidly backed their fellow-Slav Anton Cermak in 1931; the new mayor responded by appointing M. S. Szymczak city controller and later by helping elevate Szymczak to a seat on the Federal Reserve Board. Cermak's death and the subsequent reshuffling of power left the Poles insecure about their newly attained status within the party. Kelly and Nash quickly began assuaging these fears by promising not to cut back the patronage and political representation accorded the city's Polish community. Kelly further ingratiated himself by presenting a recommendation to the city council for changing the name of Crawford Avenue to Pulaski Road. This seemingly innocuous gesture raised a storm of protest, chiefly from Crawford Avenue merchants fearing a loss of business as a result of a "foreign-sounding" street name. Even after the council narrowly approved the measure, the public and press besieged the mayor to reverse the decision. He stood firm, however, and reaped considerable political capital among the Poles as a result.

In the 1935 Democratic mayoral primary, Martin Powroznik contested Kelly's nomination, but over 64 percent of the city's Poles backed the incumbent over their own countryman. Powroznik made peace with the mayor, and the Poles cast 85 percent of their votes for Kelly in the general election that followed. Although such luminaries as Benjamin Adamowski and Edmund K. Jarecki later rebelled against the machine, Chicago's Polish community continued to vote for the regular Democrats. The Polish American Democratic Organization (PADO), the party's arm in Polonia, in the words of the historian of Polish-American politics in Chicago, "gradually became more and more of a machine rubber stamp."[4]

Democratic machine leaders advise Mayor Kelly prior to a radio address. Clockwise from left: Pat Nash, Congressman Adolph J. Sabath, Kelly, Sheriff Tom O'Brien, and 24th Ward alderman Jake Arvey. (Chicago Historical Society, *ICHi-15881*.)

The large and diverse German community of Chicago had strong Republican roots and found the Anglophobic Big Bill Thompson an especially attractive candidate. Nonetheless, Cermak successfully wooed a slim majority of German voters away from Thompson in 1931, and the Democrats enjoyed similar success in the 1932 contests. As aldermen of the 43rd and 47th wards, Matthias "Paddy" Bauler and Charlie Weber were the party's leaders in the large North Side German-American community. Despite the unsavory reputations of these two saloonkeepers, whose frequent forays against the public morality were meticulously documented by the press, they gained increased stature in the new open-ended Kelly-Nash melting pot.[5]

The courting of ethnic group leaders by Kelly and Nash did not sit well with many of the Irish chiefs. They had been forced to suffer such indignities under the Czech Cermak, but the continuation of this policy under Irish leadership won no plaudits from many of the sons of Erin. Some, like Clarence Wagner and Joe McDonough, made peace with Kelly and Nash and were accepted into the organization's ruling clique; others, like Dan Ryan, John S. Clark, and John Duffy, sullenly went along but never totally accepted the new order. Ironically, it would be the Irish, not the Poles, Jews, or Germans, who would increasingly shake the foundation upon which the ethnic coalition rested. At the outset, however, the dissidents constituted a minority, and their efforts at recusancy fell on deaf ears. For most Chicago Democrats, acquiescence to the rule of Kelly and Nash proved the safest and most prosperous course.[6]

The city's business community likewise saw reason to support the Democratic machine. Kelly provided what the businessmen most coveted, a stable and unchanging environment in which investments might prosper. By keeping the city's finances in order, the mayor assured a reasonably profitable market for municipal bonds and tax anticipation warrants. Moreover, the city's image, so sullied during the cyclonic Thompson era, had undergone a considerable refurbishing. Finally, Kelly courted the favor of the city's silk-stocking crowd by tailoring taxation policies to suit its needs—both by opposing a state income tax and by "adjusting" personal property assessments. While Chicago moguls might attack the New Deal or campaign on other ideological fronts, they accepted the local Democratic regime as consonant with their interests.[7]

In any successful organization, leadership plays a crucial role, and this was the case with the Kelly-Nash machine. In the ten years during which the two men directed the fortunes of Chicago's Democratic party—Nash died in 1943—their success rested largely on their ability to perform separate tasks while avoiding each other's purviews. Each man had the specific role to which he was best suited temperamentally, and to a great extent the other respected his cohort's primacy within his own bailiwick. The difference in age between the two men, unique personality traits, and varied areas of expertise combined to define this division of labor.

Having handpicked Kelly for mayor, Nash contented himself with a rather limited role in the operation of the Democratic machine. He spent most of his time tending to his thoroughbreds at his Kentucky farm and did not concern himself with the day-to-day decision making, although he participated actively in long-term planning conferences, slate making, and electioneering. Seen as a recluse by reporters, Nash spent most of his time in Chicago sequestered at party headquarters in the Morrison Hotel. To the public, the septuagenarian appeared taciturn and gruff, seldom venturing a comment on the political affairs of the city. Apparently this reticence was a mask he donned, for party regulars held P.A., or the "Old Man," as he was affectionately called, in very high regard.[8]

Nash can best be described as a beloved patriarch, a man who commanded the respect and loyalty of Democrats of all nationalities. (While politicians differed in their opinions of Kelly, they invariably—Republicans as well as Democrats—rhapsodized about Nash.) He enjoyed the reputation of unquestioned honesty, a trait much prized in Chicago politics, where personal ambition frequently superseded honor. With the trust of the politicians and a reputation for fairness and scrupulous honesty, Nash served as the great mediator and harmonizer for the party. Benjamin Adamowski observed: "Pat Nash was revered by the committeemen. They adored him. . . . Had it not been for Pat Nash, Kelly would have been in trouble nine times out of ten."[9]

Nash worked behind the scenes smoothing over hurt feelings, massaging egos, and persuading potential dissidents to curtail their complaining, because he willingly accepted the low-profile, less glamorous role. While part of this approach can be explained by his personality—Nash was basically a diffident, retiring man who shunned the spotlight—another explanation is the county chairman's view of the distribution of power within the party leadership: He readily acknowledged that the mayor stood as the top official and that the county chairman was the lesser of equals. "You never fight with the Mayor of Chicago," Nash said, and he regularly deferred to Kelly—often against his better judgment. Nash's willingness to take a back seat to his younger, more aggressive partner kept the machine running smoothly.[10]

While the "Old Man" holed up in the Morrison Hotel, Ed Kelly maintained high visibility. As mayor, he gave speeches, cut ribbons, kissed babies, and kept reporters abreast of Democratic party affairs as well as city business. A tall, robust man in the prime of his life, gregarious, affable, and outspoken, "Big Ed" Kelly struck an imposing figure. "He looked like a mayor," one admiring Chicagoan noted. If so, he lived more like a king. The Kellys abandoned their South Side home for more plush accommodations on Lake Shore Drive and later at the Ambassador East Hotel. They maintained a summer home at Eagle River, Wisconsin, and a winter retreat at Palm Springs, California. Kelly dressed nattily—he was named the nation's best dressed mayor on several occasions—and he regularly attended the top sporting events in the Midwest, such as prizefights, football games, and horse-racing sweepstakes. Ed Kelly lived his private life much as he managed political affairs—with gusto.[11]

If Nash acted as the velvet glove, Kelly served as the mailed fist. Benjamin Adamowski said of Kelly, "Why, he could even give a lesson in bossism to Hitler and Stalin." The mayor insisted that he have control over patronage and shamelessly used it to command

Governor Henry Horner and Mayor Kelly strike an amiable pose for photographers. (Chicago Historical Society, *ICHi-15880.*)

fealty from party members. He kept close tabs on all administrative departments and especially the city council. His command of the council was so complete that, upon leaving the office of mayor in 1947, he could boast that it had never turned down one of his proposals or forced him to veto a bill. Kelly baldly admitted his autocratic methods: "These people look to me for leadership. To be a real mayor you've got to have control of the party. You've got to be a potent political factor. You've gotta be a boss!"[12]

With anyone other than Pat Nash as his co-boss, Ed Kelly's drive for power might well have resulted in recurring conflict. But Nash, who begrudged his protégé neither the trappings of power nor recognition as the organization's boss, gave Kelly great freedom to determine policy for the party. Trouble arose when other Democrats refused to recognize the mayor's supremacy. The first to balk was Governor Henry Horner, and the reverberations of their battle of wills convulsed the Democratic party in Illinois for the next several years.

Henry Horner, a lifetime resident of Chicago, was reared in the relative affluence of the German-Jewish neighborhood of Hyde Park. He turned to law as a career and won election as judge of Cook County Probate Court in 1914. During his tenure in that office over the next eighteen years, Horner established a reputation as a scrupulously honest judge who gave particular attention to the needs of the underprivileged. Widely renowned as an Abraham Lincoln scholar, the jurist became a pillar of the Jewish community and a shining light of the otherwise disreputable local Democratic party. In 1932, when party boss Cermak was casting about for a "reformer type" of impeccable credentials to run for governor against Big Bill Thompson's protégé Len Small, Horner fit the bill. His election set off a jubilee of celebration in the state's good-government circles. And though Horner acknowledged his political debts to Cermak when he awarded patronage, the new governor stopped far short of being a rubber stamp for Chicago appointments; he liberally sprinkled political independents and academicians into his administration. As governor, Horner apparently intended to remain loyal both to his party and to his lofty ideals.

Relations between Kelly and Horner had always been cordial. Both men hailed from Chicago's 5th Ward and they had known each other socially when Horner was a probate judge and Kelly the chief engineer of the Sanitary District. When Horner ran for governor in 1932, Kelly campaigned long and hard for him in their home ward. Horner, though somewhat surprised at the choice, offered no resistance to Nash's selection of Kelly to succeed Cermak. And with the exception of the flap over the liquor home-rule issue, the two men worked well together in the first two years of Kelly's mayoralty. Problems surfaced when the governor bridled at the increasingly popular notion of Kelly's primacy in Illinois Democracy: Horner insisted upon asserting his independence from the Chicago leadership.[13]

The critical event in the growing disenchantment between the two men was the governor's veto of the controversial "bookie bill" in the summer of 1935. Representative John M. Bolton of Chicago, a Kelly man in the state legislature, sponsored a betting bill that would license and tax handbooks in Chicago, limiting the number of betting parlors to twenty-five hundred. One-half of the licensing revenue would go to the schools and the other half to the city's general corporate fund. Anticipating possible resistance from conservative rural enclaves, Bolton's bill exempted the downstate area from coverage. Kelly urged passage of the measure, saying: "I cannot estimate the amount of revenue such licensing would bring to the city of Chicago, but I believe that handbook fees would bring the city a large income. It will, at the same time, permit efficient control of handbooks and provide relief for taxpayers." Kelly felt the passage of the bill so important that he attended when both houses voted on the measure; the House passed it by a vote of 89 to 53 on June 13, and the Senate followed suit a week later by a 31 to 14 margin. The bill would become law on July 11 unless Horner vetoed it.[14] In that session of the General Assembly, Kelly had sponsored several bills that passed both houses. In the following days, the governor signed into law bills giving Chicago the power to grant traction franchises and permission to build a lakefront airport, while allowing a bill providing for a permanent fair to become law without his signature. Yet Horner pointedly averted action on the bookie bill and refused to discuss his intentions. Illinois attorney general Otto Kerner, pointing out that betting on horse races had been legalized by the state legislature, advised Horner that the handbook bill met the test of constitutionality. But still Horner remained silent. An exasperated Kelly said, "If Horner vetoes the bookie bill, I'll sign his death warrant." Undaunted, the governor ended the speculation by rejecting the bill. In his veto message, he emphasized the moral questions involved with legalized gambling. The newspapers applauded this "politically courageous act of principle" and called the governor a man of deep-felt convictions. Kelly maintained an ominous silence.[15]

This incident was symptomatic of the fundamental problem between the mayor and the governor: Horner's independence and Kelly's feeling, shared with other Chicago Democrats, that Horner should pay obeisance to his "superiors." According to Horner's biographer, Kelly thought that Horner should "check in" by telephone whenever he came to Chicago. "Why should I call him?" asked Horner. "I've got nothing to say to him. I'm the governor of the state." In Illinois, however, the mayor of Chicago was frequently perceived as the equal, if not the superior, of the governor, and Horner had been picked to run by the Chicago Democrats. Kelly therefore felt justified in holding Horner accountable.[16]

Horner's insistence upon autonomy in the governor's mansion resurfaced in regard to political appointments. Chicago Democrats expected the governor to rubber-stamp their candidates for state jobs; that was, after all, one of the chief benefits of having a Democratic governor. But from the beginning of his term, Horner carefully reviewed suggestions for political appointments and frequently broke precedent by awarding jobs to Republicans. This behavior won praise in good-government circles but not among the "boys" in Chicago. According to Jacob Arvey, one incident in particular galled Kelly: The mayor wanted a close friend appointed to a state commission, and Horner promised to fulfill the request. But the governor later reneged, explaining that he had found someone better qualified.[17]

By midsummer Kelly had decided to drop Horner. "We're going to take that son-of-a-bitch out of the mansion," he said. "We're going to drop him down the chute and there's nothing he can do about it." Nash argued against such a radical course, fearing destruction of the Democratic party in the state. Kelly would not be dissuaded, and in typical fashion, Nash reluctantly went along. In August Horner revealed that he would announce his candidacy for reelection in 1936 on Democratic Day at the Illinois State Fair. Invariably, Chicago's top Democrats took the train down to Springfield for the annual affair, but that year Kelly, Nash, and the others stayed at home. Horner's speech contained no mention of the 1936 election, an omission that gave vent to rumors that he would not run without the support of the Chicago organization. Kelly underscored his absence by saying, "I have no candidate for governor."[18]

Publicly Kelly attributed his decision not to support Horner to the governor's lack of popularity and the difficulties inherent in his reelection. Kelly explained that he had been advised by many people throughout the state that the sales tax made Horner the state's most unpopular governor in memory. The mayor feared that Horner at the head of the state ticket in 1936 would be a liability rather than an asset and that he would handicap the Cook County slate in particular. Worst of all, he concluded, the dissatisfaction with Horner might drag Roosevelt down to defeat, especially since the unpopular governor had repeatedly affirmed his allegiance to New Deal policies.[19]

In view of Horner's loyalty to the Roosevelt administration, many people assumed that the Washington Democrats would stand by him. Several Illinois Democrats urged Roosevelt to do just that. Congressman Scott Lucas informed the president that without Horner "we cannot carry Illinois" and urged Roosevelt to "tell Mayor Kelly and Pat Nash to get in line for Horner." Harold Ickes took a more temperate view. While he deplored the actions of the Kelly-Nash machine, Ickes did not think much of Horner's chances without its support. "Horner is an honorable man and an able man," he observed, "but he is a poor politician and he certainly lacks guts." Perhaps this view of Horner as an inept politician, also shared by public works director Harry Hopkins, or a respect for Kelly's vote-getting strength convinced Roosevelt not to support the incumbent: On a stopover in Chicago in late November, Democratic national chairman Jim Farley denied that the administration was "going to order anybody in any state to do anything. Gubernatorial matters are local matters and should be taken care of locally." The message from Washington rang clear—Horner was on his own.[20]

Roosevelt scheduled a visit to Chicago for December 9. On December 8 a conference of state Democratic leaders met at Kelly's home to discuss the gubernatorial nomination, and although Horner was in town awaiting the president's arrival, he was not invited. After the meeting, none of the participants divulged what had transpired, but the smiling Kelly's reference to a harmonious meeting indicated that the downstate leaders had agreed to the ostracism of Horner.[21]

Minutes before the December 9 luncheon honoring the president, Kelly and Nash approached Horner and told him that they had decided not to support his candidacy. "I'll beat the hell out of both of you," Horner reputedly retorted. "I've got more friends over the state of Illinois than you realize. You'll find out." When Roosevelt arrived, Kelly and Nash escorted him into the banquet hall and sat on each side of him. (Normal protocol dictated that the host mayor and governor flank the president.) Horner came in later and sat near the end of the speaker's table, exiled to the fringes of the party hierarchy.[22]

The next day, on a train ride to Notre Dame University, where the president would receive an honorary degree, Roosevelt offered Horner a federal judgeship and hinted at a possible Supreme Court appointment. Several weeks later, when Horner visited Washington to discuss relief appropriations for Illinois, Roosevelt repeated his offer of a judgeship as an inducement for Horner to retire from the gubernatorial race. It was clear that he would not receive administration support for his renomination; the president would remain "neutral." But Horner had decided to fight the Kelly-Nash machine, and he refused the president's overtures.[23]

On January 3, 1936, the Cook County Democratic organization announced its decision to run Dr. Herman Bundesen, Chicago health commissioner, for governor instead of Horner. The choice of the little-known Bundesen came as a shock, especially to downstate Democrats, whom Kelly had led to believe that Bruce Campbell of Belleville would be the party's choice. On January 12 the state Democratic Central Committee met at the Morrison Hotel in a hotly contested session to rule on the Cook County nomination. After a long and bitter debate, a visibly disappointed Campbell withdrew his candidacy in favor of Bundesen. As a balm to ruffled downstaters, Kelly acquiesced to the selection of John Stelle as the party's candidate for lieutenant governor.[24] Commenting on the events at the Morrison, Horner accurately observed: "The slate named at Chicago was not the nomination of the democratic party, but the personal choice of one man: Mayor Edward J. Kelly. It appears to me that the meeting was a pantomime performance in which the so-called leaders were made to reflect Mayor Kelly's desires. I am being opposed in the primary solely because one man doesn't like me."[25]

The governor wasted little time in using the powers of his office to strike back at the Kelly-Nash machine. He began by swinging his political axe, removing numerous Kelly-Nash state employees from the payroll. He also used the recurring relief crisis in Illinois to his own advantage by demanding that Chicago be forced to provide more money for relief costs. Despite the fact that the state had unappropriated money that could have been used to help defray the welfare costs in municipalities, the governor called for increased responsibility in urban areas. In a move obviously directed at Chicago, which Horner charged had never paid its share for relief, a levy of $0.30 per $100.00 of assessed property valuation was mandated for cities that wished to qualify for state aid. With the passage of this "soak Chicago" tax, Kelly's city became the first in the state to be singled out to contribute more to the care of its own indigent. Kelly initially refused to adopt the new tax and allowed relief stations to close; but when Horner remained adamant, the mayor capitulated and levied the tax.[26]

Meanwhile, the Chicago Democrats geared up the campaign machinery for their gubernatorial candidate. Bundesen, a native German, had occupied the health commissioner's office since 1931 and had established a reputation as an able, if eccentric, administrator. Under his tutelage the city listed as its accomplishments the reduction of infant mortality, improvement of milk sanitation, and the curtailment of diphtheria and smallpox. He gained national renown for his books on infant care, and using city birth records, he distributed complimentary copies to all the city's new mothers. This action meant high visibility, which, along with his strong following in the German community, undoubtedly figured in his selection as Horner's opponent.[27]

"Herman the Healer," the self-professed "Savior of Babies, Friend of Mothers, Builder of Health," also possessed a reputation for outlandish behavior. He fired, or threatened to fire, Health Commission employees who failed to attend church services. A fitness fanatic, the monocled Bundesen frequently beat on his abdomen to demonstrate the firmness of his stomach. He placed glasses of milk in front of each director at the Department of Health meetings and answered critics of chlorinated water by downing daily a glass that had been treated with one hundred times the normal dosage. In later years he became enamored of venereal disease control and boasted that Chicago was the safest city in the world in which to have sexual intercourse. All of this made good copy but led many to question his suitability as candidate for the state's highest office.[28] Kelly defended the choice of Bundesen by pointing to his ethnic appeal, his high recognition factor—he had become a household name in Chicago, thanks to his books—and his effective speaking style.[29]

Despite the presence of the flamboyant Bundesen, the Democratic primary became a contest between Kelly and Horner. The governor quickly established "Boss" Kelly, not his "pawn," Bundesen, as the force behind the machine's effort to control the politics of the state. Accordingly, Horner made the struggle against bossism the theme of his campaign. He called Kelly "the latest feeble imitation of Napoleon" and, on a statewide radio broadcast, defined the major issue of the contest as "the Democratic voters of the state against Boss Kelly. . . . My biggest mistake was when I made Kelly mayor of Chicago. I will tear off his mask and with the people's help I will purge Illinois of bossism and sinister influence."[30]

The issue of bossism became a gold mine for Horner when he championed a reform bill for voter registration that Kelly opposed. The Schnackenberg-Hubbard-Brands or so-called honest elections bill provided for two permanent registration cards that would be signed by each voter, the master card filed with the election board and the duplicate kept at the polling place. On election day each voter would sign his name at the polls, and signatures would be compared before the ballot could be cast. The bill, geared to halt such election-fraud techniques as chain voting and repeat voting, applied only to Chicago and other large municipalities having boards of election commissioners.[31]

Kelly and Nash led the opposition to the bill. Knowing that small counties could not afford election commissions and the operation of a complex system of registration, Nash argued for a permanent registration bill universally applied throughout the state: "I maintain that if permanent registration is good for Chicago, it is good for all of the state." Kelly contended that such an intricate voting procedure would confuse many legitimate voters and would result in the loss of some two hundred thousand votes for Roosevelt in the November election. Most observers correctly saw the contest as Horner's effort to dismantle the Chicago Democratic organization's election machinery. And while it failed—the bill passed the House but lost in the Senate, where the Chicagoans held the balance of power—the affair undoubtedly reinforced Horner's charges that Boss Kelly opposed genuine election reform.[32]

Horner received support from Chicago's afternoon newspapers, the *Daily News* and *American,* and from much of the Chicago citizenry because of Kelly's "clock tinkering" scheme. At the mayor's urging, the city council placed Chicago on permanent Eastern Standard Time, while the rest of the state remained on Central Standard Time. This time change deprived the afternoon dailies of the late market reports from the New York Stock Exchange at the height of a newspaper war and obviously worked to the advantage of the morning *Tribune,* owned by Kelly's old friend Colonel McCormick. It also proved very unpopular with Chicago parents, who resented having to send their children to school in the dark. Horner skillfully portrayed this episode as another example of Boss Kelly's influence-peddling, public-be-damned politics.[33]

Pat Nash and other Democratic sachems warned the mayor not to take a leading role in the campaign but to let Bundesen take Horner on by himself. But Kelly, who had originated the dump-Horner move, determined to meet the charges of bossism head on.[34] In a campaign speech before five hundred party loyalists, he chronicled the governor's shortcomings:

> Horner is a fine man, but as governor he has failed miserably. . . . He sponsored the sales tax, which hits the little fellow. He vetoed the Chicago handbook licensing bill in an effort to make himself look like a high churchman and all the rest of us look like porch-climbers . . . it seemed all wrong to the governor to pass a law enabling Chicago to save two million dollars a year for its people by licensing handbooks.[35]

He further charged that enemies of President Roosevelt were backing Horner in order to weaken the state Democratic organization and elect a Republican governor. These conspirators had, Kelly detailed, pledged $5 million to the campaign to destroy Roosevelt by tricking Democrats into nominating in primaries candidates who would bring no strength to the national ticket. And Horner had agreed to go along in order to get reelected. This allegation, which Kelly never substantiated, was at least partially designed to reassure the Roosevelt administration that the Chicago machine remained the most loyal and trustworthy Democratic body in Illinois.[36]

The Roosevelt administration maintained throughout the primary campaign a "neutrality" beneficial to the Kelly-Nash forces. Roosevelt was concerned by an early report that Kelly would purge State's Attorney Tom Courtney and municipal judge James Sonsteby as well as Horner and urged Jim Farley to "talk with Ed Kelly about this but don't bring me into it." Kelly's agreement to support Courtney and Sonsteby mollified the president, who thereafter turned a deaf ear to the Kelly-Nash critics. Harold Ickes complained that Farley, won over by the Kelly organization's generous contributions toward paying off the debts of the Democratic National Committee, "has every faith in Kelly and is going along with him to the limit." Both Roosevelt and Farley were also blinded by the size of the vote they thought Kelly could deliver in the fall election. As a result, they did nothing to disavow local campaign materials linking Bundesen with Roosevelt and looked the other way as Kelly-Nash forces used New Deal agencies to further their cause.[37]

The Bundesen-Kelly forces utilized the WPA, the federal works agency created to replace the CWA in 1935, to cultivate more support for the regular Democratic ticket. While Harry Hopkins, the chief administrator of the WPA, had gone to great lengths to keep politics out of the CWA, he did not sustain that effort during the spring of 1936. WPA files overflowed with complaints from around the state that enumerated instances of politicking by Bundesen partisans on work sites, and one WPA director blatantly campaigned for Bundesen with federal money during work hours. A group of WPA supervisors told Hopkins that WPA employees were being "advised" to contribute funds to the Bundesen campaign. Lorena Hickok, Hopkins's chief troubleshooter, confirmed that members of the agency's administrative staff were under great pressure from Chicago to work for Kelly's candidate. But despite the overwhelming accumulation of evidence, Hopkins did nothing to curb the flagrant abuses.[38]

While Horner did not have access to federal patronage, he could, and did, use the governor's office to great advantage in the primary war. The *Tribune* reported that F. Lyndon Smith, Horner's campaign manager and an employee of the state highway department, admitted soliciting donations from contractors doing state road building. The Civil Service Protective Association filed a suit against several Illinois department heads who had raised $200,000 for Horner by coercing other employees to make contributions and discharging those who refused to give 2 percent of their salaries.[39]

Horner applied personal pressure also, as evidenced in the case of Judge Harry Fisher. He told Fisher, a Chicago Jew of considerable influence, that if he did not submit a letter of endorsement for Horner, his son David would be fired as an attorney in the Cook County Public Administrator's Office. Fisher wrote Horner that he had already pleaded the governor's case to Kelly but could do little else without committing political suicide. Horner refused to alter his demands, and David Fisher ultimately resigned to save his father's position. The governor's conduct showed that he could play power politics just as aggressively as the Kelly-Nash legions. The historian James T. Patterson accurately captured the essence of the bitter primary struggle by saying, "The dispute, which some described as a battle between a corrupt urban machine and a more progressively inclined governor, was really a power contest between two opponents, each of whom pined for recognition from Washington."[40]

In the end, Horner's hard-nosed politics paid off, and Kelly's gamble failed. Horner beat Bundesen in the April 14 primary by 161,092 votes. The incumbent carried downstate by a huge margin as expected, but his good showing in Chicago provided the impetus for victory. In the Kelly-Nash stronghold he lost by only 162,039 votes, amassed more than 300,000 votes, and actually carried eight wards. The vanquished leaders of Chicago Democracy had little to say in the wake of the startling upset. Kelly, seemingly unshaken, said: "Oh well, we wouldn't have had him anyway. This was the chance we had to take and we really didn't have anything to lose." The laconic Nash told Bundesen: "Well, Doc, it looks like your brigade of loyal mommies has deserted."[41]

While they publicly disavowed any incidence of panic, the Kelly-Nash insiders ardently sought the reasons for this dramatic setback. Actually, several factors contributed to the insurgent's good showing in Chicago. One was the ability of the Horner forces to keep vote stealing to a minimum. The machine spent $600,000 on election day to ensure a good turnout and employed the usual array of tricks to pad the final tally. (For example, when pro-Bundesen canvassers found voters who intended to vote for Horner, they told them to write "Please Do Not Destroy" on the bottom of their ballots; the extraneous writing would invalidate them.) To keep the machine from voting "butterflies, fence rails and ghosts," Horner enlisted the aid of county judge Edmund K. Jarecki, whose job it was to administer elections in Cook County. Jarecki, like Horner, was an independent Democrat who bridled at taking orders from the machine, and his diligence in patrolling the polls and actively seeking out fraudulent votes undoubtedly kept to a minimum the number of "extra" votes Bundesen received.[42]

Another factor in Horner's success was the defection of several leading Chicago Democrats from the Kelly-Nash fold. In addition to the maverick Jarecki, some hitherto loyal party men either failed to campaign for Bundesen or came out for Horner. Federal district attorney Mike Igoe, U.S. senator J. Hamilton Lewis, and State's Attorney Tom Courtney all maintained an imprudent silence during the primary contest. Those in outright rebellion included municipal court bailiff Al Horan, 6th Ward leader James Whalen, and 29th Ward boss Martin J. O'Brien, Irishmen all. And, more important, countless other Democrats listlessly went through the motions for Bundesen, an uninspiring and often laughable candidate. Many Democrats who had no reason to oppose Horner and did so only because of the pressure applied by the machine leadership attributed the fiasco to "Kelly getting a big head." In short, while a united Chicago Democratic party would probably have squelched the Horner insurrection, no such unified opposition materialized.[43]

Surprisingly, Horner failed to monopolize the Jewish vote. Three of the eight wards he carried were peopled substantially by prosperous German Jews. But other Jews of more modest economic status remained loyal to the political machine, which continued to provide jobs and services for the less well-to-do. Kelly made a concerted effort to appeal for Jewish votes during the campaign, de-emphasizing the religious question. He said:

> When Horner was nominated in 1932 all the Irish in town got on the firing line and battled side by side with the Jews to elect him. Now we're fighting Horner, not because he's a Jew, but because he is fighting the organization. We expect the Jews to fight for us now. I admire the man who declares his religion. Why I would kiss the Cardinal's ring at State and Madison Streets in broad daylight. But no Irishman is going to tell me to vote for an Irish candidate just because he's Irish. He can't use me that way.[44]

Jacob Arvey, alderman of the city's largest Jewish ward, the 24th, withstood great pressure from Horner and many community religious leaders and remained faithful to the Bundesen candidacy. Organization loyalty, not friendship or religious ties, he told the governor, were critical for the party. The 24th Ward went ten-to-one in favor of Bundesen.[45]

To a great degree, Horner's victory constituted a personal triumph, for no one else on the unofficial "Horner slate" defeated a regular party candidate. The primary results could be viewed no less as an affirmation of the incumbent governor than as a repudiation of the machine. The Kelly-Nash forces still controlled Chicago, if not as totally as before, and certainly no one made the mistake of sounding the death knell for the Chicago Democratic organization. The primary results underscored the fact that although the Kelly-Nash machine held the balance of power in the state, its might fell short of total dominance. As the winner, Horner would have to be granted his independence and the spoils of victory; certainly he had established himself as the Chicago boss's peer, if not his superior. Thus the possibility of a reconciliation between Horner and Kelly depended upon the latter's willingness to adapt to an altered political balance of power and to share the top spot, at least partially, with his former foe. The continued turmoil demonstrated Kelly's denial of the need for such concessions.[46]

Immediately after the primary Pat Nash moved to shore up relations with Horner. On April 26 the Cook County Democratic Convention met and reelected Nash county chairman. He told reporters that the Cook County Democrats would go all out for the governor in the fall election. Kelly, still out of town since the primary two weeks before, would not jump on the bandwagon so rapidly. When he returned from his vacation, the mayor struck back at those dissidents in the local organization who had supported Horner. Disregarding Nash's pleas for fence mending, Kelly transferred the lucrative city bonding business from the firms of Al Horan and Martin J. O'Brien to one represented by loyal machine members. Scoffing at newspaper reports that Kelly had buried the hatchet, Horner replied: "Kelly would love to bury the hatchet, right in this bald pate of mine."[47]

At the Democratic State Convention in Springfield, the Cook County contingent greeted the governor's appearance with a prolonged chorus of boos and catcalls. When Kelly entered later, bedlam broke loose, launching a ten-minute-long demonstration of piety. One zealot fired a revolver. Another Kelly partisan, an appellate court clerk, scrambled over the typewriters in the press section to reach the stage, where he waved his arms to lead the cheering. When Kelly and Nash stood up and shook hands on the dais, the din was deafening. The perfunctory business that followed, including the endorsement of the party slate, seemed anticlimactic.[48]

For his part, Horner did not sit idly by. He called the legislature into a special session and successfully forced the passage of a permanent registration bill. Then he vetoed a bill sponsored by Adamowski to use half instead of one-third of the state sales taxes for relief. This action would again force Chicago to spend more of its own money, an estimated $1.4 million more per month, for relief appropriations. Kelly responded by charging the governor with playing politics with the relief of unfortunate citizens and by reaffirming his conviction that the state was responsible for relief.[49]

At the Democratic National Convention in Philadelphia, the Horner legions stayed at the Bellevue-Stratford Hotel, the Kelly-Nash loyalists at the Benjamin Franklin Hotel. The two groups sat separately on the convention floor, and messages had to be carried between their leaders. As a compromise, the delegation chose Nash as national committeeman and Horner as state chairman. While reporters observed Nash and Horner talking occasionally during party caucuses, Kelly and Horner did not speak at all during the entire convention—or even nod. Any reports of harmony had clearly been exploded, and this churlish behavior alarmed members of the Roosevelt campaign staff, who feared the inability of a divided Democratic party in Illinois to deliver in November.[50]

In his communications with Democratic chief Farley, Kelly blamed Horner for the sustained hard feelings in Illinois. "It is difficult to understand just why any Democratic candidate would act so independently," he wrote Farley in June. "We are honestly striving to promote genuine harmony, but his actions in every way and the suspicious attitude he displays at times hamper our efforts seriously." Kelly told Roosevelt that Horner insisted on running as a downstate candidate; Mike Igoe countered that Horner had to do so because of the treatment afforded him by the Cook County Democrats. When the carping and backbiting continued, Roosevelt instructed Farley to force a rapprochement between the combatants. On August 26 Farley called an impromptu press conference for the purpose of announcing peace on the Illinois political scene. He introduced Kelly and Horner, who stood at opposite ends of the room and later reluctantly shook hands for photographers. In their remarks to reporters, neither referred to the other, though both pledged unity in working for the reelection of the president.[51]

While it is doubtful that such a lukewarm reconciliation totally satisfied Roosevelt, he nonetheless felt confident that the political situation in Illinois had been improved. All reports indicated that his prospects for doing well in Chicago, the key to offsetting Alf Landon's support in Republican downstate Illinois, were quite good. Kelly assured the president in September that the Cook County organization would carry Chicago handily for Roosevelt. Lorena Hickok wrote Harry Hopkins that "everybody, including the Republicans when they are not talking for publication, concedes that the Kelly organization will put Chicago over for the President in a great big way." And Kelly predicted to Farley that, despite the negative effects of Horner's miserly relief policy and politically disastrous voter registration law, Cook County would stake Roosevelt to at least a two hundred thousand-vote lead in the Illinois contest.[52]

In fact, Kelly's prediction proved modest. Roosevelt carried Chicago by an overwhelming 555,689, winning 65.1 percent of the vote. In the state as a whole, the president won by 714,606 votes, with a 57.7 percent plurality. Horner did not fare as well, running 152,539 votes behind Roosevelt in Chicago. While some vote "trimming" had occurred in the machine wards, Horner still did achieve a 319,690 plurality in Chicago. The machine may not have put forth the effort for Horner that it had for Roosevelt, but it did work hard enough on behalf of the Democratic ticket for the governor to receive some residual benefit.[53] On election night Kelly left the Morrison Hotel victory party before Horner arrived; the lingering bitterness precluded their joint celebration of the Democratic triumph. For while the Roosevelt landslide in Chicago vindicated the Kelly-Nash machine in part, the decision to dump Horner and the failure to do so had proved a major disaster. Kelly would now have to deal with four more years of a governor bound to be even more independent and assertive. The year 1936 had been one of turmoil, and for that Kelly had his own hubris to thank. The next year would be tumultuous because of events generated elsewhere.

In the middle thirties, as organized labor assumed a more active role in Chicago, clashes between trade unionists and police became commonplace. Chicago's policemen broke up picket lines, drove sit-down strikers from plants they had occupied, and inflicted severe punishment on those who resisted. Chicago achieved a reputation as a tough anti-union town, and Kelly defended the police policy of taking a hard line against strikers. "The people of Chicago want law and order," he said, "and insist that the laws be obeyed by everyone, regardless of who he is." By early 1937 the conflict had intensified; in February workers at the Fansteel Metallurgical Corporation conducted a sit-down strike abetted by fellow workers, who brought food and medicine from the outside. The police brutally suppressed the strike by using "siege towers" to storm the plant. This was a fateful harbinger of the inevitable strike in Chicago's steel industry, long a target of Congress of Industrial Organizations (CIO) unionizers.[54]

Notified of an impending strike at the South Chicago Republic Steel plant, corporation counsel Barnet Hodes notified Police Commissioner James Allman on March 31 of his office's opinion that peaceful picketing should be allowed as a lawful enterprise under Illinois statutes. On May 27, newspapers carried a statement from Kelly affirming the right of picketers to assemble and march peacefully. Subsequently, the Steel Workers' Organizing Committee and the Amalgamated Association of Iron, Steel and Tin Workers of North America called for a strike at the Republic Steel mill along Burley Avenue between 116th and 118th streets. The police established headquarters inside the mill entrance gate and prepared for confrontation. On Friday, May 28, the police intercepted marching strikers near the plant, and a brief skirmish ensued. Neither side reported heavy casualties, but the battle lines had been drawn.[55]

On Sunday, Memorial Day, between 1,000 and 2,500 protesters, including women and children, gathered a few blocks from the plant to criticize police refusal to allow picketing. After the meeting, the protesters, led by two men carrying American flags, headed for the mill; 26 policemen met them two blocks north of the main entrance and blocked their advance. Accounts of what happened next

Chicago police pursue fleeing strikers, beating them with clubs and guns, during the Memorial Day massacre. (Wide World Photos.)

differed, but a general outline can be sketched: Picketers threw rocks and clubs, while police opened fire with revolvers and lobbed tear gas into the crowd. As the picketers broke ranks and fled, the police followed, firing their guns and beating the fallen with billy clubs. When the smoke cleared, ten marchers had been killed and thirty wounded by gunfire. Sixty suffered injuries from beatings and clubbings. Thirty-five policemen reported injuries, none from gunfire; three required hospitalization, but none died.[56]

Vacationing at his home in Eagle River, Wisconsin, at the time of the incident, Kelly announced that he backed the actions of the police totally. He said: "From what I know of the situation, I feel sure that the riot was caused by outside mobs who came into Chicago for the purpose of making trouble. We can settle our own troubles if we are let alone." The Republic Steel Corporation hired a public relations firm, Hill and Knowlton, to present its side of the incident. It charged that the strike, Communist-led, had as its goal the seizure of the mill and that the strikers were armed with guns. Having been fired on first, it alleged, the police shot back in self-defense. A Cook County coroner's jury exonerated the police, ruling justifiable homicide. The *Tribune* concurred and praised the swift work of the authorities: "Owing to the strong hand the police exercised during the wave of sitdown strikers, Chicago escaped the disorder and bloodshed that other large cities experienced. A tight rein was kept on the strikers and the disputes were settled in comparatively short order."[57]

But not everyone accepted the verdict so completely. On

June 8 approximately forty-five hundred citizens attended a meeting at the Civic Opera House to question the "whitewash." From this gathering came the Citizens' Joint Commission of Inquiry to Investigate the Facts of Memorial Day, contributors to which included such notable Chicagoans as Paul H. Douglas; Professor Earl Dean Howard of Northwestern University, former deputy administrator of the National Recovery Administration; Professor Malcolm P. Sharp of the University of Chicago; and Arthur Goldberg, who submitted a brief on the legal questions involved. The committee report, issued in September, disputed the city's account and held the police culpable for the violence that erupted on Memorial Day.[58]

A subcommittee of the U.S. Senate Committee on Education and Labor, chaired by Senator Robert M. LaFollette, Jr., of Wisconsin, corroborated these conclusions, finding that "the force employed by the police was far in excess of that which the occasion required." Basing its conclusions on interviews with eyewitnesses, still photos, the trajectories of bullets lodged in the bodies of the slain strikers, and newsfilm provided by a Paramount Newsreel cameraman, the subcommittee further concluded that "the entire effort of the police was directed not toward an impartial investigation of the event but to an attempt to build up a case against the marchers." It also turned its guns on city hall: "The action of the responsible authorities in setting the seal of their approval upon the conduct of the police not only fails to place responsibility where responsibility properly belongs but will invite the repetition of similar incidents in the future."[59]

Kelly's reaction to the incident suggested, however, that he sought to avoid any such repetition. Although he refused to discipline the police as the citizens' committee demanded, his actions indicated a desire to patch up relations with organized labor. In a move widely interpreted as a peace offering, he intervened successfully in a dispute between the Packinghouse Workers Organizing Committee and the Union Stockyards and Transit Company to engineer a settlement beneficial to the workers. Moreover, the leaders of the Democratic organization so feared retaliation by working-class voters that they met with CIO officials to discuss ways of improving their rapport. Conscious of the CIO's successful South Side organizing effort for the Democrats in 1936, and fearful that that influence might be used against them in the 1939 mayoral primary, Kelly offered the CIO future exemption from police interference in return for official forgiveness of Kelly's role in the Memorial Day affair. The CIO complied by working for the machine in the 1938 elections and the 1939 mayoral primary. Amazingly, a steelworker whose eye had been shot out in the Memorial Day battle gave Kelly a radio endorsement during the 1939 campaign.[60]

In subsequent years Kelly enjoyed much better relations with organized labor. At his behest, Chicago police assumed a more circumspect stance during labor-management confrontations. Shortly after his reelection, Kelly used his influence in the state Senate to help defeat the Lantz bill, a measure forbidding mass picketing, secondary boycotts, and sit-down strikes. In May 1940 Phillip Murray underscored the mayor's resurgent reputation by naming him to address the Steel Workers' Organizing Committee conference to aid Roosevelt's reelection campaign. In 1944 the Communist *Daily Worker* even praised the mayor for his solicitude toward organized labor, singling out his stand against Montgomery Ward president Sewell Avery in the latter's dispute with the War Labor Board. In short, while the Memorial Day incident was at first thought disastrous for the Kelly-Nash machine, the long-range effect was to strengthen the uneasy ties between the city's Democratic organization and its awakening labor movement.[61]

As 1938, another election year, approached, Kelly prepared to launch another salvo against his foes within the party. Rumors abounded that Horner would run his own slate of candidates in that year's elections and that state's attorney Courtney would ally himself with the governor. The impending clash heated up in December 1937, when Kelly proposed to license handbooks in Chicago, a scant two years after this same proposal had been vetoed by Horner. In order to circumvent the state law prohibiting off-track betting, the new bill referred to bookies as "betting brokers" and provided that all money taken from patrons had to be transported to the tracks for wagering. On December 23 the city council approved the bill by a vote of 43 to 4, and Kelly signed the ordinance on Christmas Eve. Horner exploded: "The Chicago Council has no authority to take such action. The ordinance means nothing. It is anarchy. It is nullity." Hours after state attorney general Otto Kerner filed suit against the city in circuit court and corporation counsel Hodes apprised Kelly of the likelihood of defeat, the mayor announced the withdrawal of the bill.[62]

The battle between city hall and the governor's mansion raged on another front as well: The continuing struggle over the payment of relief flared anew with the coming of the "Roosevelt recession" in late 1937. Welfare applications in Chicago tripled in the autumn months of that year, while the WPA steadily reduced its allotments. The two hundred thousand people on relief in the city received 15 percent less than the amount authorities set as an absolute minimum. By May 1938 some ninety-one thousand persons received no relief payments whatsoever, despite the fact that, according to Howard Hunter, Illinois was "in very good financial condition." Horner simply refused to bail out Chicago, and even when the state legislature provided more funds for relief, he insisted that a specific limit be placed on appropriations designated for Cook County. The crisis in Chicago remained critical into 1939—although it was alleviated somewhat by a resumption of WPA spending—and Kelly bristled at Horner's penuriousness. In retaliation, the mayor turned his guns on a new target in the Horner camp.[63]

The Kelly-Nash forces resolved to oust county judge Jarecki from office. His record of independence during the previous sixteen years in that office and his strict enforcement of election laws in the 1936 primary, which had favored the Horner candidacy, marked him as a threat to the machine. Kelly offered Jarecki a circuit judgeship as an inducement not to seek reelection, but the obstinate jurist refused. On February 1 the Cook County Democratic Central Committee announced its slate of candidates, and the list excluded Jarecki. Kelly approached Benjamin Adamowski about replacing Jarecki on the ticket; when he declined, the mayor authorized a city council subcommittee of Adermen Frank Konkowski (26th), John Szumnarski (35th), and James Bowler (25th) to request Polish organizations to agree on a replacement candidate. On February 5 the Polish American Democratic Organization ratified the machine's decision to dump Jarecki, and circuit court judge John Prystalski was chosen to replace him. To no one's surprise, Horner and Courtney quickly endorsed Jarecki.[64]

The other major office to be filled that year was the U.S. Senate seat previously held by William H. Dieterich. In January Kelly and Nash told President Roosevelt that they had selected Mike Igoe to replace Dieterich. Horner adduced that one of the senators must be from downstate, and since Senator J. Hamilton Lewis hailed from Chicago, Igoe would be unacceptable. The governor chose Scott W. Lucas of Havana as his candidate. But while the battle over the senatorship involved prestige and some federal patronage, the competing factions saw the Jarecki-Prystalski contest for the county judgeship as the spearhead of the campaign.[65]

The Kelly-Nash partisans charged that Jarecki bore the responsibility for the 1932 tax muddle, as a result of which one-third of Chicago real estate taxpayers still owed 10 percent of that year's tax bill. They argued that he cost the regular Democratic organization 100,000 votes by his ruling that Republicans could vote in the Horner-Bundesen primary with freedom to return to the Republican column in the next election. And they claimed that he had been excessively severe in his punishment of minor violators of election laws who offended chiefly through ignorance. Jarecki campaigned as a courageous independent who opposed the crass bossism of Kelly and his cronies. Predictably, he basked in his association with such reform-minded politicians as Horner and Courtney.[66]

As in 1936, Horner was again ready to mix it up with his Chicago enemies. In 1938 the Horner forces prepared to battle the machine with its own tactics: For a month before the April primary, 450 additional men were employed by the state in Cook County at a cost to the taxpayers of $23,268. Many of them performed no work at all but spent their time toiling for the Horner-Jarecki-Lucas ticket; their work cards were signed by the campaign manager for the Horner slate in northern Illinois. At the same time, several state employees complained that they were being required to donate thirty-six dollars annually to the Horner organization.[67]

On the eve of the election, Jarecki warned that "the Kelly-Nash machine is attempting the greatest vote steal ever conceived in the history of Cook County." To counteract this expected perfidy, he announced that, in addition to the thousand policemen assigned to county polling places, he had hired six thousand college students (many of them "husky athletes") to forestall any electoral depredations. State's attorney Courtney contributed 155 more "watchdogs" (35 state highway patrolmen, 100 retired Chicago policemen, and 20 off-duty suburban policemen), to the patrol of notorious trouble areas.[68]

These precautions paid off: Jarecki defeated Prystalski to retain his office. The key to his victory was the support of the Polish electorate. While Polonia's voters had remained loyal to the regular Democratic organization two years earlier, they broke ranks in large numbers in 1938. All three Polish-language dailies endorsed Jarecki, and two-thirds of the voters cast their ballots for the incumbent.[69] Another important factor was the substantial cross-over vote by Republicans; GOP leaders, citing Jarecki's incorruptibility and fearing that Kelly would gain control of the county voting machinery, urged their charges to vote in the Democratic primary. When billboards went up all over town warning Chicago Republicans that cross-over votes would cost them the right to vote in the next Republican primary, Jarecki took out a full-page ad in the newspapers affirming the right of all citizens to vote in either primary.[70]

For the second time in two years, Kelly had mustered the resources of the Chicago Democratic organization to vanquish his political rivals—and failed. Not only had he been unable to remove Jarecki from the county judgeship, but Horner's candidate had defeated his own in the senatorial primary. Again the list of defectors included a large number of the Irish, including Martin O'Brien and Al Horan of the 29th Ward, John Egan of the 13th Ward, city clerk Peter J. Brady, and municipal court judge Charles Dougherty. At the request of Nash and U.S. attorney general Homer S. Cummings, however, Kelly pledged to support the entire Democratic ticket actively in November—including Scott Lucas. He promised Horner that Chicago precinct captains would not engage in "trimming" of Lucas votes, and election returns in Cook County substantiated his claim. Lucas lost the downstate area and suburban Cook County, but his margin of victory in Chicago enabled him to win the election. So, while another of Kelly's ill-conceived power plays had backfired, he had been able to salvage something. If political conditions in Illinois seemed as uneasy as ever, Kelly's stock in Washington had risen again with the realization that the Chicago Democrats' strong showing had saved Illinois from disaster in a largely unsuccessful election year. Roosevelt partisans felt that they needed Kelly's support in order to hold Illinois in 1940.[71]

But before the national election of 1940 came the Chicago mayoral contest of 1939. In the four years since his last election, Kelly had attempted to establish his already-considerable power within the state Democratic party as total. The result had been just the opposite: Dissidents found common cause and came together in opposition to his dictatorial rule. By 1939 the regular Democratic organization faced challenges not only from its traditional foes, the Republicans and the reform-minded independents, but from the Horner-Courtney-Jarecki Democrats as well. Clearly, 1939 would not be a repeat of the utterly one-sided contest of 1935.

In Tom Courtney the dissident Democrats readily found their man to oppose Kelly in the mayoral primary. Kelly and Courtney had been friends for many years, frequently attending prizefights, horse races, and political fund-raisers together; and Courtney had supported Kelly for mayor in 1933. But over the years the ambitious state's attorney drifted away from the Kelly-Nash inner circle. Like Horner, Courtney exhibited a strong desire for independence and bridled at taking orders from the Morrison. In 1935 an attempt on Courtney's life, generally assumed to be ordered by the underworld in retaliation for one of the state's attorney's infrequent crackdowns on gambling, elicited a desultory response from the mayor. Kelly's indifference—he even hinted that it might have been a fake attack staged to arouse sympathy—irritated the indignant Courtney. Although he did not actively campaign for the Horner ticket in 1936, his refusal to endorse Bundesen convinced Kelly and Nash that he was no longer one of the boys. In 1938 rumors abounded that Courtney would be dumped by the machine, and although Kelly and Nash took no steps to blackball Courtney, he took the initiative and made the break, supporting Jarecki and Lucas. Their victories launched Courtney into his drive to unseat Kelly in the February 1939 primary.[72]

While Courtney went to great lengths to portray himself as a crime-busting reformer, many Chicagoans regarded "Fighting

Tom" as a machine politician whose break with the organization had more to do with opportunism than with moralistic fervor. Before becoming state's attorney, Courtney had violated Illinois law by simultaneously holding four public jobs. (As a state senator, he was prohibited from occupying other state or municipal positions.)[73] As the county's top law enforcement official, Courtney protected certain interests at the expense of the general populace: He prosecuted no tax or receivership cases, ignored election fraud, and largely overlooked gambling and prostitution, except for occasional forays around election time. He also achieved a reputation for union busting that earned him the concerted opposition of the Labor's Nonpartisan League and the Chicago Federation of Labor. In short, the candidacy of Tom Courtney left few Chicago progressives excited about the alternative to Boss Kelly.[74]

As a result, several leading Chicagoans approached Secretary of the Interior Harold Ickes to suggest that he return to run for mayor as an independent Democrat. John Fewkes, president of the Chicago Teachers Union, led a delegation to Washington to woo him. Professor Charles E. Merriam told Ickes of his support in the CIO, and Professor Paul H. Douglas repeatedly harangued him about his obligation to the people of Chicago. Ickes, anxious to oust Kelly but reluctant to resign his cabinet post for such a risky venture, urged Roosevelt to prevail upon Kelly to step down in favor of a candidate more philosophically attuned to the New Deal. In a meeting with Fewkes, Kelly dismissed alternative candidates Adamowski and Judge John Gutknecht as unelectable and affirmed his commitment to "liberalism" and "concern for the under-privileged." When Roosevelt refused to become further involved, Ickes declined to enter the mayoral race, choosing to help the New Deal "by staying in harness where I am." He urged defeat of the machine but stopped short of endorsing Courtney. With Ickes's decision, the Democratic primary reverted to a two-man race.[75]

Courtney resolved to make use of his office in his campaign against the incumbent mayor; by making Kelly's acceptance of gambling and obeisance to organized crime the major issues of his campaign, Courtney could offer as a contrast his vigorous anti-vice operations. Beginning in August 1938 he dispatched his police to smash syndicate-owned gambling joints throughout the city. Under the leadership of Courtney's top aide, Captain Daniel Gilbert, the police descended upon several handbooks daily; armed with axes, they reduced the premises to kindling and arrested the attendants and patrons. When the courts turned them loose, pointing out the absence of warrants, the police moved on relentlessly to the next target. Some places were raided as often as ten times in two weeks. In all, Courtney's police conducted over six hundred raids and made over twelve thousand arrests, yet no convictions resulted. The crusading Courtney vowed to continue his solitary war on crime. He intoned: "The mayor is part and parcel of the Syndicate which controls gambling. No syndicate could operate here under the eyes of the mayor if he wanted it stopped. . . . The fact that Kelly permits a hoodlum syndicate to control gambling in itself establishes that he is part and parcel of it. The fix is in at the top."[76]

Courtney counted on assistance from a number of Chicago Democrats dissatisfied with Kelly's leadership. The increasingly unwieldy Irish bolted in greater numbers than ever before; joining the 1938 rebels (O'Brien, Horan, Egan, Brady, and Dougherty) was powerful 27th Ward boss John Touhy. Leading Polish politicians Adamowski and Jarecki quickly fell into line behind Courtney as well, but all of the Polish ward committeemen, the PADO, and the Polish-language press backed Kelly. The mayor further strengthened his hand by choosing a Pole, Thomas Gordon, to run for city treasurer and by convincing the Polish ambassador to the United States to award him the Polina Restituta, Poland's highest honor. More disappointing to the Courtney legions than the sustained loyalty of the Poles to the regular Democratic organization, however, was the absence of one crucial endorsement: They did not receive the support of Henry Horner.[77]

Two days before the November 1938 election, Horner fell victim to a cerebral thrombosis. On doctor's orders, he went to Miami for a recuperation period that dragged on for months, well past the date of the mayoral primary in Chicago. In the governor's absence, the Kelly-Nash forces spread the word that Horner had intended neutrality in the contest. One of Horner's key political advisers, Illinois Commerce Commission chairman James M. Slattery, diverted some of the resources of the Horner machine to its Kelly-Nash counterpart. Lieutenant Governor John Stelle, who assumed the role of acting governor in Horner's absence from the state, had long been a Kelly admirer and used the opportunity to help the mayor against Courtney. Stelle signed a bill enabling Chicago voters to switch party affiliations and vote in either mayoral primary on February 28—a move that would enable the many Republicans who voted in the 1938 Democratic primary to cast a GOP ballot in 1939. Courtney lamented: "If anyone put Governor Horner into a sickbed it was Mayor Kelly and Lieutenant Governor Stelle." Later, after he had lost the election, Courtney charged bitterly that "the Jew took a dive under the bed." Kelly acknowledged his debt by sending Horner a telegram thanking him "for the wonderful support from your close friends Slattery et al. which I know came indirectly from you."[78]

Despite a bitter struggle, the Courtney crusade fell short.

Kelly defeated him by a margin of nearly two to one: 604,190 to 317,054. This unexpectedly easy victory relieved some of the anxiety in the Kelly-Nash circle, but a great deal of trepidation remained. The Republican primary had also produced a landslide winner and in a change from 1935, the opposition party gave every indication of putting up a tough fight. Staggered by the recent setbacks and still breathing hard from a fractious primary that left party unity in doubt, the Democrats seemed more vulnerable than at any time since the Cermak victory in 1931. The Republicans, basking in their successes nationwide in the 1938 elections and unified behind an attractive, dynamic candidate, saw this election as a golden opportunity to crack the Democratic stranglehold on Chicago politics.[79]

The man inspiring so much enthusiasm among the Republicans was Dwight H. Green, an able young lawyer and reformer. Green had easily dispatched Big Bill Thompson in the Republican primary, and he quickly forged his strategy for the battle with Kelly. Unlike Courtney, Green came well prepared to challenge the mayor on the issue of corruption in municipal government; as an assistant district attorney, he had helped build the income tax evasion case against Al Capone that resulted in the gangster's imprisonment. When District Attorney George E. Q. Johnson retired, Green succeeded him and remained in that office until the Democratic administration ordered his replacement. In 1939 Green left his private law practice to launch a career in electoral politics by crusading against lawlessness in Chicago and by charging that the Capone gang had returned to power in the good graces of Mayor Kelly.[80]

Responding to newspaper reports that the Kelly-Nash organization spent $2.5 million on the Democratic primary, Green asked why the machine would approve such an expenditure to secure an $18,000-a-year job. The reason, he explained, was that the mayor controlled the purse strings to a billion dollars of taxpayers' money. And what was the source of the $2.5 million? Much of it came from the underworld, he alleged, some from wealthy taxpayers who had had their taxes reduced, some from favored contractors, and part from the huge assessments on city jobholders.[81]

Green also raised the issue of Chicago's delay in collecting 1938 city taxes. The city typically mailed the tax bills in February, and April 1 stood as the traditional deadline for payment. But in this election year, no mention of the tax levies had been made and county clerk Flynn refused to make public the rates for the previous year. The reason, Green averred, was that Kelly did not want known before the April 4 election that taxes had increased by 4.5 percent, a fact later confirmed by the Chicago press. The delay in collecting the taxes would also force taxpayers to pay interest on tax anticipation warrants that could not be returned on time. The mayor was playing politics with the finances of the city and ignoring the well-being of the individual taxpayer.[82]

Kelly, steadfastly maintaining that he ran on the merits of his six years in office, refused to discuss these issues. He pointed to the wealth of federal relief funds his administration had procured, the city's sound financial outlook, and the fact that, under his enlightened leadership, Chicago had "progressed fifty years in the last six." Kelly's claims were summarized in a booklet, *Out of the Red, Into the Black: The Truth about Chicago's Municipal Government,* issued by the Citizens' Committee on Public Information, an ad hoc organization composed of State Street merchants and bankers. The committee lauded the mayor's reduction of the municipal debt and curtailment of expenditures while holding taxes to a minimum. The booklet failed to deal with charges that real estate taxes had reached an all-time high, that the public payroll had increased every year of Kelly's mayoralty, and that the number of city workers was continuing to rise. Kelly ignored the charges, emphasizing the savings to Chicago taxpayers that had resulted from federal largess.[83]

The mayor benefited from the announcement before the election that the federal government had agreed to finance the building of a subway in Chicago. Business leaders of the Loop desired improved mass transportation, and their support could be important for Kelly. The construction of the subway would also provide jobs and stimulate related industries. Kelly originally approached the WPA for funds, but when that agency could not fulfill his request, he turned to the Public Works Administration (PWA). Harold Ickes, head of the PWA, recognized the public relations coup the approval of the subway would be for the Kelly administration and hesitated to approve it for that reason. But when a commission of PWA engineers endorsed the proposal, Ickes reluctantly acquiesced. Roosevelt telegraphed congratulations to Kelly, noting that the subway would represent a "fine achievement for the city of Chicago and for your administration." Once again, Kelly could boast that his connections in Washington had worked for Chicago.[84]

In spite of a vigorous, impassioned campaign, Dwight Green failed to defeat the Kelly-Nash election machinery. Kelly managed to hold the Democratic party together—even Courtney grudgingly supported the entire ticket—and again received considerable aid from the formerly antagonistic Hornerites. Even so, Green managed to make the final outcome extremely respectable; his vote total of 638,068, the highest ever compiled by a Republican, constituted an increase of 470,962 over the total amassed by Emil Wetten four years earlier. Green managed to carry fifteen of the city's fifty wards, principally residential wards on the city's periphery where homeowners were sensitive to spiraling real estate taxes. Map 1 illustrates this pattern. Furthermore, as Map 2 shows, the wards in which Kelly accumulated the largest vote totals were located near the city center, clumped around the 1st Ward. The wards furthest removed from the city core yielded Kelly his narrowest victories.[85]

For the incumbent mayor the margin of victory came from the city's "river wards." He carried Chicago by 185,000 votes while netting a plurality of 186,000 in the sixteen wards located at the core of the inner city, which contained high concentrations of first- and second-generation immigrants, blacks, the unemployed, and unskilled workers. These wards also boasted the highest relief and WPA rolls in the city. And, as Green pointed out, these wards most frequently fell victim to the illegal voting practices perpetrated by the machine operatives.[86]

Although Kelly basically succeeded in keeping the Democratic coalition together, Green's surprisingly strong showing indicates that defections must have occurred. While the Jews turned in a victory margin for Kelly equal to the 1935 standard (a whopping 90 percent in the city's premier Jewish ward, the 24th, for example), the other ethnic groups did not prove as loyal. The Polish vote on the Northwest Side split, undoubtedly as a reflection of the Jarecki-Adamowski insurgencies of recent years. The Democrats also received diminished pluralities from blacks on the South Side and Germans on the North. The Irish, though they supported the party, turned out in smaller numbers than before.[87]

Despite Kelly's many advantages, Green managed to throw a scare into the Democratic leadership. The vanquished Republican commented on his loss: "With all of the regimentation of their payrollers, the most lavish campaign fund in history, and the intimidation, coercion, and regimentation of people in the ranks of the WPA and those on relief, the Democratic Party of this city was able to garner only fifty-six per cent of the votes." Indeed, the talk in national Democratic circles centered around the narrow Democratic victory in Chicago and what the resurgent Republican party might be able to accomplish in 1940.[88]

In the years 1936 to 1939 the fortunes of the Kelly-Nash machine plummeted. Electoral defeats in 1936 and 1938 and a surprisingly narrow victory over a supposedly impotent Republican party in 1939 caused considerable consternation among Democrats. The debilitating illness of Henry Horner, from which he would die in 1940, left Kelly the most powerful of the state's Democrats, but the mayor clearly presided over a weakened party primed for a setback. In fact, Dwight Green would use his surprising showing in the mayoral con-

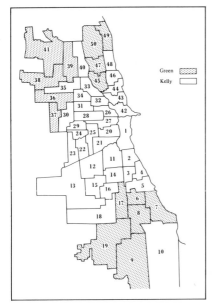

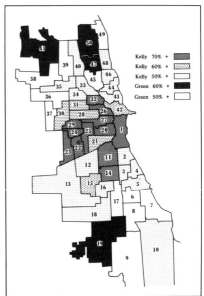

Map 1. Chicago Mayoral Vote—1939   Map 2. Chicago Mayoral Vote—1939

test as a springboard to the statehouse in 1940, besting Kelly's candidate, Harry B. Hershey.[89]

In Chicago the mayor's hold on the machine was equally tenuous. Since Kelly's election in 1935, more and more Democrats, chafing under the mayor's iron rule, had dared to bolt the party ranks to support insurgency movements. Rumors circulated that Kelly and Nash, once close friends as well as co-workers, had drifted apart because of the mayor's heavy-handedness. Even though Kelly maintained control of the machine for the next eight years, it would be a constant battle to suppress the periodic outbursts of rebellion—acts of insurgency that had been encouraged by Kelly's failed attempts at securing party hegemony. As the decade came to a close, the Kelly-Nash organization was at least able to depend upon one constant: the continuing support of the New Deal apparatus, particularly Harry Hopkins's WPA. Weakened though it may have been, the Kelly-Nash machine still held a favorable position in the nation's capital.

4 Kelly, Roosevelt, and the New Deal

 BY THE end of the 1930s, the New Deal's relief and public works programs faced extinction at the hands of a hostile Congress. In the wake of a Senate investigation into the politicization of the WPA in the 1938 primary elections, Congress passed the Hatch Act, which prohibited any political activity by federal employees. When President Roosevelt requested an emergency appropriation for the WPA in January 1939, the legislative branch approved a substantially lower amount and required local sponsors of WPA projects to furnish 25 percent of the funds. Representatives of the U.S. Conference of Mayors, threatened by the apparent emasculation of this vitally important federal works agency, testified before a House Subcommittee on Appropriations, and while the mayors pleaded their case for continued federal assistance, the congressmen interrogated them about inefficiency, graft, loafing, and political maneuvering in the WPA. The congressmen ardently questioned Mayors Fiorello LaGuardia of New York City, Maurice Tobin of Boston, and Harold Burton of Cleveland, but the man attracting the most attention was Chicago's infamous boss, Edward J. Kelly.[1]

"It is not a question of 'How can we afford relief?' It is a question of 'How can we afford not to provide relief?' " Kelly told the subcommittee. "Human want is nonpartisan. Starvation knows no party label. Balancing of the human budget comes first. . . . Chicago is at the wailing wall, like any other city in desiring the continuation of Federal relief assistance." Acutely queried about the use of the WPA for political purposes in Chicago, Kelly repeatedly assured his questioners that the Cook County Democrats had not interfered in any way. Furthermore, he asserted, "at no time was any man put to work on WPA by the Chicago administration in the city of Chicago or any of its connections throughout the county of Cook."[2]

Kelly's remonstrations notwithstanding, the relationship between the Chicago Democratic organization and the New Deal institutions concerned with unemployment relief, particularly the WPA, was extremely political. WPA projects meant vast sums of money, employment opportunities for otherwise jobless citizens, new avenues for patronage, and a stockpile of political capital that could be translated into votes on election day. It could not be said, as many Kelly critics maintained, that the Chicago Democratic machine received carte blanche authority to manipulate the WPA in any manner. The mayor could not, for example, stop layoffs during times of general employment reduction. During the surprisingly close 1939 mayoral race, the WPA reduced its work force in Chicago by twenty-two thousand—a step Kelly would have delayed until after election day if he had possessed the necessary authority. But in return for their faithful support of the Roosevelt administration, the Chicagoans were allowed considerable autonomy in certain areas. The key to understanding the relationship between the Democrats in Chicago and those in Washington lies in identifying the ground rules by which the two operated: The Kelly-Nash boys had to observe certain amenities, and some practices were clearly prohibited, but the machine could avail itself of opportunities in less sensitive areas while the Roosevelt administration practiced a policy of benign neglect.

The question of eligibility for relief or federal public works employment gave pause to those fearful of undue political machine influence; if city hall could determine the identity of those awarded jobs or money, the potential for political coercion would be enormous. From all indications, however, WPA officials insisted that the certification process be free from political influence. While many party workers received WPA jobs, federal officials denied that any consideration other than need had been used to certify employment recipients. When asked about the need for political influence in securing WPA employment, one official said: "I have been in touch with the preparation of bulletins, the formulation of policies, the handling of correspondence, and even with the telephone complaints, and have never received or given a suggestion or instruction that preference should be shown to any group or individual." Harry Hopkins's top troubleshooter, Lorena Hickok, toured WPA projects in Chicago to see "if we were being made victims of the political spoils system." She found no evidence of widespread nepotism, and concluded that "someone apparently had put up a fight to keep politics out of this Chicago show—and pretty successfully too."[3]

With more unemployed than WPA jobs available, the potential for favoritism always existed and some undoubtedly went undetected. But for the machine, the perception that it controlled the certification process could be just as beneficial as the power itself. While WPA administrators worked vigilantly to maintain an objective certification process, the Kelly-Nash operatives cultivated the notion that those in good graces downtown could expect jobs in the federal work force. This notion became even more popular when the Chicago papers printed Democratic Congressman Arthur W. Mitchell's reply to a constituent seeking a WPA job. Mitchell said:

> It is an unbroken rule of the Democratic Organization in Chicago that each person seeking help from his Congressman must first get a letter from his ward committeeman requesting the Congressman to take care of the matter. I must, therefore, insist that you get a letter from your committeeman first, and I shall be very glad to do everything in my power to help you.[4]

Unquestionably the Kelly-Nash machine fostered the idea among needy Chicagoans that public employment and relief checks came to them as a result of the Democratic party's control of city hall. But claiming that power did not necessarily make it actual: If Mitchell's supplicant produced a letter of recommendation from the appropriate ward committeeman and received WPA employment, regardless of the effect of the endorsement, the machine would seem to have produced. If no job was forthcoming, the applicant could simply be told that there were no openings at the time; if he received a position later, it could be attributed to his having previously gone through channels. So while the Kelly-Nash machine could not totally control the certification process, it was in a position to benefit from the number of jobs created by the Democratic-controlled WPA program.[5]

Similarly, the administration of relief in Chicago was relatively immune from spoils politics. While politicians tried to penetrate the relief apparatus, the county agencies designated to award relief stipends, peopled by trained social workers, successfully maintained their autonomy. Edith Abbott, a Republican social worker and persistent Kelly-Nash critic, wrote the *Chicago Tribune* that appointments made by the Cook County Bureau of Public Welfare and the Chicago Relief Administration (CRA) were made strictly on a civil service basis. She further asserted that Kelly had maintained a "hands-off" policy with the CRA. Wayne McMillen, president of the local chapter of the National Association of Social Workers, concluded that the CRA was "free from graft and from political spoilsmanship." And Leo Lyons, director of the CRA, wrote, "At no time has the mayor or other city officials attempted to direct the formulation of policies or the selection of personnel by the Chicago Relief Administration."[6]

In addition, some of Kelly's oldest and most vehement foes gave the machine credit for honesty in Chicago relief operations. Paul H. Douglas, while campaigning for a city council seat in 1939, admitted that Kelly had kept the administration of relief "nonpolitical." Harold F. Gosnell, Douglas's colleague at the University of Chicago and a leader of the ongoing drive to form an independent Democratic party in Chicago, concluded that relief had been kept "relatively free from direct political interference."[7]

While both WPA officials and local relief administrators strove to keep political influence out of the certification process, they also feared coercion of voters receiving federal assistance. Republicans and independents complained throughout the decade that the success of the Kelly-Nash machine rested upon the captive votes of those on the relief rolls. According to the Better Government Association, "Chicago . . . has hundreds of thousands of unemployed whose votes are controlled by the party that now feeds them." The Kelly-Nash enemies correctly perceived that, just as in the case of certification, potential coercion could be effective regardless of the power of the machine to deliver; the mere threat of rescinding a destitute family's relief assistance could be intimidating enough to secure its compliance. And many examples of such threats can be uncovered.[8]

As previously noted, during the 1934 election, Republican Frank Knox reported to Harold Ickes that Democratic workers distributed thousands of affidavits to relief recipients by which they claimed inability to mark a ballot but affirmed their desire to vote a straight Democratic ticket. Harold F. Gosnell noted that Democratic precinct workers threatened to withhold relief funds from Chicago blacks if they voted Republican in the November 1933 and April 1934 elections. The 1936 primary between Horner and Bundesen produced numerous complaints of political coercion against both sides; WPA files abounded with letters attesting to the Kelly-Nash machine's willingness to threaten loss of employment for failure to support the organization candidate. A Women's Civic Council study of political coercion told of a polling place where "seventy per cent of the voters voted by assistance, and the men received from the Democratic precinct captain a blank filled out which consitituted an 'OK' for the voters to go back upon their WPA jobs the day after election." And the machine employed a subtler form of influence by placing near the polling place a sign reading, "Don't bite the hand that feeds you."[9]

The apex of criticism came in the 1939 mayoral contest with Dwight H. Green's endless complaints about the WPA as an arm of the Kelly-Nash machine. Following the February primary, Green charged that the "Kelly-Nash machine forced men in the ranks of the WPA, the PWA and the people on relief to vote its ticket. They made a chain gang of the unfortunates of our city and under the lash made them protect their bread by voting Kelly-Nash." In the heat of the campaign against Kelly, Green charged that city hall wanted people unemployed "because then on election day they coerce, intimidate and buy their votes in order to elect their machine candidates." And according to reports of such civic groups as the Better Government Association and the Civic Federation, the machine "encouraged" thousands of relief clients to vote for Kelly.[10]

Although Kelly-Nash politicos used federal relief and work programs to attempt to influence Chicago voters, these attempts did not mean that all those receiving aid voted Democratic for that reason. Many factors undoubtedly contributed to the heavy Democratic vote in 1930s Chicago, with political coercion one of the least significant. The popularity of Franklin D. Roosevelt and his New Deal reinforced the trend in urban America toward establishing the Democrats as the nation's majority party. Equally critical was the attitude of the Republican party toward the New Deal relief program. Leading GOP figures in Chicago, in conjunction with the city's Republican newspapers, spoke derisively of the "dole" and referred to relief recipients as "parasites." Constantly attacking the WPA as a shameless boondoggle, they allowed Kelly and the Democrats to portray themselves as the friends of the common man, the unemployed, and the dispossessed. It is little wonder that the apparently callous Republicans did not receive the vote of Chicagoans whose livelihood depended upon Democratic-inspired programs.[11]

The real importance to the Chicago Democratic machine of federal assistance lay not in the manipulation of relief roles nor in the intimidation of voters but in the financial support provided in a time of economic disaster. Because of this economic windfall, Kelly could keep the city's head above water and continue to provide essential city services; at the same time, extra funds meant that the politically vital patronage roles need not be pruned. The ability to provide jobs and money for the needy and maintain employment for municipal workers proved to be politically beneficial, so it comes as no surprise that a machine politician like Kelly donned the cloak of an ardent New Dealer.

Kelly repeatedly maintained that the city of Chicago could not contribute any significant amount to the care of its indigent and unemployed. The local welfare dispensers, the social workers, countered that patronage, graft, and waste took first priority in the Kelly scheme and accounted for the dearth of funds available for the truly deserving. Governor Horner had long said the same thing, and throughout the decade a suspicious Illinois legislature frustrated Kelly's demands for more state aid to Chicago. Kelly flatly refused to raise municipal taxes or trim patronage rolls, and he could get away with such intransigence because of federal largess. And, by any standard, Kelly's administration contributed very little to the welfare program.[12]

From July 1933 to December 1935, for example, the federal government provided 87.6 percent of the funds for emergency relief in Chicago, the state 11 percent, and the city 1.4 percent. For the entire period prior to July 1936, when the state finally compelled Chicago to increase its contribution, the city provided only 0.6 percent of the total relief cost. While New York City allocated $85 million for relief in 1938, Chicago provided a mere $5 million. The local chapter of the National Association of Social Workers concluded that "the chief effort of Mayor Kelly has been to avoid paying any part of the relief bills."[13]

Kelly's securing of WPA projects reflected the same philosophy. Because the local sponsors of projects had to provide tools and supplies, Kelly concentrated on proposals that called for a maximum of labor and a minimum of equipment—things like street repair, park improvements, and sewer construction. These projects also made for good politics: Highly visible, lasting, and practical, they were everyday reminders of the Kelly administration's commitment to make work programs. The premium placed on labor inevitably resulted in overmanning at project sites, so much so that the state WPA admitted that the use of excessive numbers of workers constituted a serious problem in Chicago.[14]

Prior to 1939, when Congress mandated that sponsors provide one-fourth of the cost for projects, the division of costs between the WPA and local sponsors was negotiable. Harry Hopkins argued that allocations should be approved case by case on the basis of need. Consequently, Hopkins approved low sponsor contribution for expansion of the Chicago municipal airport because the city had to purchase land and remove railroad tracks from the existing facility. Aubrey Williams defended the city's paltry contribution to a street repair project by noting its great need for work relief. On yet another occasion, a congressional committee investigation uncovered a building demolition project in Chicago in which the city had not only failed to contribute any funds to the WPA but had actually made $45,000 by the sale of salvage materials. With a lenient, friendly WPA administration, public works projects constituted a "can't miss" proposition for the frugal Kelly administration.[15]

Capitalizing on the public works bonanza, Kelly claimed the credit for improvements around the city engineered by federal monies. In *Chicago's Report to the People,* Kelly argued that his program of public works, in conjunction with WPA support, saved the city's taxpayers $6 million annually. He further claimed sole credit for ending payless paydays for schoolteachers, greatly reducing the city's floating debt, painting and repairing 450 schools, and saving $44 million for the corporate fund—all without mention of the role played by the WPA.[16]

Moreover, besides maintenance and refurbishing of city

property, Kelly could point to an impressive list of development and construction projects—all courtesy of WPA money. He enlarged Chicago's antiquated municipal airport, adding four sets of dual runways so that for the first time, two planes could land simultaneously, and installed the most modern lighting system in the nation. Under the aegis of the Chicago Park District, Chicago's lakefront was given a much-needed facelift: WPA labor landscaped all of Lincoln Park between Foster Avenue and Belmont Street, totally revamped approximately half of the park south of Belmont, and reconstructed the lakefront park area south of Roosevelt Road. Under the joint sponsorship of the city and the park district, the WPA launched an Outer Drive Improvement program that finished the construction of a continuous seventeen-mile drive from Foster Avenue to Jackson Park, including the Outer Drive Bridge over the Chicago River. The most noteworthy achievement, however, was the PWA-funded State Street subway, which won plaudits as the "safest and fastest subway yet constructed" in the world.[17]

The new subway, the modernized airport, the expanded Lake Shore Drive, Outer Drive Bridge, the acres of beautiful new parkland, and the ubiquitous road and sewerage improvements—all of these accomplishments were made possible by Kelly's political clout and the resultant good relations with New Deal administrators in Chicago and Washington. Kelly benefited from the outset of the WPA program by the selection of Robert Dunham, head of the Chicago Park District and a longtime friend, as the state director. Not surprisingly, Dunham continually supported Kelly in his dealings with Washington and allied his office with the mayor in Illinois's political struggles, most notably in the 1936 contest with Horner. Kelly's other major contact in Chicago, WPA regional administrator Howard Hunter, not only worked well with the mayor but also achieved a personal intimacy with him. Hunter, well aware of the need for rapport with the local Democratic organization, explained his cultivation of the goodwill of such a notoriously Machiavellian boss: "We'd never get to first base if we didn't work with and through him and his gang."[18]

For Kelly-WPA relations, Harry Hopkins set the tone, and he was friendly to the Chicago machine from the outset. After Kelly established himself as the most powerful Democrat in Illinois with his landslide victory in 1935, a position threatened but never destroyed by electoral disappointments in subsequent years, Hopkins turned his back on the mayor's rivals. Governor Horner complained to Harold Ickes that Hopkins ignored him, even refusing to return his telephone calls; Ickes, in turn, lamented Hopkins's blind worship of Kelly to President Roosevelt, but to no avail. Hopkins went out of his way to support the Kelly administration, funneling extra money to the

Mayor Kelly (second from left) and WPA Chief Harry Hopkins (third from left) greet the Washington press corps after a private conference. (Chicago Historical Society, ICHi-15879.)

Chicago office; in December 1936, for example, he phoned Dunham to tell him: "The Treasury has suddenly found a little more money, and I don't want to put you and Ed in a hot spot. If there is any money here and it will do some good, I want you to have it."[19]

Hopkins decided to court Kelly's favor in part because of his own political aspirations. Assuming that Roosevelt would retire from the presidency at the close of his second term, Hopkins set his sights on becoming the successor and sought the support of Kelly and his fellow bosses. Jim Farley, who harbored presidential aspirations of his own for 1940, suspected that Hopkins hoped to get Kelly and Frank Hague of Jersey City to manage his campaign in the cities, a view shared by Senator Joseph Guffey of Pennsylvania. Ickes observed that Hopkins was "playing politics all along the line" and that he saw his presidential candidacy as "undoubtedly tied up with Mayor Kelly." Hopkins discussed his strategy for securing the Democratic nomination in 1940 with Hunter, who assured him that if Roosevelt chose not to run, Kelly would "go all the way down the line" for Hopkins. The Hopkins boom waned, however, when a duodenal ulcer necessitated the surgical removal of much of his stomach, and he spent the better part of 1938–40 convalescing.[20]

Along with Hopkins, Kelly could count on the support of Roosevelt's political right hand, Postmaster General Jim Farley—at least until Farley became convinced that the Chicago mayor had hitched his star to the Hopkins-for-president movement. Farley, like many others, assumed that Roosevelt would step down in 1940; as chairman of the Democratic National Committee, Farley occupied an excellent position from which to launch his own campaign. And, like Hopkins, Farley ignored the other politicians of Illinois to focus all his attention on Kelly. A disgruntled Tom Courtney told Ickes that "Farley never talks with anyone in Chicago except Mayor Kelly." To affirm their exclusive contact, Farley wrote Kelly that the Democratic National Committee would "do nothing in your County with references to speakers or meetings without first consulting Pat." With these members of Roosevelt's coterie jockeying for position in the expected race for succession in 1940, Kelly enjoyed an enviable position. At the same time, he benefited from a favored position with the president himself.[21]

Kelly's first contact with Roosevelt came during the 1932 election campaign. Following the national convention at which Roosevelt secured the nomination, Kelly accompanied Mayor Cermak to Hyde Park to discuss the Chicago Democrats' belated support of the victorious candidate. In September Kelly sent a letter to Roosevelt advising him on strategy for the campaign: He urged Roosevelt to make Hoover, not the Republican party, the focus of his attack. Roosevelt's view of this suggestion as "very helpful" portended the beginning of a relationship in which the Chicago boss served as an adviser and barometer of public opinion for the president. As Samuel Rosenman, one of Roosevelt's speech writers, observed, Roosevelt valued Kelly's opinion because he knew the mayor to be totally candid. In subsequent years, Kelly would frequently regale the president with results of public opinion polls he had conducted in Chicago and advise him on topics ranging from practical politics to foreign affairs.[22]

Besides establishing his reputation as a sagacious and candid politician, Kelly also made himself a worthy Roosevelt lieutenant by performing some sensitive tasks for the Democrats in Washington. He championed administration initiatives in Illinois and frequently aided WPA chief Hopkins in his struggle to compel Governor Horner and the Illinois General Assembly to assume greater financial responsibility for the state's relief program. Furthermore, Kelly used his influence on other Illinois politicians to force them into line with presidential initiatives: On two occasions, Kelly had to lean on U.S. senator William H. Dieterich to ensure such compliance.

When Roosevelt launched his court-packing scheme to subvert the obstructionism of the Supreme Court, Kelly took to the stump to defend the president's position. Hopkins, acting on orders from Roosevelt, used Kelly to guarantee Dieterich's support for the ill-fated proposal. Hopkins again approached Kelly about securing Dieterich's vote during the contest for Senate majority leader, in which Roosevelt's choice, Alben Barkley of Kentucky, was pitted against Pat Harrison of Mississippi. Dieterich had promised his allegiance to Harrison, but Kelly provided the leverage necessary to swing the crucial vote to Barkley. These demonstrations of loyalty and power clearly enhanced Kelly's reputation as a "good soldier."[23]

Most important, of course, in explaining the president's esteem for Mayor Kelly was the power wielded by Illinois's political kingpin. Despite the performance of the Chicago Democratic machine in 1934, Roosevelt found the idea of supporting Kelly in the 1935 mayoral contest singularly distasteful. Kelly's landslide victory that year undoubtedly altered his opinion, as did the mayor's impressive demonstration of statewide influence in breaking the legislative log-jam over taxes that same month. Kelly's political achievements contrasted sharply with the stubborn recalcitrance of Governor Horner, who continued to obstruct New Deal policies in the last months of 1935. Roosevelt cast his administration's lot with the Chicago Democrats in the 1936 gubernatorial race and in subsequent contests spearheaded by antimachine reformers in the prairie state. And because of the huge Democratic vote turned out by Chicago throughout the thirties, the president's decision to back Kelly paid off handsomely.

There also developed between the president and the mayor a mutual respect and friendship. Roosevelt not only thought enough of Kelly's political prowess to rely upon his counsel but also socialized with him, inviting him to luncheons in Hyde Park and Washington. While Roosevelt stayed on the good side of many big city bosses whose support he coveted, men like Ed Crump of Memphis and Frank Hague of Jersey City, Kelly was one of a select few—Ed Flynn of the Bronx was another—who penetrated into the inner circle. Even Eleanor Roosevelt, who looked upon the urban bosses as anathema, thought enough of Kelly to defend him publicly when journalists labeled him a corrupt boss of the Hague-Pendergast stripe.[24]

As for Kelly, he could not have been more effusive in his praise of the president. "Roosevelt Is My Religion" was the title of his standard campaign speech in the thirties. Privately, Kelly called Roosevelt one of the greatest Americans of all time, not to mention the country's finest chief executive. According to many Kelly intimates, the mayor became so enamored of Roosevelt Democracy that he took up the New Deal mantle in earnest. It appears logical that a man in

Kelly's position would at least pay lip service to New Deal tenets—
urban bosses profited from both the nationwide success of the Democratic party and the provision of large quantities of federal funds—but
there exists some evidence that he came to be, at least in part, a
believer in the Roosevelt brand of liberalism.[25]

Kelly adduced that "politics is people" and emphasized
the importance of aiding the underprivileged of society. While many
of his critics denounced him for his ruthless brand of bossism, they
also recognized his genuine commitment to aiding the poor during the
depression. Benjamin Adamowski, whose liberal proclivities explained
in part his break with the Kelly-Nash machine, opined: "Kelly had the
milk of human kindness. He understood the poor and was genuine in
his warm feelings toward them and in his efforts to help them." The
mayor's conversion to liberal ideas led him to surround himself with
progressive young advisers who administered some limited reforms in
Chicago government; one of these young Democrats, Gael Sullivan,
founded the Altgeld Forum, a discussion group that met to ponder
new directions for the Illinois Democracy. Kelly lent the Altgeld
Forum his moral and financial support and helped it attract guest
speakers to its meetings. In later years, Kelly reveled in the success of
Sullivan, who progressed from mayoral speech writer to the executive
directorship of the Democratic National Committee.[26]

Kelly never repudiated the tactics of bossism that sustained his rise to power in the mid-thirties, but his excesses became
less conspicuous under Roosevelt's influence. Clearly not an ideo-
logue, Kelly did commit the prestige of his administration to Roosevelt
policies. While he never totally transcended the narrow, parochial values of his Irish political background, his exposure to the New Deal
crowd did somewhat broaden his intellectual horizons. Unlike the
cruder bosses of the Curley-Hague-Pendergast ilk, Kelly never embar-
rassed Roosevelt as a presence in the New Deal coalition—at least not
to the extent that the president felt it necessary to terminate the relationship. Indeed, the mayor's relative respectability, coupled with his
staunch loyalty, made him the ideal choice to lead the controversial
move to draft Roosevelt for an unprecedented third term as president.

More than a year before the 1940 Democratic conven-
tion, Kelly began to trumpet Roosevelt's candidacy. A week after his
own successful reelection in 1939, he met with the president in the
White House to discuss the upcoming contest. According to the Chicagoan, Roosevelt argued against a third term, quoting George Washington on the benefits of limiting the presidency to two terms. Kelly
rejoined, "George Washington wouldn't make a good precinct captain
in these days," and he further argued that Roosevelt could not step
down at a time of international crisis, that the incumbent's experience

in foreign affairs was critical to the nation. Roosevelt remained non-committal, but Harry Hopkins felt that Kelly's arguments had struck home. Immediately after the Washington meeting Kelly launched an extensive speaking campaign designed to advocate a draft-Roosevelt initiative, and the president never instructed him to cease.[27]

In February 1940 the Democratic National Committee met to choose the site of its nominating convention, and Kelly aggressively lobbied for Chicago. At one point it seemed that Philadelphia, the choice of Chairman Farley and other presidential hopefuls who feared a Kelly-controlled convention in Chicago, had the inside track. Philadelphia offered $150,000 to the committee, an offer that Kelly lacked authorization to match; so despite the politicking of Kelly, Nash, and their ally, Frank Hague, it seemed that the much more lucrative Philadelphia bid would win. At the last moment, however, Kelly matched the $150,000 offer—although he later admitted to reporters that he had no resources to justify his bid—and the Democrats awarded the convention to Chicago by a 47 to 46 vote.[28]

According to Bronx boss Ed Flynn, "A majority of the delegates were not enthusiastically for the renomination of the President." Nonetheless, there was no other clear-cut favorite for the nomination; only Jim Farley went to Chicago with a well-publicized commitment to opposing the incumbent. Working with Kelly in Roosevelt's behalf were several other urban bosses: Flynn, Crump, Hague, and James Pendergast. Kelly also made it possible for Harry Hopkins to manage the president's forces; since Hopkins was not a delegate, Kelly gave him a courtesy badge as a deputy sergeant-at-arms to allow him access to the convention floor. And with the proceedings held in Chicago, Kelly could pack the galleries with the foot soldiers of his own Cook County machine.[29]

At the opening session of the convention, Kelly delivered, as the welcoming speech, an unabashed paean to Roosevelt. While the mayor reportedly hoped to stampede the convention at the outset, the audience responded desultorily, a reflection of the feelings of many delegates that such partisanship by the host smacked of poor taste. When Senator Carter Glass of Virginia addressed the convention on the pitfalls inherent in a third-term presidency, the galleries, packed with Kelly-Nash patronage workers, shouted him down. Amid the boos, catcalls, and epithets, Glass could barely be heard and had to cut short his peroration.[30]

A few days before the convention Roosevelt had met with Kelly, Ed Flynn, Harry Hopkins, James Byrnes, and Frank Walker in the Oval Office and told them of his plan to send a letter, in which he denied his desire for reelection, to the delegates. The pols advised him against such action, arguing that he would surely be nominated "almost by acclamation." Nonetheless, the president drafted a letter that was originally designed to be read by Speaker of the House William Bankhead at the opening session. With Bankhead's speech scheduled for 10 P.M., however, Roosevelt decided to let Senator Alben Barkley, the convention chairman, read the statement early on the evening of the second day. Barkley told the stunned delegates:

> Tonight, at the specific request and authorization of the President, I am making this simple fact clear to the Convention. The President has never had, and has not today, any desire or purpose to continue in the office of President, to be a candidate for that office, or to be nominated by the Convention for that office. He wishes in all earnestness and sincerity to make it clear that all the delegates to this Convention are free to vote for any candidate. That is the message I bear to you from the President of the United States.[31]

Forewarned of the president's message, Kelly was prepared. As the delegates sat transfixed by Barkley's address, a voice boomed forth, "We want Roosevelt!" from loudspeakers around the hall. As delegates began marching in the aisles, the loudspeakers bellowed, "Everybody wants Roosevelt!" Spectators from the gallery poured onto the floor to join in the demonstration as the loudspeakers roared, "The world needs Roosevelt!" The parade became a frenzied mob, pushing over chairs, toppling tables, jostling observers. "Chicago wants Roosevelt!" "The party wants Roosevelt!" "Illinois wants Roosevelt!" "America needs Roosevelt!" The demonstration lasted just minutes short of an hour, when finally the mysterious voice subsided. Thomas Garry, Chicago superintendent of sewers, had been stationed in the basement with a microphone hooked up to the hall's public address system. Thus concealed, the "Voice from the Sewers" bellowed Roosevelt's name as a signal to the Kelly legions and launched the hour-long show of devotion. A flustered, yet stubborn, Jim Farley regained control of the floor and defeated efforts to designate Roosevelt the nominee by acclamation. But the next day, the convention chose the incumbent on the first ballot with 936 votes to 72 for Farley, 61 for John Nance Garner, 9 for Millard Tydings, and 5 for Cordell Hull.[32]

After the delegates had all gone home, many Democrats reacted negatively to Roosevelt's apparent duplicity in coyly accepting a synthetic draft and to the Chicago machine's overt manipulation. Farley enunciated some of these feelings when he told Roosevelt: "It was just too silly for words the way Kelly and Hague acted. Kelly acted as if he was running a ward caucus. The performance of 'the voice of the sewers' was beyond all decency." But the reaction of the pro-Roosevelt forces proved laudatory. Hopkins wired Kelly, "Dear Ed, you did more to swing it than anybody else." Roosevelt sent the mayor a warm note of thanks for his handling of the convention in which he said: "I want to send you this letter to tell you of my real appreciation for your loyalty. You know, of course, that I consider you one of the archconspirators in the placing of this millstone around my neck, even though I appreciate the motives which impelled you."[33]

Kelly's assiduous labors for Roosevelt, exemplified by the 1940 Democratic convention, and the special perquisites that the president granted to the Chicago machine do indeed make it seem indisputable that the Kelly-Nash organization thrived as a result of its association with the New Deal. In fact, the operation of the New Deal in Chicago contradicts many of the tenets of the "Last Hurrah" thesis, which attempts to explain the demise of the big city political machines. Based upon Edward O'Connor's novel, *The Last Hurrah,* this thesis suggests that the New Deal destroyed the urban political machines by terminating the dependence of the poor upon city hall and substituting federal suzerainty. Kelly's experiences called into question the notion that the machine bosses were at odds with Roosevelt; clearly, the relationship between Kelly and Roosevelt was both cordial and mutually beneficial. No evidence indicates that Roosevelt set out to subvert the influence of the Chicago politicians, nor did he attempt to de-emphasize the achievements of the local Democrats in favor of his own federal programs. In the battle between a "reformist governor" and a corrupt local boss, Roosevelt sided with the latter. Clearly, the ties between Chicago and Washington grew stronger, not weaker, during the New Deal; for a variety of reasons, the Kelly-Nash machine enjoyed a much more secure position than had Cermak's fledgling model on the eve of Roosevelt's inauguration.[34]

O'Connor's thesis also contended that the New Deal eliminated one of the keys to the machine's success, the social welfare function. By reorienting the populace toward Washington via the Social Security Act, labor legislation, federal employment programs, and unemployment relief, Roosevelt supposedly stripped the local political organizations of their hold on a once-dependent voter. This argument lacks credibility for Chicago, because the Roosevelt administration granted the Kelly-Nash forces a great deal of autonomy in directing the federally sponsored welfare programs. The WPA, from Hopkins to Hunter to Dunham, worked hand in hand with the Kelly government and did not attempt to supersede its authority. Kelly benefited tremendously from federal programs, so he had every reason to cooperate in their application. Moreover, the Chicago machine continued many of its own "welfare" programs and even created some new ones during the thirties.

Owing to the severity of the depression, the machine

took every opportunity to provide social services for its constitutents, financing this charity in a number of ways. The Kelly-Nash regime instituted first a football and later a basketball game between the public high school and Catholic league champions, games that produced as much as $125,000 annually. Kelly enlisted the aid of Chicago Musicians Union chief Jimmy Petrillo to put on a musical benefit, the "Night of Stars," at Chicago Stadium. A host of famous musicians and show business celebrities, including Tommy Dorsey, Glenn Miller, Amos and Andy, Francis X. Bushman, and Xavier Cugat, appeared free of charge to boost the sale of tickets. The proceeds, totaling as much as $470,000 in 1941, went toward the purchase of clothing for needy children, and Kelly boasted that some seventy-five thousand youths received free apparel as a result. Other benefits, fund-raisers, and solicited contributions made it possible for Chicago's Democracy to grandly display its generosity to the city's unfortunate.[35]

In the first three decades of the twentieth century, Democrats and Republicans alike fought with varying success to gain control of Chicago's political terrain. Before Anton Cermak's victory in 1931, no political machine was able to establish such a large measure of dominance; certainly the sustained success of the Democratic machine into the eighties surpassed any standards of electoral control established before the depression. As caretaker of the machine's fortunes, Ed Kelly profited from the expanded role of the federal government. At a time of unsettled social relations and financial chaos, the New Deal helped to bolster the Chicago Democratic machine in its infancy. Kelly's ability to assure a good standing for his organization in Washington, along with his dramatic coup of swinging the black voters of Chicago from the Republicans to the Democrats, constituted his greatest contribution to the growth and sustenance of Chicago Democracy.[36]

5 "Big Red" in Bronzeville

 IN CHICAGO, as elsewhere, blacks voted Republican in overwhelming numbers prior to the 1930s. A popular saying of the early twentieth century—"The Republican party is the ship, all else the sea"—accurately described the passionate commitment of the nation's blacks to the party of Lincoln. As one of the first politicians to court the black vote actively, Chicago mayor William Hale "Big Bill" Thompson, a Republican, amassed huge majorities in the city's Bronzeville. In the bitterly contested campaign of 1919, Thompson's narrow victory was attributed to his support by black voters, and in 1927 he received an amazing 93 percent of the black vote. Though he lost to Democrat Anton Cermak in 1931 and received only 42 percent of the popular vote, Thompson still garnered a formidable 84 percent of the Bronzeville tally. In wrenching the mayoralty away from the Republicans, the Democrats still failed to disengage the GOP's stranglehold on the city's black electorate.[1]

Aware of the party's ineffectiveness in the black South Side, Cermak immediately went to work to alter the political balance of power there. The day he took office, he fired 2,260 temporary employees, many of whom were black. At the same time he served notice that gambling, prostitution, and other illegal activities, ignored by the Thompson administration, would cease in Bronzeville. The *Chicago Defender*, the city's most influential and widely read black newspaper, observed that the city was "closed up like a drum. The lid went on five minutes after it was certain that former Mayor Thompson had lost his fight for a fourth term as Chicago Mayor."[2]

Cermak transferred police captain John Stege to the South Wabash station in the middle of the black community, telling him to "raise all the hell you can with the policy gang." Stege's men arrested some two hundred a day, cramming them into jail cells so tightly that no one could sit down. They randomly stopped automobiles to search for evidence of gambling and raided private homes to break up games of whist and bingo. Police arrest records for 1931 showed that 87 percent of the locations raided that year fell within the black belt; the number of blacks arrested that year tripled. The *Defender* called the South Side raids "political persecution" and Cermak's police "Cossacks," but the mayor replied that such actions would cease if blacks switched their allegiances to the Democratic party.[3]

In addition to implementing these heavy-handed tactics, Cermak also began the task of constructing a black Democratic political organization on the South Side. The mayor served notice of his intentions by installing Michael Sneed, a precinct captain in the Thomas Nash organization, as the first black Democratic committeeman of the 3rd Ward. Joe Tittinger, the white committeeman of the heavily black 2nd Ward, also received instructions from city hall to organize a black Democratic contingent in his domain. Cermak's death after only two years in office cut short his plan, however, and left to his successor the bulk of the task yet undone.[4]

Kelly took a tack different from that of his predecessor. He quickly repudiated the coercive methods employed by Cermak's police and allowed a return to a policy of benign neglect regarding gambling and vice on the South Side. Despite his repeated and vehement protests to the contrary, Kelly's police allowed the black vice lords a free hand. Originally a nickel and dime operation, by the thirties the policy game had become a multimillion dollar operation and the chief source of capital within Bronzeville. Correspondingly, some of the richest and most powerful men were policy kings who operated through the sufferance of the local authorities. Just as it had achieved a comfortable working relationship with the previous Republican administration, so did the black underworld reach a rapprochement with its Democratic successor.[5]

Evidence that leading figures in the black underworld had totally cast their lot with the Kelly-Nash machine surfaced by the mid-thirties. The Jones brothers, the South Side's most powerful gambling kings, actively participated in the operation of the 3rd Ward Democratic organization and became precinct captains as well. Illy Kelly, noted policy chieftain and the son-in-law of former Republican alderman Louis B. Anderson, ran unsuccessfully for 2nd Ward Democratic committeeman in 1934. And as the leaders of black syndicates offered their allegiance to the Democratic machine, they brought with them considerable sources of manpower; as Harold F. Gosnell reported, one gambling operation dispatched fifteen hundred policy writers to the South Side streets to canvass for the Democratic ticket at election time. With their considerable financial and human resources, the black underworld bosses exerted a significant influence on the political participation in Chicago's Bronzeville.[6]

Even as he cultivated the seedier elements of the South

Mayor Cermak, third from left, listens to the grievances of Chicago's black community leaders. (Chicago Historical Society, *ICHi-09766*.)

Side, Kelly accelerated the process of constructing a black Democratic organization. Spurning threats and intimidation, he sought to attract blacks by demonstrating that as the party in power, the Democrats had much to offer those who enlisted; he did this by making available more patronage jobs than the number previously offered by the beloved Big Bill Thompson. The subsequent advent of New Deal–created federal jobs would increase the patronage Kelly could offer black Chicagoans, but even before then the city's blacks received government jobs in unprecedented numbers.[7]

In addition to increasing the quantity of jobs, Kelly also improved the quality. He appointed blacks to prestigious committees and panels and elevated them to high positions in city government, for example, civil service commissioner, assistant corporation counsel, assistant city prosecutor, deputy coroner, assistant traction attorney, assistant attorney general, assistant state's attorney, chairman of the Chicago Housing Authority, member of the school board, and judge of the municipal court. He also broke down the barriers to advancement within the police department, paving the way for blacks to rise to the rank of captain. And the mayor appointed Robert S. Abbott, editor of the *Chicago Defender,* to several prestigious positions, including the Board of Commissioners of the Chicago World's Fair, the Committee on the Chicago Exposition, and the Chicago Jubilee Committee.[8]

Kelly worked assiduously to present a good image to black voters and succeeded in establishing a reputation as a friend of "the Race." The mayor censored the showing of the film "Birth of a Nation" in Chicago because of its explicit racism. He honored successful black Americans for their achievements—he made Joe Louis "mayor for ten minutes" in an elaborate city hall ceremony, for example—and made numerous personal appearances at South Side functions. "Big Red," as blacks affectionately called the mayor, attended the annual Tuskegee-Wilberforce football games at Soldier Field and endorsed Governor Horner's refusal to extradite a fugitive black man to an almost certain lynching in Arkansas. He espoused his belief in integration and pledged to expedite the process:

> I am afraid that the colored people have segregated themselves too much and have not taken advantage of the opportunities offered them to mingle freely in different public places of amusement that would contribute to their culture and refinement and general betterment. . . . As long as I am mayor of the city of Chicago I intend to be mayor of all the people and not any particular group of people, and I expect to see to it that each and every person and every group of people have an equal opportunity, as far as I am able in my capacity as executive of the city.[9]

At the dedication of the new Wendell Phillips High School, Kelly affirmed his intention "that the public school system in Chicago, so long as he is mayor, shall be conducted in accordance with law and order applicable alike to all nationalities." He concluded by pledging his administration to the quest for racial justice, saying, "The time is not far away when we shall forget the color of a man's skin and see him only in the light of intelligence of his mind and soul."[10]

In the second year of Kelly's mayoralty, events on Chicago's South Side tested his ambitious rhetoric. In October 1934 he met with a grievance committee of Morgan Park blacks to discuss the de facto segregation of the local high school, a supposedly integrated facility. The black parents protested to the mayor that two branch schools set up near the high school, ostensibly to relieve crowded conditions, actually were being used to separate black and white students. (White freshmen went to Clissold, while their black counterparts attended Shoop.) At the same time, they complained, school officials brought hundreds of white pupils into the Morgan Park district, while neighborhood black students could not attend the local school. Amid howls of protest from whites, Kelly rescinded the Board of Education's edict commanding black students to attend Shoop and ordered them readmitted to Morgan Park High School.[11]

On the Monday following Kelly's action, over two thousand white students, a majority of Morgan Park High School's enrollment, walked out in protest. When an estimated two hundred

Mayor Kelly "appoints" heavyweight boxing champion Joe Louis "mayor for ten minutes" in a well-publicized city hall ceremony. (Chicago Historical Society, *DN* #78,179.)

aggrieved white parents stormed the mayor's office demanding segregation, Kelly dispatched them and refused to reconsider. Following his threat of police action against the strikers, the protest died out and the recalcitrant white students returned to school. The *Defender* praised Kelly for his courageous stand: "In this answer the Mayor of Chicago vindicated his right to the respect and confidence of every citizen and every color and creed whose mind is not blinded by hate, prejudice, and bigotry." In 1945 white students struck at Englewood and Calumet high schools in opposition to integration, and again Kelly stood firm in his commitment to open schools.[12]

Kelly's soaring popularity in the black community showed in the political realm. The first indication came in 1934 when the Democrats selected a black candidate, Arthur W. Mitchell, to contest Oscar DePriest's congressional seat from Illinois's 1st District. The popular DePriest, a three-term incumbent who was nationally renowned as the first black Republican to sit in Congress since 1901, had the endorsement of the black press, including the influential *Defender*. But with the aid of the Kelly-Nash machine, Mitchell won a narrow victory and became the first black Democratic U.S. congressman.[13]

On the heels of this electoral triumph came the 1935 mayoral election, the outcome of which substantiated Kelly's tremendous popularity among black voters. The mayor received the enthusiastic endorsement of the *Defender,* which observed, "Black people believe in Kelly and in fact say that the only difference between him and Bill Thompson in respect to them is the name." He enjoyed the support not only of Bronzeville Democrats but of many black Republicans as well: Both William L. Dawson, alderman of the 2nd Ward, and Robert Jackson, alderman of the 3rd Ward, ran for reelection that year as Republicans but publicly backed the incumbent mayor. Berthold Cronson, Republican alderman of the 4th Ward, came out for Kelly as well. The mayor, in turn, endorsed these three black South Side Republican aldermen. Kelly's margin of victory far exceeded even the Democrats' expectations: He received 80.5 percent of the vote in the black 2nd, 3rd, and 4th wards.[14]

The dramatic change in the voting of Chicago blacks from 1931 to 1935 reflected not only a burgeoning attachment to Kelly but also a realistic assessment of political facts in the city. The blacks' desertion of the Republican party in 1935 represented only part of a larger, citywide defection as Republicans and independents alike forsook the hapless GOP candidate, Emil Wetten. Recognizing the certainty of the outcome, South Side blacks determined to jump on the victorious Kelly bandwagon well in advance of the post-election reckoning time. As the *Defender* reminded its readers: "If you leave it to the West, North, and far South Side to elect the mayor then don't be surprised when those things you are likely to want are left to them. Politics is a business; there is no sentiment involved; support is given for support."[15]

In the 1936 gubernatorial primary, black voters demonstrated their fealty to the Kelly-Nash machine by supporting the organization candidate, Dr. Herman Bundesen. In the predominantly black 2nd and 3rd wards, Bundesen's plurality exceeded eighty-three hundred votes; in nearby wards in which blacks constituted a minority of the population, the 5th, 6th, 7th, and 8th, Horner defeated the challenger by over four thousand votes. The *Defender* explained, "Members of the Race who voted in the Democratic primaries had nothing personally against Governor Horner, they were following the leadership of Mayor Edward Kelly, who had proven himself their friend." In the general election later that year, South Side blacks followed the lead of other Chicago Democrats and supported Horner against his Republican opponent.[16]

In 1939 black support for Kelly failed to equal the standard set four years earlier, but the South Side vote remained substantially Democratic. Kelly's appointments of Wendell Green to the Civil Service Commission and Robert Taylor to the Chicago Housing Authority elicited praise from the black community. Again the *Defender* gave Kelly its hearty endorsement, saying that "Mayor Kelly has faced all issues fairly and squarely when the rights of our race are involved." Republican mayoral candidate Dwight Green argued that little progress had been made in combating the school board's segregationist policies, but Kelly's stand for open schools, most notably in the Morgan Park incident, negated the attack. Kelly received 59.5 percent of the black vote, as compared to 56.1 percent of the total city vote. In a reasonably close, hard-fought contest, Kelly's success in Bronzeville exceeded his citywide performance.[17]

Kelly critics groused that his following among black voters resulted primarily from the popularity of the national Democratic party and of Franklin D. Roosevelt in particular. Certainly blacks throughout the nation found much to their liking in Roosevelt's New Deal; hard hit by the depression, urban blacks found make-work and relief programs sponsored by the federal government a godsend. A popular blues song of the time illustrated the black dependence upon such programs:

> Please, Mr. President, listen to what I've got to say:
> You can take away all of the alphabet, but please leave that WPA.
> Now I went to the poll and voted, I know I voted the right way—
> So I'm asking you, Mr. President, don't take away that WPA![18]

The exhortation of one black preacher—"Let Jesus lead you and Roosevelt feed you!"—typified the high regard in which Roosevelt came to be held by black Americans in the thirties. Indeed, by 1940 the previously Republican *Defender* had become a staunch supporter of the Democratic party, repenting its earlier "blind, child-like faith" in the GOP and lauding Roosevelt as the "greatest champion of the cause of the common people." As one political analyst wrote, "Harry Hopkins really turned Lincoln's picture to the wall."[19]

But to assume that Roosevelt's popularity—and Kelly's, in turn—depended solely upon federal welfare programs would be to oversimplify and distort a complex phenomenon. In the 1932 presidential election Roosevelt and his vice-presidential running mate, southerner John Nance Garner, received only 23 percent of Chicago's black vote. In 1936 that percentage more than doubled to 48.9, and it rose again to 52 in 1940. While the popularity of relief programs undoubtedly accounted for much of the increase, the existence of such programs was only one of a number of factors coalescing in the decade to attract blacks to the Democratic party. As Harold F. Gosnell and Elmer W. Henderson have detailed, other considerations were also vitally important: The urbanization of blacks in the preceding decades engendered psychological changes that broke down traditional allegiances. There was a mounting dissatisfaction with the Republicans, who failed to respond to the support they took for granted from blacks. A growing class consciousness among blacks resulted from increased exposure to labor movements and radical ideology. The more enlightened Democratic party of Roosevelt benefited from the reputations of such noted "race liberals" as Eleanor Roosevelt, Aubrey Williams, and Harold Ickes. The president, like Kelly, broke new ground by appointing blacks in ever-increasing numbers to prestigious federal positions. And finally, the successful wooing of black votes by local Democratic leaders aided the quest of the national party.[20]

This last point underscores the fact that Kelly's support in the South Side of Chicago was not simply a microcosm of Roosevelt's national following. While the vote totals for the president rose steadily, Chicago blacks never supported the national Democratic ticket as completely as they did Kelly. The Chicago Democratic machine's attempts to recruit blacks predated the Roosevelt administration's similar actions. Clearly, efforts by local and national Democrats complemented each other, and each benefited from the successes of its counterpart. Kelly brazenly claimed the virtues of the Roosevelt administration as his own and never ceased to emphasize the importance of federal relief to depression-stricken blacks. But heralding the Roosevelt connection was but one firearm in the mayor's arsenal; his sustained success with black voters rested upon the construction of a robust organization in the South Side subservient to, and patterned after, the larger city Democratic machine.[21]

The man who ultimately came to rule the black Democratic submachine was William L. Dawson. Kelly did not start out to choose a black lieutenant to whom he could entrust the administration of the party's interests in the black community; he initially chose Dawson for a very specific purpose, to take control of one troublesome ward. In the words of a politician close to Dawson: "Kelly did not build Dawson by pre-arranged plan into the South Side boss; he made him head of the second ward, and after that Dawson just grew. In each showdown, Dawson was seen to be the better man and was supported."[22]

Born in Georgia, William Levi Dawson attended Fisk University and Northwestern University Law School, served with distinction in the army during World War I, and settled in Chicago, where he became a lawyer. He entered politics as a Republican, becoming a precinct captain and eventually, in 1933, with the backing of Congressman Oscar DePriest, alderman of the 2nd Ward. In the city council he acquired a reputation as a maverick who frequently voted against his fellow Republicans. Dawson and the Democratic mayor became good friends, and the 2nd Ward alderman became known as "Kelly's man" in the council. Along with several other Republicans, Dawson openly supported Kelly-Nash candidates in municipal elections. Many disgruntled South Siders charged that he was a Republican in name only.[23]

Events within the Republican party on the South Side served to blunt Dawson's ambitions. William E. King, the 2nd Ward committeeman, feared that Dawson intended to assume complete control of the ward and therefore disavowed any connection with him. With the control of patronage for the ward and the support of Congressman DePriest, King staved off Dawson's challenge in 1936 and kept the office of committeeman. The year after his successful reelection as alderman in 1937, Dawson shifted his sights to the congressional seat taken away from DePriest by Arthur Mitchell. In the Republican primary, Dawson bested Louis B. Anderson and Oscar DePriest, thanks in part to the aid of 1st Ward Republican committeeman Daniel Serritella, who operated under the orders of Democratic county chairman Pat Nash. In the general election, however, he lost to the popular Mitchell by a 30,207 to 26,396 vote. By the end of the 1930s with avenues for advancement blocked within the GOP, an inability to assume control of the 2nd Ward organization, and a healthy relationship with the powerful Kelly-Nash machine, Dawson had begun to look at the Democratic party as the political promised land.[24]

Fortunately for Dawson, an upheaval in the 2nd Ward Democratic organization created an opening for someone of his ambitions. For several years blacks had complained of the dictatorial, insensitive leadership of the white committeeman, Joseph Tittinger. He distributed almost all of his patronage jobs to the few whites living in the eastern edge of the ward and even imported whites from neighboring wards to supervise employment assignments. He had a black precinct captain removed from a patronage job to make way for his son, kept "colored" office hours at party headquarters, and moved his personal residence to an area governed by a restrictive covenant. Impervious to complaints by his black constituents, Tittinger pledged to remain committeeman as long as there remained "a single white vote in the ward."[25]

In June 1939 fifty-three precinct captains from the 2nd Ward presented Kelly and Nash with a petition of grievances requesting the removal of Tittinger as committeeman. The *Defender* warned that if the Democrats failed to take action, "the belief is current that the Republican forces will come back into power in the next election." Tittinger responded to the criticism by firing the precinct captains from their patronage jobs; many of them then banded together to form an independent organization to oppose him in the upcoming 1940 election. Faced with a disintegrating ward organization and the threat of a black Democratic faction hostile to the Kelly-Nash regime, the mayor resolved to oust Tittinger and replace him with a black politician.[26]

Speculation about the new boss of the 2nd Ward revolved around three men: Christopher Wimbish, Bryant Hammond, and William Dawson. Wimbish, a former Republican assistant state's attorney, had joined the Democrats in the mid-thirties as a member of the Courtney faction, and he had been instrumental in challenging Tittinger's control of the ward. Hammond, a Democrat of longer standing, supported Cermak in the 1931 mayoral election and ran a strong race against William E. King for state senator in 1934. Unlike Wimbish, Hammond had long been a staunch Kelly loyalist and an outspoken critic of Courtney in the 1939 primary. But as Kelly's champion in the city council, Dawson held the inside track, the only drawback being his party affiliation. He was, after all, still a Republican—at least until 1939.[27]

In the February elections for alderman that year, Dawson finished third behind Democrat Earl B. Dickerson and Republican William E. King. When the closeness of the contest necessitated a runoff between the top two finishers, Dawson threw his support to Dickerson, who subsequently won the election. Dawson then met with Kelly, informing him of his decision to switch to the Democratic party. Kelly, who had been advised to choose Dawson as Tittinger's replacement by several influential black citizens, solicited Dickerson's approval and announced the change in late November.[28]

Not everyone among the Democrats welcomed Dawson with open arms, and the chief obstructionist was Pat Nash. Always a stalwart party man, Nash did not trust anyone who would switch parties for what he suspected to be personal gain. He remembered Dawson as an enemy in the bitter struggle for control of the 2nd Ward, and while it was permissible to help a friend from the city council in a Republican primary, it seemed quite another matter to aid the same individual against lifelong, proven Democrats. Therefore, Nash stood by Tittinger and promised him continued control of the ward's county patronage. Kelly stuck with Dawson, granting the new Democrat access to state and local patronage and finally winning the Cook County Central Committee over to his side. By December 1939 Dawson had officially received the blessing of the Democratic machine; his biggest difficulty lay in consolidating his power within the 2nd Ward.[29]

Initially, Dawson faced two complex problems—how to convince his former Republican supporters to follow him into the rival camp and how to assuage the fears of 2nd Ward Democrats that they would be supplanted by a wave of renegade Republicans. By his own account, the first problem proved the more difficult. For years Dawson had been preaching partisan loyalty to black Republicans and denigrating Democrats. Now he had to explain his dramatic reversal and encourage others to make the same move. He pointed to bankrupt Republican promises, the Democratic record as the party of the downtrodden, the friendly Kelly administration, and the great progress enjoyed by blacks during Roosevelt's two terms. Many followed Dawson into the Democratic ranks, a situation that gave pause to established Democrats in the ward. Dawson reassured them that they would lose neither their high standing in the party hierarchy nor their jobs; they had, in fact, few jobs to lose, and after the dictatorial reign of Tittinger, Dawson readily won over the fearful.[30]

In a short period of time, the new ward chief proved himself an able and energetic administrator. He instituted strict discipline into what had always been a loosely structured ward organization, formed women's and young people's Democratic clubs, and made his office open at all times to all residents of the ward. Recognizing the great number of women working as precinct captains, he appointed three blacks as senatorial committeewomen. He made former rival Christopher Wimbish president of the ward organization. And to appease the few white residents of the ward, Dawson slated Tittinger for state representative. The newcomer was securing his hold on the 2nd Ward, but his uneasy alliance with Alderman Dickerson prevented his control from becoming total.[31]

Trouble between the two men commenced even before Dawson's official acceptance by the Cook County Central Committee. Kelly named Dawson and Dickerson to co-chair a fund-raising drive for his annual Christmas charity. Dawson's workers sponsored a benefit raising $5,000 to buy clothes for distribution at Christmas. Dickerson, however, claimed credit for work that Dawson felt had been done by his staff alone. The incident, in which both men strove to impress the mayor, indicated the tension between them. Dawson's refusal to endorse Dickerson in his bid for the 1940 Democratic nomination for congressman further exacerbated their uneasy relationship. Although Dawson had promised that support in exchange for the alderman's backing against Tittinger, in 1940 he stood behind the incumbent, Arthur Mitchell. Meanwhile, Dawson worked to isolate Dickerson from the center of power in the 2nd Ward; he "forgot" to invite the alderman to meetings and regularly called him to the podium to speak at political rallies with only a few minutes left on the program.[32]

Dickerson also found himself increasingly alienated from city hall. Feeling betrayed by Dawson in 1940, he refused to campaign for Mitchell—a decision very unpopular with Kelly and Nash, who demanded complete support of the ticket by all Democrats. Kelly also disapproved of Dickerson's incipient radicalism: The alderman became an outspoken proponent of organized labor, a more militant spokesman for black rights, president of the Chicago Urban League, and, worst of all, along with Paul Douglas and John Boyle, a persistent critic of the Kelly administration in the city council. Particularly galling to the mayor was Dickerson's opposition to a traction ordinance favored by Kelly, on the grounds that it allowed unions to discriminate on the basis of color. Dawson observed, "He was always raising the race issue and antagonizing people. . . . Me, I never raise the race issue, even in Congress, and I certainly didn't in the Council."[33]

The events of 1942 sealed Dickerson's fate as a pariah. Congressman Mitchell decided not to run for reelection that year; although he gave as the reason his wife's failing health, many believed that his decision reflected a surrender to the expanding Dawson machine—and the Democratic organization chose Dawson to replace him. Dickerson resolved to run as an independent in the primary, finally severing the cord that bound him to the Kelly-Nash machine. He campaigned ardently as a New Dealer and criticized Dawson for replacing Democratic jobholders with his formerly Republican cronies. Defending his radicalism, Dickerson predicted that Dawson "can at best be another weak-kneed Mitchell owing allegiance to a machine rather than the people." But despite a valiant campaign, Dickerson lost to Dawson by an overwhelming margin, 14,628 to 4,521. Dawson's subsequent victory over the Republican candidate, William E. King, elevated him to a new pinnacle in the South Side political arena.[34]

In 1943 Dickerson lost his city council seat to Dawson's

cohort, William H. Harvey, so that Dawson was assured complete control of the 2nd Ward. That same year Benjamin Grant, elected as the first black Democratic alderman from the 3rd Ward in 1939, lost to Republican Oscar DePriest, a loss that signaled the death knell for Edward Sneed's decaying 3rd Ward organization. It also paved the way for Dawson, whose subordinate, Christopher Wimbish, succeeded Sneed as ward committeeman. Secure in his own bailiwick, Dawson added the neighboring ward to his expanding fiefdom.[35]

In the following years Dawson would repeat this pattern of infiltration, so that by the mid-fifties his domain would span five wards on the predominantly black South Side: He installed Kenneth Campbell as committeeman in the 20th Ward; in the 4th, Claude Holman; in the 6th, Robert Miller and later, when Wimbish faltered, Ralph Metcalfe in the 3rd. As blacks moved into these previously white wards, Dawson's men, political organizers and canvassers, came in as well, laying the groundwork for the take-over. When the white bosses lost an election, Dawson approached the city Democratic leaders—Kelly, Nash, and later Jacob Arvey and Joe Gill—and pleaded to try his hand. In each case his superior organization produced healthy vote totals for the machine and vindicated his claims.[36]

Dawson built within the larger Chicago Democratic machine a submachine through which he controlled the votes of an estimated quarter of a million people by 1950. His success can only be explained as a by-product, and not the intended result, of Kelly's decision to install the former Republican in the seat of power in the 2nd Ward. Dawson's ability to produce for the machine, the electoral success in each of the wards he controlled, guaranteed his continued support from city hall. As James Q. Wilson noted, "Had a weaker or less effective man than Dawson set out to be the Negro leader, it is possible that in a series of challenges others would have triumphed and no single Negro machine would have emerged." Despite the fact that Kelly had not foreseen the direction in which Dawson's leadership would take the South Side, his strategy must be viewed as successful: Dawson, an organizational genius, brought discipline and order to a traditional trouble spot, so that Kelly and countless other Democrats reaped the rewards on election day.[37]

In short, Kelly's successful cultivation of the black vote proved a great boon to the electoral success of the Chicago Democratic machine. Unlike Cermak, who chose the stick rather than the carrot, Kelly astutely proselytized blacks by offering them unprecedented recognition and increased patronage. He used the availability of federal jobs and the popularity of Franklin D. Roosevelt to add to the luster of the local machine. And while some machine critics questioned his sincerity—Dickerson maintained that Kelly really "was never a friend of the Negro people"—and skeptics called the mayor's commitment to blacks solely political, his administration struck a positively progressive chord in the realm of race relations. His sustained advocacy of integrated schools and defense of open housing, reaffirmed in the post–World War II years, rankled much of his predominantly white constituency in Chicago. Though Democratic politicians coveted the black vote, Kelly's "liberalism" on the race question often exceeded the bounds of political expediency. Clearly the black community, as well as the Democratic organization, benefited from the alliance forged by Kelly.[38]

6 An Imperfect World

 IN THE 1920s Chicago acquired a reputation as the nation's wickedest city. Most shocking was the revelation that the tentacles of organized crime extended even to city hall, where Big Bill Thompson presided over a wide-open town. Al Capone, exiled to suburban Cicero when reformer William Dever assumed the mayoralty in 1923, moved his headquarters back into downtown Chicago upon Thompson's reelection in 1927. (Capone reputedly contributed over $100,000 to Thompson's campaign that year.) Several factors linked Thompson himself to the underworld: For example, Capone henchman Daniel Serritella also served as a Thompson ward committeeman and a member of Big Bill's cabinet, and the gangland slaying of *Chicago Tribune* crime reporter Jake Lingle uncovered other ties between the mayor and noted mob figures. With Thompson's defeat in 1931, the question remained whether his successor would be any less susceptible to the lures of organized crime. During Anton Cermak's tenure as county board president, he allegedly enjoyed close contacts with the underworld, and certainly Cermak's avid "wetness" gave cause for concern to Chicago's reform-minded citizenry.[1]

As mayor, however, Cermak vowed to clean up Chicago. He succeeded in reducing the amount of street violence attributed to gangland warfare and, in so doing, earned the plaudits of the city's leading crime-fighting organization, the Chicago Crime Commission. In the 1933 annual report of its operating director, the commission stated that "Chicago has advanced in its war with the criminal enemy," thanks largely to the efforts of Cermak. But more perceptive was the analysis of the head of the Secret Six, a private crime-fighting agency largely responsible for the incarceration of Al Capone:

> There has been a marked improvement in crime conditions in the city since Anton J. Cermak became mayor and James P. Allman commissioner of police. But the old alliance between politics and crime, so flagrant under the former city administration, still exists and is strong. The political-crimi-

nal alliance has been severely jarred on several occasions, but the same old "fix" is still working.[2]

      While Cermak cracked down on the policy game in the South Side in hopes of changing the political allegiances of black Chicagoans, he ignored gambling in other areas of the city. He overlooked the traditional gamblers' practice of paying off the police in exchange for immunity and turned his back on the graft accumulated by Democratic ward committmen. The changes spawned by the brief Cermak administration were largely cosmetic, while the substructure of crime in Chicago remained untouched. In fact, as the era of Prohibition ended with the passage of the Twenty-first Amendment, the heirs to the Capone empire—Jake "Greasy Thumb" Guzik and Frank "The Enforcer" Nitti—began to expand their enterprises into new, more lucrative areas. Gambling, prostitution, narcotics, and labor racketeering became the avenues for development when Chicago's city council approved the selection of the martyred Cermak's successor.[3]

      Reformers who felt cause for optimism with a new mayor recoiled at an incident that occurred just months after Kelly took office. In what seemed a return to the violence-laden Thompson era, newly elected alderman Paddy Bauler shot a policeman during an argument outside his tavern. The altercation began when Bauler refused to admit the policeman and his friends to a private party long after closing time; in the ensuing struggle, Bauler shot his antagonist, who, in turn, accidentally gunned down a bystander. Although the newspapers cried for swift retribution, Kelly, who had been with Bauler earlier in the evening at a 43rd Ward banquet, soft-pedalled the incident. In a perfunctory and biased trial, Bauler was rapidly found not guilty. Shortly afterward, the mayor welcomed Bauler back to the city council and brought the house down when he lauded the acquitted alderman as "a real straight shooter."[4]

      The good government advocates suffered another shock when Kelly revealed his philosophy on gambling. The new mayor explained that gambling and vice would prevail in any large city and that the only answer to the problem was regulation, not abolition. Moreover, he added, there was nothing intrinsically wrong with the pastime:

> Gambling isn't a violation of divine law, and you'll find it wherever there are human beings, beginning with kids who play marbles for keeps. All you can do is keep the strong-arm boys, the muscle, from moving in. And the strong-arm boys always move in where an activity is illegal. That's why gambling ought to be under state control like the race tracks, where betting is legal. It's the only way to keep out the gambling syndicate.[5]

As noted previously, on two separate occasions Kelly's men in Springfield introduced legislation to legalize handbooks in Chicago, but both times Governor Henry Horner intervened to defeat the plan. Undaunted, the mayor swore that Chicago would not become a "bluenose" town where a workingman could not enjoy his leisure time. Gambling flourished in Chicago, as the police conveniently looked the other way. Kelly, who boasted publicly of his own gambling prowess, asserted that "people want all the liberty of action and personal conduct they can get within the limits of public safety." And the Kelly-Nash machine allowed them a remarkable amount.[6]

In a 1934 editorial, the *Chicago Daily News* estimated that seventy-five hundred gambling joints existed in Chicago, permeating every part of the city, even the downtown Loop area. Many operated within the shadow of city hall, including the main establishment of syndicate chief Jake Guzik at 123 North Clark Street. One journalist counted nearly thirty within a few blocks of city hall. According to Virgil Peterson, former director of the Chicago Crime Commission, cigar stores commonly fronted for betting parlors; inside, people wearing headphones and tabulating results were visible from the street. Used gambling tickets were discarded outside the cigar stores and covered the floors inside. A former Republican ward committeeman recalled that slot machines could be found operating in every ward of the city.[7]

On the South Side the policy wheel still reigned supreme. The operation grossed millions of dollars annually and employed an estimated six thousand persons. The policy game operated in the machine wards not only with immunity but with the approval of Bronzeville Democratic sachem William L. Dawson. On several occasions Dawson explained his acceptance of gambling in the black wards, saying, for instance:

> If they are going to make gambling illegal, then it's up to the police to keep it out of business; it's not up to Bill Dawson. . . . I think it's rank hypocrisy anyway. They tell the little man that he can't go across the street to the cigar store and place a bet with a bookie, yet the big people can go down to Arlington Park and bet all they want. . . . If they are going to enforce the laws, let's enforce them on everybody, not just on my people.[8]

Dawson went even further; he admitted, first to the *Chicago Daily News* and later to investigators for the Chicago Crime Commission, that he accepted financial contributions from South Side policy kings. He asserted that he used them for political purposes only and never for personal gain and added that he operated with the tacit approval of the Democratic organization; he praised Mayor Kelly, who "was always willing and ready to assume responsibilities." And on the city's West Side, an area of gradually expanding black population, operation of the lucrative policy game fell to James Martin, one of Pat Nash's political lieutenants in his home ward, the 28th.[9]

The tolerance of gambling and other "victimless crimes" emanated from many official sources. Cook County sheriff Thomas J. O'Brien, a protégé of Pat Nash, so frequently denied the existence of gambling despite overwhelming evidence to the contrary that he became known as "Blind Tom." As chief of law enforcement for the county, O'Brien had the responsibility of ferreting out illegal gambling operations; his laxity, combined with the inaction of the Chicago police, guaranteed virtual autonomy to well-connected gamblers.[10]

Gambling also thrived because of a judiciary unwilling to punish the few criminals brought into the courtrooms. Armed with technicalities and demonstrating considerable arbitrariness, judges dismissed cases for lacking evidence and placed impossible demands upon prosecuting attorneys. Judge Oscar Caplan insisted that a policeman had to make a bet, then secure a search warrant, and finally place another bet before making an arrest. Judge Eugene McGarry ruled that a bet had to be placed to prove gambling, but that if it were placed, the bookie would be a victim of entrapment and therefore not subject to arrest. Municipal court judge Eugene Holland, notorious for dismissing gambling cases at the rate of seven hundred per month, held that "scratch sheets, hard sheets, and registers of bets, as kept in handbook joints, are not evidence of racetrack gambling." Holland, who owned stock in dog racetracks and entered into a partnership with a bookmaker for real estate dealings, survived an attempt by the Chicago Bar Association to place him on probation and won reelection to the bench with the support of the Kelly-Nash machine.[11]

Ultimately, however, culpability for relaxed enforcement of the anti-gambling statutes rested with the Democratic administration. Throughout his tenure as mayor, Kelly dismissed charges of widespread gambling in Chicago despite the obvious visual evidence to the contrary. In response to complaints in 1937 Kelly maintained, "We are making a drive against gamblers, but every time we arrest them the judges turn them out." An incensed jurist, Chief Justice James Sonsteby of the municipal court, responded for the press by enumerating the sins of the Kelly administration: The police, when they bothered at all, arrested only small-time handbook operators and neglected the more affluent gamblers; the city showed no zeal for securing convictions in the few cases in which arrests ensued; the city refused to appeal cases that it lost; and while mere possession of a roulette wheel constituted sufficient evidence for conviction, none had ever been confiscated. Characteristically, Kelly reaffirmed his faith in Police Commissioner James Allman and dismissed the notion that gambling existed on a wide enough scale to constitute a major problem.[12]

The reason for the complicity of the Chicago Democratic organization, and all those in government beholden to it, was money. Tribute paid to the organization by the gambling interests in return for protection became a vital source of revenue for the Kelly-Nash machine, variously estimated at $12 to $20 million annually. A particularly prosperous handbook operator might pay up to $1,000 a month, whereas for a more modest hole-in-the-wall crap game the fee might have commanded $300 per month. While rates varied by wards, gambling proprietors typically had to split their profits equally with the local political representative.[13]

The Kelly-Nash machine entrusted the supervision of the gambling revenue to each ward committeeman. A portion of the money collected went to Democratic headquarters downtown, while the rest stayed in the ward to be used to defray the expenses of campaigning and electioneering. (In the 42nd Ward, for example, 40 percent of the money collected stayed in the ward organization, and the remaining amount went to the Morrison Hotel.) Ward committeemen chose police captains, who were usually placed in charge of collections. If a ward committeeman became troublesome to the organization, a new police captain would be dispatched to that district with orders to enforce the gambling laws. Thus cut off from his source of revenue, the penitent committeeman would get back in line and gambling would again flourish in the area.[14]

The *Chicago Daily News*, mindful of the vast sums of money available to the Kelly administration by virtue of its acceptance of gambling, touched on an even more important factor in Kelly's decision to sanction protection for the underworld:

> Cynics, viewing the mixed picture of the mayor's good financial administration in contrast with his tolerance of protected vice and gambling, are tempted to ask whether the two are not somehow related. The question arises whether it is not because the mayor has courageously denied his henchmen the opportunity to exploit the city's finances directly that he allows them to exploit vice and gambling on so lucrative a scale.[15]

Just as massive doses of federal funds aided Kelly's administration in a time of extreme economic scarcity, so did the millions of dollars procured from illegal sources. But while Kelly presided over an organization saturated with graft and corruption, there is little evi-

dence to suggest that he profited personally—at least after his elevation to the mayoralty. His apparent decision to spurn emoluments from
gambling may have been the result of several considerations: Having
once fallen victim to an Internal Revenue Service investigation, he
cautiously avoided any hint of fiscal impropriety while mayor. Another
explanation lay in the mayor's already healthy financial state. Since he
had allegedly stockpiled a fortune during the Whoopee Era at the
Sanitary District, he could bypass this second wave of graft. In the
parlance of Chicago politics, "Big Ed already had his." Some observers
suggested that Kelly's abstinence reflected a change in his character
triggered by exposure to New Deal principles. Though the money
generated from gambling seemed too important to the party organization to spurn, Kelly, with one eye on what would go on his gravestone,
insisted upon a higher standard for himself. As one student of Chicago
politics wrote, Kelly tolerated the corruption around him "in the familiar style of Irish Catholic politicians who went to mass, led lives of
personal fidelity, and were not scandalized by an imperfect world." In
all likelihood, all of these factors contributed.[16]

By acquiescing in the provision of gambling and other
forms of vice, Kelly and the other members of Chicago Democracy
entered into a covert partnership with the primary purveyors of these
services, the Capone syndicate heirs. As legatees of the Capone dy-
nasty, Jake Guzik and Frank Nitti enjoyed control of virtually all vice
operations in Chicago; only some parts of the black community remained outside their control, and that exception would be removed
within a generation.[17]

In the 1st Ward, the downtown district historically the
focus for syndicate vice operations, the Democratic leadership
remained subservient. Alderman "Bathhouse" John Coughlin and
Committeeman Mike "Hinky Dink" Kenna profited handsomely themselves and always turned in sizable majorities for the Democratic
ticket on election day. They did little in the way of governing, however;
syndicate boss Duke Cooney ran the ward with an iron fist, seldom
asking Coughlin or Kenna for their advice. When Coughlin died in
1938, Guzik ordered Kenna, by then a senile octogenarian, to assume
the alderman's post. Kenna was carried to city hall for the swearing-in
ceremony and said very little else for the duration of his term. When
Guzik decided to support Kenna again in the 1943 elections, Kelly
balked, demanding that at least a younger, healthier man should par-
rot the syndicate's views in the city council.[18]

Things ran so smoothly in the 1st Ward because of the
cooperation of the Republican ward organization, led by state senator
Daniel Serritella. Serritella, a close friend of Capone's and a member
of the syndicate hierachy, granted the Democrats political mastery of

the ward in exchange for a healthy cut of the gambling take. As a result of his association with Kenna, the Democratic Central Committee failed to select a candidate to oppose Serritella in the campaigns of 1934 and 1938. A strikingly similar situation unfolded in the senatorial district enveloping the "Bloody Twentieth" Ward, where Republican James B. Leonardo, also reputed to enjoy syndicate connections, won election in 1934 and 1938 when the Democrats withdrew his opponent.[19]

In the West Side 24th Ward, home of city council finance committee chairman Jacob Arvey, there was an equally strong tradition of cooperation between politics and gambling. Moe Rosenberg, Arvey's political benefactor and one of the few party dignitaries invited to Ed Kelly's first inaugural, served as a member of the Sanitary District Board as well as 24th Ward committeeman. Shortly after Kelly became mayor, the Internal Revenue Service accused Rosenberg of failure to pay income tax on approximately $500,000 earned the previous two years. In his testimony before U.S. Treasury Department officials in Washington, Rosenberg, who ostensibly made his income from a junkyard he owned, revealed his alternative source of income: He purchased iron, copper, and other discarded materials from utilities czar Samuell Insull at extremely low prices and then resold them as scrap at market prices. This revenue went to judges, legislators, and other public officials to ensure goodwill for the Insull concerns. By his own estimate, Rosenberg passed out over $500,000 to politicians, including a $30,000 gift to Mayor Cermak to pay the Cook County deficit. Under Arvey, precinct captain Ben Zuckerman assumed control of political protection and gambling payoffs in the ward, a post he held until his slaying at the hands of gunmen outside his home in 1944.[20]

In other sections of the city, Billy Skidmore and Big Bill Johnson controlled the gambling payoffs. Skidmore, a junkyard and saloon owner, had at one time headed a pickpocket cartel; he owned a saloon west of the Loop where the pickpockets gathered to divide their spoils and pay protection dues. In 1902 Democratic leader Roger Sullivan brought Skidmore into politics, and from 1908 to 1933 he served as the chief clerk and purchasing agent for the party. In 1912 and 1916 he was the sergeant-at-arms at the Democratic National Conventions. From these positions, and from his post as a bail bondsman, Skidmore became well acquainted with politicians, judges, and police administrators. Johnson, the acknowledged king of gambling on the city's West Side, gained admission into the Democratic inner circle through the efforts of his longtime friend Anton Cermak. While many suspected throughout the thirties that Skidmore and Johnson held important positions in the underworld, the extent of their influence was not known until the federal government brought them to trial for income tax evasion in 1940.[21]

At Skidmore's trial the federal government charged that he failed to report income totaling $1,103,545.26 for the years 1933–38. Trial testimony revealed that the major portion of that income hailed from gamblers paying for police protection. Ten gamblers, witnesses called at the trial, testified that both policemen and politicians sold protection to gamblers through Skidmore at his junkyard at 2840 South Kedzie Avenue. Other bookies named two ward committeemen who had approached them on Skidmore's behalf. The defendant admitted his role as "bagman" for the gambling interests and further revealed his financial ties to the Chicago Police Department—including a $10,000 loan to a police captain. Found guilty and confined to a federal penitentiary, Skidmore died two years later. Johnson's trial, though less sensational, revealed the same connections between the underworld and Chicago's officialdom and also resulted in a guilty verdict.[22]

As a result of the publicity generated by the Skidmore and Johnson indictments, members of the press and the general public questioned the involvement of Kelly-Nash officials. State's Attorney Tom Courtney publicly demanded that U.S. district attorney William J. Campbell subpoena Mayor Kelly to testify at the Skidmore trial, but the prosecutor spared the mayor the embarrassment of such an appearance. The trial proved damaging for Kelly, nonetheless. From his newly appointed post as Democratic national committeeman for Illinois, replacing the infirm Pat Nash, who decided to limit his duties to those of Cook County chairman, Kelly tried to bring pressure to bear upon Campbell to drop the case against Skidmore. He even approached Roosevelt about the possibility of having the attorney general "settle" the case out of court, but that attempt also failed. The revelations from the Skidmore-Johnson trials confirmed what the crusading *Daily News* had long claimed—that gambling could thrive in Chicago only with the consent of the mayor and his administration.[23]

Concurrently, a scandal concerning the police department erupted. Frank Konkowski, Democratic alderman and committeeman from the 26th Ward, accepted payoffs in exchange for jobs or promotions within the local police district. He customarily took money from all applicants and refunded it to those who did not receive the job or promotion desired. After several years, however, an emboldened Konkowski began keeping the money from all the aspirants, including those who failed to receive positions. The disgruntled job seekers ran to the state's attorney, and a jury subsequently found Konkowski guilty. In the course of his trial the true nature of advancement in the police ranks became known: Promotions to higher ranks cost increasing amounts of money. Each rank carried a price tag, and the ideal of promotion by merit had long been abandoned.[24]

Following these disclosures came a series of equally damaging excavations, which cast further shadows on the integrity of Chicago government and law enforcement officials. First was the *Chicago Tribune*'s publication of the secret bookkeeping records of the Capone syndicate. In October 1941 the *Tribune* printed the Guzik-Nitti organization's records for the previous July, detailing profits from gambling in suburban Cook County and payoffs to police for protection. Next came a massive scandal involving the Chicago Police Department, the Chicago Civil Service Commission, and Mayor Kelly himself—all generated by the unwillingness of the police to enforce the anti-gambling laws.[25]

The state's attorney's office filed charges before the Chicago Civil Service Commission, claiming that four city policemen from the department's morals division (Captain Martin McCormick, Sergeant Thomas Lee, and Patrolmen James Kehoe and Fred Trauth) were guilty of neglect of duty and of filing falsified reports. Despite the presentation of "voluminous and damaging" evidence by the state's attorney, the three-man Civil Service Commission ruled in favor of the policemen. Material evidence of particularly damaging nature was excluded on technical grounds, and the belligerent conduct of the hostile committee toward the prosecutor left no question that the case had been decided long before the trial began.[26]

The identities of the three men on the commission helped to explain the blatantly prejudicial treatment afforded the defendants. Joseph P. Geary, chairman of the commission and one of the most powerful ward committmen in the Kelly-Nash machine, should actually not have been serving. His term of office had expired two years before, but the mayor had conveniently forgotten to replace him. The second member, Wendell Green, had originally been appointed as a Republican to meet the legally mandated bipartisan composition of the committee; during the trial, however, Kelly placed Green on the Democratic ticket for a municipal court judgeship. The third member, William P. Ronan, also held a position in the local Democratic party hierarchy. Thus, the supposedly bipartisan Civil Service Commission included three Democrats, all linked closely with the Kelly-Nash machine.[27]

A public outcry at the decision, fueled largely by such civic groups as the Chicago Crime Commission and the Cook County League of Women Voters, forced Kelly to appoint a blue-ribbon panel of prominent lawyers and judges to review the proceedings. This panel included federal judge William J. Campbell, state supreme court justice Francis S. Wilson, appellate judge Kickham Scanlon, former federal judge George E. Q. Johnson, and attorney Lloyd D. Heth. To no one's surprise, they reported that the four defendants should have been found guilty and that the Civil Service Commission "acted improperly and was biased in favor of the policemen." By that time Geary, whose term had long expired, had been replaced on the commission and given a patronage job elsewhere. Wendell Green had won election to the municipal court and had likewise been replaced. Shortly after the decision of the investigating committee, the third member, William P. Ronan, resigned. Kelly suspended the four policemen temporarily, and the furor subsided.[28]

But the episode raised important questions about not only the tolerance of gambling but also the operation of the civil service in Chicago. The Kelly-Nash machine regularly circumvented civil service regulations by employing "temporary" help indefinitely. Many of these "temporary" employees, of whom the Cook County League of Women Voters counted over seven thousand, were also precinct captains in the Democratic organization; in order to keep their jobs, they had to produce acceptable vote totals on election day. The League of Women Voters also found a number of civil service positions not reclassified since 1915, examinations not graded for years at a time, and legally required annual reports not submitted. The publication of the league's findings in late 1942, though damaging enough, paled in comparison with the spate of scandals that befell Kelly's regime in 1943.[29]

On January 14, 1943, Edward "Spike" O'Donnell, a low-level underworld figure, confronted the commissioner of streets, Joseph Butler, outside his office on the seventh floor of city hall. O'Donnell, who claimed to have arranged some lucrative asphalt-paving contracts between the city and certain unnamed contractors for a promised fee of $70,000, demanded his "commission." When Butler refused, O'Donnell battered him so severely that he required hospitalization for several months. The imprudent O'Donnell, who boasted of his close association with Mayor Kelly, threatened to uncover a scandal that would "blow the lid off city hall" if he did not receive his money. Shortly thereafter, unknown assailants machine-gunned O'Donnell in front of his home in broad daylight, a classic gangland slaying.[30]

Five days later syndicate chief Frank Nitti committed suicide subsequent to his indictment by a federal grand jury, which charged that Nitti and others had extorted over $2 million from the four largest motion picture studios and their thousands of union employees. These deaths led the *Chicago Tribune* to ask "how it happened that hoodlums like Nitti and O'Donnell have been allowed all these years to terrorize citizens of Chicago and rob them without effective opposition from the mayor of Chicago and the police department he commands."[31]

Later that year a grand jury convened for the purpose of answering the *Tribune*'s question. The most sensational testimony came from Michael J. Flynn, county clerk and Democratic committeeman of the 13th Ward, who detailed Kelly's role in circumventing civil service procedures. "Everybody knows how promotions are made in the police department," he explained. "Most captains are appointed by the mayor on recommendation of the ward committeeman. Every ward committeeman knows that civil service examinations for promotion are mostly a sham—it's all handled through the mayor."[32]

The grand jury subpoenaed Kelly, who testified for over four hours on October 27. Kelly maintained that he left police affairs to Police Commissioner Allman, just as he granted total autonomy to the heads of other city departments. Furthermore, the mayor added, he had had no idea of the seriousness of the situation before reading about it in the newspapers. A spokesman for the grand jury bluntly told Kelly that its findings revealed either incompetence or corruption in the Chicago Police Department, to which charge the mayor responded by promising increased vigilance in the future. The next day the gambling establishments in the city closed en masse, and the police hauled in a covey of idle gamblers. In a few weeks, however, the police relaxed their dragnet, the gambling joints reopened, and it was business as usual.[33]

The same phenomenon recurred when a gangland slaying over control of the national racing wire spawned a public outcry in 1946. James M. Ragen, who had teamed with Moe L. Annenberg to gain control of nearly every racing information service in the country, staged a rebellion against the Capone gang when it demanded 40 percent of the income from his business. Ragen vowed to "fight the gangsters to the bitter end" and submitted to the state's attorney a statement in which he disclosed his knowledge of gambling in Chicago: He asserted that the Capone mob owned every Loop handbook except one; that many Kelly-Nash precinct captains worked in gambling joints; and that even some municipal court attachés moonlighted in mob-owned emporiums every day after court adjourned. The indiscreet Ragen was mortally wounded by several gunmen on June 24, 1946, and died a few weeks later. Again, in the advent of public indignation, the lid went on gambling in Chicago; Kelly and his new police commissioner, James Prendergast, vowed to stop it altogether—and did for a while. The resumption of gambling weeks after Ragen's death served to underscore the fact that the administration could indeed control vice in the city when it cared to, but that most of the time it looked the other way.[34]

The gangland killings and broad-daylight gunplay that besmirched Chicago's reputation in the Roaring Twenties recurred infrequently in the years of Edward J. Kelly's mayoralty, most notably in the few instances mentioned here. Yet it would be a mistake to assume that organized crime took a holiday in the thirties and forties, for another kind of lawlessness prevailed: The repeal of Prohibition meant new areas of involvement for the underworld. While in the days of Big Bill Thompson open conflict between warring mob factions never let Chicagoans forget the existence of organized crime, the ubiquitous gambling dens served the same purpose during the Kelly years. Occasional forays against gamblers stilled periodic outbursts of public vexation, but the Kelly-Nash machine generally turned its back on the duty of law enforcement. The reason for this policy of benign neglect was the vast amount of money—and to a lesser extent, the votes— essential to the well-being of the Democratic machine. It seems a paradox that Kelly, in many ways an enlightened liberal and genuine New Dealer, was at the same time inextricably linked with the darkest elements of the Chicago underworld. This connection is best explained as the mayor's practical response to political exigencies. Firmly committed to the preservation of personal liberties and opposed to pietistic crusades to enforce bluenose laws, Kelly also realized the indispensable contributions made to the machine by the agents of organized crime. And so the Kelly-Nash machine, beholden to both Harry Hopkins and Frank Nitti, Franklin D. Roosevelt and Billy Skidmore, straddled the line between respectability and ignominy.

7 War and Politics

 THE COMING of the Second World War found Kelly secure in his position as one of the most powerful and influential Democrats in the nation. Owing to his successful reelection campaign in 1939 and his orchestration of the 1940 Democratic National Convention, the mayor remained a favorite of President Roosevelt. As chief executive of the nation's second largest city and one of the country's most vital industrial centers, he held an important position in the United States' mobilization effort. The war years proved successful for Kelly: His administrative skills in the crisis period earned him the plaudits of Washington bureaucrats and military personnel alike. Similarly, Kelly achieved noteworthy triumphs in the political realm, turning back yet another Republican effort to unseat him by winning the 1943 mayoral election and continuing to exert an influence on national politics, as witnessed by his role in the 1944 Democratic National Convention. Kelly maintained his customary forceful, aggressive leadership during the hostilities and anchored it to a staunch support of Roosevelt's conduct of the war.

Prior to the U.S. entry into the war, Kelly manned an internationalist outpost in the generally hostile terrain of isolationist mid-America. As Roosevelt's envoy, he took the initiative of speaking out often against the aggression practiced by Hitler and the Axis powers. Significantly, Roosevelt chose the dedication of the federally funded Outer Drive Bridge in 1937 as the occasion to deliver his "Quarantine Speech"; despite favorable comment by Kelly, the speech met with fierce criticism, led by the isolationist *Chicago Tribune*, and Roosevelt gingerly backtracked to reaffirm his commitment to American neutrality.[1]

But while Kelly came early to accept the inevitability of the United States entry into the war and labored to prepare the American people for the unavoidable, he did not approve of Roosevelt's refusal to inform the public of the harsh foreign policy realities. "You're going at this all wrong," he told Roosevelt. "Your secrecy and double-talk have confused the people." Although he did not oppose the use of political chicanery in principle, he nonetheless argued that too much deviousness can be self-defeating and that a healthy dose of candor would prove more effective in this case. Furthermore, the working class had little interest in world affairs but supported Roosevelt because of what he had done for them in dollars and cents. Since the people would soon discover that war was inevitable and sacrifice inescapable, the mayor urged Roosevelt to tell them so. He further suggested that the president

> assure the working people and the little fellows that they won't do all the sacrificing. You've got to give everybody the feeling that the fellow making one thousand dollars a year more than himself will be making more sacrifices. Right now, most people suspect that everyone with more money will have to sacrifice less. The voters want to be told the truth—and, if it's as grim as they suspect, they will want you to put the Emergency program into the hands of a man who commands your respect and who can win theirs.[2]

In the months before Pearl Harbor, Kelly initiated the preparations for wartime emergency government. On December 20, 1940, the city council established the Chicago Commission on National Defense as an official city agency, with Kelly as its chairman. In May of the following year Roosevelt appointed Fiorello H. LaGuardia, mayor of New York City, the director of the U.S. Office of Civilian Defense (OCD); LaGuardia subsequently declared the Chicago metropolitan area a special defense unit, with Kelly as its administrative coordinator. Because of the concentration of heavy industry in the metropolitan area and the fact that, as Kelly repeatedly pointed out, northeastern Illinois was more accessible than the east coast to enemy bombers from Europe via Greenland and Canada, the army declared the Chicago region a critical area and gave it a priority rating for OCD protective equipment.[3]

Kelly immediately set to work to ready Chicago and its environs for wartime conditions. Long before the beginning of U.S. involvement, the Chicago Commission on National Defense established the first of many servicemen's centers, sponsored the collection of aluminum and other vital materials, and registered more than one hundred thousand civilian volunteers. With the goal of securing as many wartime contracts as possible for Chicago manufacturers, the commission held conferences on production techniques and, in cooperation with the Illinois War Council, sponsored the Defense Production Clinic in October 1941. The mobilization effort intensified as war became imminent: "This is not 'playing soldier,' " Kelly warned. "This is war!"[4]

One of the most acute problems confronting Chicago at the outset of the war, and one that would continue to prove nettlesome for the duration, was the labor shortage. The War Manpower Commission (WMC) designated Chicago a "Group One" city, one that exhibited a critical shortage of labor. (A "Group Two" city anticipated labor shortages in the future but temporarily met WMC standards.) Industrial centers strove to avoid Group One classification, which mandated stricter governmental control of labor management and also provided that government orders could be placed only when facilities for their production could not be found in Group Two cities.

Kelly named the Committee for Patriotic Action to publicize the manpower shortage and recruit workers: Civilian defense volunteers rang doorbells to recruit part-time and full-time workers, actively sought women to fill job vacancies, and staged elaborate parades to advertise the urgency. The highlight of its effort came on February 21, 1944, when the mayor led a massive torchlight parade down State Street. WACs, WAVEs, war veterans, military bands, tanks, and other war equipment moved through the downtown area as committee members signed up workers on the spot. But despite Kelly's efforts, the labor conundrum proved insoluble. Paul V. McNutt, chairman of the WMC, chastised Chicago industry for "overdrawing its manpower bank account," race discrimination, reluctance to employ women, and hoarding skilled labor. Chicago remained a Group One city until the close of the war in Europe.[5]

Like the labor shortage, which beset all large industrial areas, the debilitating effect of the war on small businesses constituted another sticky problem in city after city. While the exigencies of rapid, large-scale matériel production favored big business, the same conditions worked to the detriment of the nation's small businesses, which found it increasingly difficult to compete. In his defense of Chicago's endangered merchants, Mayor Kelly emerged as the leading spokesman for the country's small businesses. During the war years he spoke before congressional committees on seven different occasions to plead his case. Testifying before the Senate Committee on Naval Affairs, Kelly explained his concern for Chicago:

> Although Chicago has a few outstanding large industrial corporations, nevertheless more than 125,000 city workers are employed in plants of under 500 employees. This represents 31.7% of the total industrial manpower of the city. Yet, on the basis of careful estimates, it is shown that only 400 million dollars of defense production work so far has been sub-

contracted by the large plants in the Chicago six-county area.[6]

Kelly admitted that placing government contracts with small business concerns would be costly, but the additional expenditures, he argued, would be rewarded in healthy morale. The alternative would be bankruptcy, widespread unemployment, and the emergence of a "roving irresponsible population of floaters . . . which will make these rootless workers easy prey to false doctrines, destroy their confidence in their existing government and render them susceptible to subversive influences and violence." The mayor presented a specific plan for the allocation of large volumes of defense contracts, based upon the following guidelines: a certain percentage open to all plants on a competitive basis, a percentage open only to small plants on a competitive basis, a percentage open to small "distressed" plants on a "cost plus guaranteed profit" basis, and a percentage open only to larger plants in distress, also on a "cost plus guaranteed profit" basis. Small business, he concluded, "must survive if our economic structure is to survive." Congress rejected Kelly's plan, and despite some concessions, the federal government continued to favor the larger industrial and business concerns.[7]

Kelly's inability to resolve the vexing problems of small business and the manpower shortage belied notable successes in other areas. He could boast that at no time during the war years did a labor dispute prevent a Chicago-based corporation from meeting its shipment schedule. Indeed, no major strikes broke out during that time, a remarkable fact ascribed to the spirit of cooperation pledged by organized labor on the eve of U.S. involvement. A series of prolonged and violent strikes initiated by the CIO in March 1941 against the International Harvester works led Kelly to attempt mediation. After lengthy negotiating sessions with American Federation of Labor (AFL) president William Green and several top CIO officials, the mayor proudly indicated that a compromise settlement had been reached. His crowning achievement, announced on January 6, 1942, was the adoption of a resolution by twelve hundred representatives of AFL and CIO unions pledging no strikes and no jurisdictional disputes that would deter war production. As a result of that compact, Chicago could claim a record of labor tranquility unmatched by any other U.S. city.[8]

Under Kelly's driving leadership, Chicago led all cities in sales of war bonds, total number of enlistments, and salvage collection. The Windy City produced more war goods than any other metropolis, and one-seventh of all plasma donated to the American Red Cross came from Chicagoans. In fund raising the Kelly-Nash machine stood second to none, as exemplified by its 1942 Flag Day extravaganza, billed as the largest and longest parade ever: Four hundred thousand people marched fifty-one miles (from Howard Street on the north to the Indiana border) for seventeen hours. The parade and War Show at Soldier Field raised a total of $565,000. After the war, Mayor and Mrs. Kelly received the Award of Merit, the army's highest honor paid to civilians for service during the conflict, for their efforts in behalf of the armed forces. Chicago was the only city where servicemen and women could ride streetcars and buses free of charge. The outstanding feature of the city's hospitality to the soldier, however, was the Servicemen's Center.[9]

In August 1941 Kelly opened the main Servicemen's Center in the Loop at 176 W. Washington. "Mr. Kelly's Night Club" occupied twelve floors of a building previously owned by the Chicago Elks Club. In order to finance the center, Kelly applied to the Federal Works Agency for assistance. President Roosevelt, hesitant to set a precedent that would obligate the federal government to help fund such centers in all cities, concurred in the decision to deny the request. Thus rebuffed, Kelly resorted to other sources, utilizing the labor of WPA workers and city personnel to renovate the old building. The Chicago Park District supplied the staff, city hall the elevator operators. Mrs. Kelly became chairman of the canteen—often putting in twelve-hour days, while her volunteer helpers ranged from society matrons to maids given time off. Approximately thirty-five hundred women, many of them members of the USO, acted as hostesses.[10]

The Servicemen's Center, open twenty-four hours a day and completely free of charge, provided virtually every amenity desired by a soldier on leave. The canteen served hot meals as well as box lunches. Quieter floors near the top contained rows of beds and a public library, and there were recreational facilities for bowling, card playing, and dancing on the lower levels. Well-known bands performed nightly, and Kelly occasionally dropped in to sing along. An average of ten thousand soldiers passed through the center on a week night, with as many as forty thousand counted on a weekend. In 1942 Kelly opened a spacious outdoor facility on twelve acres in Lincoln Park and an auxiliary catering to black servicemen on the South Side. The centers constituted such an unqualified success and engendered such goodwill for the city—soldiers from across the nation spoke glowingly of their time spent in Chicago, even years later—that reporters called their operation one of Mayor Kelly's finest achievements in office.[11]

The splendid overall performance of Chicago, coupled with the high visibility of its energetic, patriotic mayor, led political pundits to speculate that Ed Kelly might be intending to ride his rekindled popularity into a higher office. The focus of that speculation came to center on the Democratic senatorial nomination in 1942. Kelly had been mayor for almost a decade, the reasoning went, and might be searching for new challenges; furthermore, Dwight H. Green, who had been elected governor by a landslide in 1940, was building a statewide political organization of such power that it might soon threaten even the mighty Chicago Democratic machine. Finding relations with Springfield increasingly difficult and facing the possibility of a swing in the political balance of power, the sixty-five-year-old Kelly might have concluded that a six-year tour of duty in Washington would constitute the perfect finale to his political career. Kelly's refusal either to confirm or to deny these conjectures served only to fuel the fires.[12]

During the months of speculation prior to the selection of a candidate, Kelly proved equally noncommittal to his fellow Democrats. He found objections to all candidates mentioned: Tom Courtney, the choice of much of the state party's hierarchy, had not announced his strong support for Roosevelt's foreign policy before Pearl Harbor; neither Paul Douglas nor Benjamin Adamowski was well enough known throughout the state. Harold Ickes, feeling that "apparently his technique is to knock down everyone who is suggested, leaving only himself as a possibility," led a coterie of Illinoisans, including Secretary of War Frank Knox and Senator Scott Lucas, to urge Roosevelt to veto a possible Kelly candidacy.[13]

The mayor's reluctance to commit himself undoubtedly reflected an ambivalence born of uncertainty. Judge William Campbell and Lucas reported that Pat Nash, growing increasingly disenchanted with his co-boss, urged Kelly to run in order to find out how much power the mayor actually possessed on his own. Kelly harbored serious reservations about his influence outside Cook County and noted that four previous Chicago bosses who had sought to top off their careers with senatorships ran aground downstate. (Roger Sullivan failed in 1914, Big Bill Thompson in 1918, George Brennan in 1926, and Anton Cermak in 1928.) Kelly repeatedly told all who would listen that he would bow to the president's desires on the matter and informed Roosevelt that he allowed his name to be used "to keep the aspirants down." Finally, the opposition from within the party, the absence of Roosevelt's blessing, and the prospects of tackling a resurgent Republican party in an off-year election convinced Kelly not to pursue whatever senatorial ambitions he held.[14]

On February 5 Kelly read to the Cook County Democratic Central Committee a letter declining to run for the U.S. Senate; the committee then endorsed Raymond S. McKeough as its candidate. The selection of the little-known McKeough, a congressman from the 2nd District on Chicago's South Side and a reliable member of the

Kelly-Nash machine, raised a howl of protest from Democrats around the state. Tom Courtney vowed to oppose the machine candidate in the primary, but the decision of Benjamin Adamowski, his frequent partner in anti-machine crusades, to accept the regular organization's endorsement for congressman-at-large dissuaded the state's attorney from running. Paul Douglas, Chicago alderman and Democratic reformer, did contest the nomination but lost the primary when the Illinois Democratic Central Committee supported the Chicago machine's candidate; the disgruntled Douglas, though fifty years old, enlisted in the Marines, where he served for the duration of the war.[15]

Kelly's selection of McKeough, a laconic man of little stature, to oppose incumbent Republican C. Wayland "Curly" Brooks, the darling of Colonel McCormick, paved the way for charges of duplicity. After similarly questionable nominations in the past—the machine chose Dr. Herman Bundesen to oppose Brooks in the 1936 gubernatorial contest and James M. Slattery in the 1940 senatorial race—McKeough shaped up as another straw man for Brooks to topple. Kelly denied such motives, promising an all-out campaign against the isolationist Brooks, whom he referred to as the "spearhead of the opposition" to Roosevelt's war program. "Nazis and Bundists will be voting for Mr. Brooks on election day and not for Mr. McKeough," the mayor predicted, adding that a Brooks victory would cause "rejoicing in Berlin."[16]

The McKeough-Brooks contest, the only senatorial election in any of the three largest states that year, stirred a considerable amount of interest nationwide. The *Tribune*'s incessant references to McKeough as "small potatoes" led the Democrats to adopt the tuber as their symbol. Delegates carted baskets of them to political rallies and contended that McKeough was the friend of the common man, the real "small potatoes" of the elitist Republicans. The *Tribune,* depicting McKeough as a subservient machine underling, turned his initials, R.S., into the sobriquet "Rubber Stamp." The Democrats pointed to their candidate's prescient support of Roosevelt's preparedness program in 1940–41 and hammered at a Brooks speech, delivered in the Senate shortly before Pearl Harbor, entitled "This Is Not Our War."[17]

The outcome of the election confirmed the Democrats' fears of a Republican victory, for Brooks won by a plurality of two hundred thousand votes. Republicans did remarkably well across the board in Illinois, winning the elections for state treasurer and superintendent of public instruction and gaining three additional seats in Congress. Adamowski, the machine candidate for congressman-at-large, lost to Republican Stephen A. Day. McKeough carried Cook County by a relatively few sixty-five thousand votes and lost badly downstate. Lacking a mandate to run himself, Kelly denied nomination to any of the other strong, but independent, candidates. If he had judged the cause to be completely lost, he would probably have offered up as a sacrifice a Courtney or Douglas rather than a lesser party loyalist. He saw the defeat of Brooks by McKeough as highly unlikely, yet palatable. But because Kelly was not himself running, and because more important local offices were contested, the senatorial race lacked immediacy. With the Republicans likely winners, the Democrats had little to lose and therefore gave McKeough only tepid support. Like other Democrats throughout Illinois, he fell victim to a resurgent Republican party but also suffered as a result of the machine's fatalism and indifference.[18]

The Republican triumphs in 1942 raised the question of Kelly's ability to secure reelection in the next year's mayoral race. In fact, following the disappointing performance of the Illinois Democrats, Kelly refused to say if he would seek to remain in office. A pair of fortunate political developments, however, paved the way for his decision. The first concerned the threat that Tom Courtney would repeat his 1939 challenge in the Democratic primary; in that earlier election, Kelly narrowly survived a heated intraparty fight and an equally spirited battle with a strong Republican candidate. As Benjamin Adamowski noted, any leader, especially one as ruthless and opportunistic as Kelly, naturally accumulated enemies in office, and Kelly had been in the eye of the storm for a decade. The concerned mayor, fearful that Adamowski would support a Courtney insurgency again, promised him the position of corporation counsel in return for his support. Adamowski refused the offer, declaring his lack of interest in the office, but added that he had broken with Courtney and would not campaign against Kelly.[19]

The second of these lucky circumstances involved the Republican party's choice of a mayoral candidate. On December 21, 1942, the *Tribune* announced that Roger M. Faherty, a wealthy lawyer whose father had been Big Bill Thompson's commissioner of public works, would oppose Kelly. This announcement, rendered before the Republican Central Committee had met in slate-making session, revealed the unknown Faherty as Colonel McCormick's handpicked sacrifice to Kelly. After reading about Faherty's selection in the newspapers, the Republican nominating committee hastily called a meeting and issued a perfunctory endorsement. The fledgling candidate shocked the members of his party by saying that he did not have "the slightest idea what the issues will be." When he boasted of his close personal relationship with Kelly, Republicans from around the state, led by Governor Green, protested. As the Cook County Central Committee rebelled—county chairman John T. Dempsey refused to serve as Faherty's campaign manager—Faherty finally withdrew, and the Republicans chose George W. McKibbin, Green's state director of finance, as their new candidate.[20]

The choice of McKibbin, a little-regarded figure only slightly better known than Faherty, raised a few eyebrows as well. (Informed of McKibbin's selection, one city hall reporter said, "Oh, I remember him. He's the guy the Republicans send out for coffee at their meetings.") Moreover, McKibbin, whose father-in-law, Bernard E. Sunny, headed the Chicago City Railway Company and held a seat on the board of operations of the Chicago Surface Lines, was termed a tool of the powerful traction interests. With such a vulnerable and inexperienced opponent, Kelly's decision to run for reelection became easier.[21]

As in past years, reform-minded Democrats attempted to unseat Kelly in the primary. In 1943 Alderman John S. Boyle of the 16th Ward, with the proxy support of Paul Douglas, bore the anti-machine standard. But with Courtney and Adamowski otherwise engaged, the anti-Kelly drive never materialized. Likewise, McKibbin, riding the endorsement of Governor Green, suffered little competition in the Republican primary. Well before primary election day, both candidates ceased to comment on their intraparty competitors and turned their attention to their certain opponents in the general election.[22]

McKibbin, like Wetten and Green before him, based his campaign on an all-out attack on bossism and machine politics. "Pendergast is out in K.C.," he proclaimed at the outset of his campaign. "Hague, in Jersey, and Tammany, in New York, have been cleaned out. Now it is time to clean out the Kelly-Nash machine." And like his unsuccessful predecessors, McKibbin returned repeatedly to the theme of the underworld-politics connection. Events during the campaign proved timely for the Republican claims and provided McKibbin with additional ammunition. He said: "The bullet that wounded Spike O'Donnell on Monday and the self-inflicted wound that ended the career of Frank Nitti on Friday forcibly reminded the voters that the taxpayers and the reputation of our city alike are suffering because of the gangsters' deals with higher-ups in the Kelly machine."[23]

To a lesser extent, McKibbin attempted to get at Kelly through criticism of the Roosevelt administration. A favorite target was the new rationing program effected by Washington; the Republicans warned that, under a Kelly government, the time would come when Democratic "snoopers" began invading pantries to check rationed food supplies. Speaking for McKibbin, Governor Green suggested that "a vote for Kelly is a vote for four more years of domination and arrogant control of every individual effort and of throttling every attempt of free enterprise. I tell you now that if Ed Kelly is re-elected, within one week after the ballots are counted he will again raise the 'Voice From The Sewer' for four more years of bureaucratic control." McKibbin scored Kelly for other shortcomings as well, including the deteriorating situation of the Chicago public schools—a criticism that, as the events of the next few years would demonstrate, could have been used to much better advantage.[24]

Kelly, as had become his custom, conducted a low-key campaign, one in which he largely refused to answer the charges of his opponent. Affirming his respect for McKibbin, a fellow South Sider, Kelly refused to use any of the critical information he claimed to possess about his rival. "I am not here," he proclaimed, "to warp any one's mind." Rather than delivering speeches or rushing around the city making personal appearances, the mayor virtually refused to take an active role in his own fight for reelection. He declined to involve the national administration in his campaign; Democratic National Committee chairman Frank Walker confirmed that Kelly had neither asked for nor received any help from national headquarters. To wrap up what there was of a campaign, he took a ceremonial "first ride" in the nearly completed, PWA-funded State Street subway, as a reminder of the public works improvements brought to Chicago by the Democratic administration.[25]

In the closing days of the campaign, the machine resorted to a bit of chicanery to ensure the loyalty of the black voters. On the Saturday before the election, the *Defender* hit the streets with a front-page headline: "McKibbin Signed Jim Crow Covenant!" complete with a large facsimile of a restrictive covenant that McKibbin and his wife had allegedly signed, barring blacks from residence in their Hyde Park neighborhood. McKibbin denied knowledge of any such document and charged that the Democrats had falsified the charges. The *Defender*, ignoring McKibbin's pleas of innocence, advised its readers not to vote for him.[26]

The next day the Republicans sent into the black community thousands of copies of a handbill charging that Kelly harbored sympathy for restrictive covenants. They commissioned a white real estate agent, a known advocate of segregated housing, to deliver leaflets to the home of Oscar DePriest. As the agent ascended the steps of DePriest's home, a group of men seized him and pirated him off to a nearby police station, insisting that he be arraigned on charges of inciting to riot and that the leaflets be impounded as evidence. On Monday the daily newspapers relayed the story of his "kidnapping by a band of Negro Democrats," but the Kelly-Nash machine denied any complicity and denounced such lawlessness. Unfortunately for the Republicans, the publicity created by the "kidnapping" backfired: The entrusting of the delivery of the handbills to a man of such unsavory reputation among blacks proved disastrous when the newspapers revealed his identity and therefore cast doubt on the veracity of the accusations against Kelly. The *Defender* later attributed much of Kelly's success in the black belt to the incident.[27]

In a very light voter turnout, Kelly bested McKibbin by a plurality of 114,020. In many respects, the outcome was disappointing for the mayor: Against an acknowledgedly weak candidate, his margin of victory fell substantially below that of his 1939 victory. (Four years earlier he defeated Green by 184,401 votes.) Moreover, he carried thirty-one wards in 1943, compared to thirty-five in 1939. McKibbin won the same fifteen wards carried by Dwight Green in 1939 while adding the 5th, 18th, 44th, and 46th. Map 3 shows a repeat of the voting pattern established in the previous mayoral election: Kelly's opposition centered in the Far South Side, the residential Northwest area, and the Lake Shore wards extending from Lincoln Park northward to Evanston. Again Kelly's strength lay in the inner city wards, although, as Map 4 shows, many of the machine wards turned in substantially less lopsided returns than they had in 1939.[28]

Nonetheless, despite machine apathy and overconfidence, Kelly's refusal to campaign, and the untimely deaths of O'Donnell and Nitti, the incumbent still won by a comfortable margin. As a *Chicago Sun* editorial noted:

> The reduction of the mayor's majority from that which he attained against Governor Green in 1939 thus seems no worse than legitimate wear and tear, chargeable to the four years in office which intervened. In view of the heavy artillery which the Republicans levelled against him, his 54.5 per cent looks pretty solid. Above all, it shows that heavy income-tax payments, rationing, price controls and other supposed burdens of war did not create in Chicago a state of political unrest and blind opposition to our new leadership.[29]

Flush from his successful reelection, Kelly had to deal with a problem that threatened to engulf many large American cities in the summer of 1943. Racial antagonism erupted in dozens of locations, including Buffalo, Harlem, Los Angeles, and, most violently, Detroit. These cities, like Chicago, attracted millions of workers, both black and white, during the war years; conflict over jobs and competition for scarce housing, a vital concern for the hundreds of thousands of blacks who moved to industrial centers during the war years, brought racial tension to a flash point in the heat of that summer. All told, 242 racial battles broke out in forty-seven cities. The violence in nearby Detroit, eventually quelled by the importation of U.S. Army

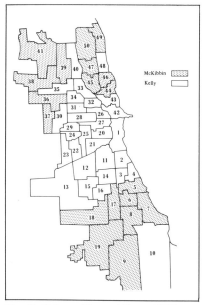
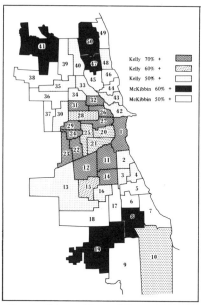

Map 3. Chicago Mayoral Vote—1943   Map 4. Chicago Mayoral Vote—1943

troops from Chicago, resulted in the deaths of twenty-five blacks and nine whites and sent a shock of alarm through the citizenry of the Windy City. Kelly responded immediately, telling the *New York Times,* "we are not going to have what happened in Detroit."[30]

The first steps taken by the Chicago administration were designed to discourage any thought of rioting. In a widely reported display of force, the army shipped twelve thousand tear gas and smoke grenades and ten thousand twelve-gauge shotgun shells to nearby Fort Sheridan "for use in the event of disorders in Chicago." Police on the South Side implemented a policy of "unexpressed, expedient segregation" by encouraging members of both races to avoid "known areas of conflict." In the event of interracial confrontations, police were ordered to hustle troublemakers off to station houses and disperse crowds. Kelly articulated his administration's pledge to discourage racial violence: "The vast majority of our Negroes and our white people are law abiding citizens, and we are going to remove every cause of friction between the great peaceful elements of the two. As to law violators and criminals, that is another story. They are going to be dealt with—in all races—with the full strength of our law enforcement facilities."[31]

Meanwhile, a group of approximately two hundred Chicagoans met to consider possible action aimed at deterring a repetition of the Detroit incident. They urged Mayor Kelly and Governor Green to form a biracial commission similar to the one appointed by Governor

Frank Lowden after the 1919 race riot in Chicago. At their request, Kelly appointed five blacks and five whites to the Mayor's Committee on Race Relations (later renamed the Mayor's Commission on Human Relations) and charged them with locating and alleviating sources of racial friction. Specifically, he urged the committee to look into such concerns as the immediate improvement of housing in the black belt and the breaking down of racial discrimination in employment, the two primary causes attributed to the outbreak of violence in Detroit.[32]

The Mayor's Committee on Race Relations became an immediate success, both as a palliative and as a public relations coup. Originally funded by the mayor's contingency fund and existing as an ad hoc body operating out of the mayor's office, it became an official department of the city government in 1947. After the war Kelly championed expansion of the newly renamed commission, securing a 100 percent budget increase and the hiring of six new experts for the staff. As the first interracial commission of its kind, the Chicago model became the standard imitated by countless cities in the post–World War II era. For its creation and for his firm guidance through the troubled summer of 1943—Chicago escaped an outbreak of racial violence that year—Kelly received widespread acclaim. Detroit mayor Edward J. Jeffries, Jr., in contrast, came in for much criticism for his handling of the riot, particularly for his indecisiveness. Once a popular figure among black voters, he barely won reelection later that year when blacks deserted his candidacy en masse. A number of post-riot studies criticized Jeffries for failure to take firm action as Mayors Kelly and LaGuardia had done.[33]

Having escaped the trauma of civil disorder, the Chicago Democrats were shaken by another event in the autumn of 1943. The death of eighty-year-old Pat Nash on October 6 gave vent to much speculation about the future of the Democratic machine in Chicago. Before any ambitious Democrats could launch a move to succeed Nash as party chairman, however, Kelly set out to take control. Since no replacement for Nash could be chosen before the 1944 primary, Kelly named himself the head of a thirteen-member special advisory committee to administer party affairs. This ploy, based upon a similar arrangement devised by George Brennan years before, made it possible for Kelly to assume the role of party chairman without actually holding the title.[34]

Several months later Kelly completed his usurpation by convincing 50th Ward alderman James R. Quinn to relinquish his post as the ward's committeeman and then assuming the position himself. (Kelly told a 50th Ward Democratic gathering that he would be ward committeeman in name only and that Quinn would continue to serve in fact.) Thus ensconced as a member of the Cook County Central

Committee, Kelly became eligible for selection as chairman. Despite some rumblings of rebellion, the party chiefs bowed to the force of the mayor's power play and elevated him to the top spot.[35]

Although the aged Nash had slowed down dramatically in later years and exerted only a nominal influence on the operation of the machine, his death constituted a watershed in the history of the Democratic organization in Chicago. Even though Kelly had undisputed control of the machine, he no longer could rely upon the counsel and temporizing influence of the party's elder statesman. Moreover, for Kelly, by then a septuagenarian himself, the change meant additional responsibilities and duties. The new party chief's prospect of absolute control was tempered by the threat of increased vulnerability.[36]

In the immediate future, however, Kelly's priorities centered on the presidential election of 1944. As expected, he spoke early and often of the need for a fourth term for Roosevelt. Utilizing the slogan "Roosevelt and the World," Kelly explained: "His duty is clearer now than ever before. Make no mistake about it, that guy's got the world in mind. He's truly a delegate-at-large now." Kelly ran into serious difficulty in Illinois because of the opposition of the resurgent Republican party. The situation became critical when the state Senate appeared to be on the verge of passing a resolution condemning a fourth term, but the Chicago Democratic bloc, led by young Richard J. Daley, managed to avoid a roll call vote. This show of strength by the Republicans, indicative of their growing stature throughout the Midwest, convinced Kelly that a fourth election of Roosevelt would be difficult. He did, however, foresee relatively few problems in securing for the president the Democratic nomination; his chief concern at the convention was thus the selection of a suitable vice-presidential candidate.[37]

The current vice-president, Henry A. Wallace, lacked popularity generally among the big city political bosses. Thought too liberal and ridiculed as a "visionary," Wallace had refused to enter into détente with the leading urban Democrats. The Chicago mayor publicly explained his opposition to Wallace by pointing toward the vice-president's unpopularity in the corn belt since his days as secretary of agriculture. Privately, Kelly told Philip Murray, chairman of the CIO, that his opposition to Wallace stemmed solely from Roosevelt's instructions. Whatever his reasons, Kelly quickly fell in step with the group aiming to deny Wallace renomination.[38]

On July 11, a few days before the opening of the convention in Chicago, Roosevelt hosted a secret White House meeting to discuss the vice-presidential situation. Of those present—Kelly, Democratic National Committee chairman Robert Hannegan, Democratic

National Committee treasurer Ed Pauley, and Roosevelt's son-in-law, John Boettiger—all voiced objections to the retention of Wallace. Kelly, who had spent time in the Library of Congress earlier that day checking on the public record of California's William O. Douglas, enthusiastically suggested his name as an alternative. Speaking for the others, who lacked Kelly's enthusiasm for Douglas, Hannegan boosted his fellow Missourian Senator Harry S Truman. Roosevelt offered no objection to either man. Hannegan asked the president for a letter they could show the delegates demonstrating the acceptability of the two men, and Roosevelt penned the following note: "You have written me about Harry Truman and Bill Douglas. I should, of course, be very glad to run with either of them and believe that either of them would bring real strength to the ticket."[39]

On July 15 Kelly and Hannegan met with Roosevelt when his train stopped briefly in Chicago en route to California for a tour of naval installations. Hannegan, who had spent the intervening days lining up support for Truman, tried to convince the president to repudiate a letter of endorsement he had given to Wallace on July 13. Roosevelt refused but confirmed his acceptance of Truman. Thus reassured, Kelly told a meeting of Cook County Democrats on July 16 that Wallace was out and that his replacement would be an "organization man." That same day, Kelly and Hannegan met with vice-presidential aspirant James F. Byrnes of South Carolina, who sought their backing at the convention. They disingenuously promised their support until Hannegan said, "Ed, there is one thing we forgot. The President said to clear it with Sidney"—that is, with Sidney Hillman, chairman of the CIO's Political Action Committee, who almost certainly would raise a strong objection to the conservative Byrnes. On July 17 Kelly hosted a dinner for Hannegan, inviting influential delegation chairmen and national committee members. The host and guest of honor took turns regaling the assembled party dignitaries about the president's "choice" of Harry Truman to succeed Wallace.[40]

On July 19 the Illinois delegation caucused to discuss the vice-presidential matter. According to Harold Ickes, a great deal of pro-Wallace sentiment existed, but Kelly managed to persuade the delegates to vote for Scott Lucas as a favorite son in the early ballots before switching to Truman. (Kelly argued that the Illinois delegation should grant the president the running mate he wanted, Truman.) On July 20 Hannegan, Kelly, Ed Flynn, Frank Walker, and a bewildered Truman, who refused to accept that Roosevelt wanted him as vice-president, gathered in the Blackstone Hotel to telephone the president in San Diego. "Have you got that fellow lined up yet?" asked Roosevelt. When Hannegan reported Truman's reluctance, Roosevelt exploded: "Well, tell the Senator that if he wants to break up the Democratic party by staying out, he can; but he knows as well as I what that might mean at this dangerous time in the world. If he wants to do it anyway, let him go ahead." A chastened Truman relented and prepared to jettison his plans to support the candidacy of Byrnes.[41]

On the afternoon of the twentieth, Wallace seconded the nomination of President Roosevelt and gave an inspired speech that ignited a massive demonstration. A short time later, when Kelly ascended the platform to nominate Scott Lucas, the delegates, recognizing the mayor's move as a detriment to Wallace, shouted him down. Whenever he took advantage of a lull to resume, the boos would rise again to drown him out. Finally Kelly managed to be heard, asserting his right to speak as chairman of the Illinois delegation. The crowd quieted to allow him to place Lucas's name in nomination, but the mayor prudently declined to give a speech of any kind.[42]

With the pro-Wallace gallery primed to stampede the convention, the Truman supporters resolved to terminate the day's proceedings. As Florida senator Claude Pepper tried to fight his way to the podium to deliver Wallace's nominating speech, Kelly urged the chairman to adjourn for the day because of the violation of city "fire regulations." When a voice vote was taken, convention chairman Samuel D. Jackson ignored the resounding chorus of no's and ruled that the aye's prevailed. The next day Kelly closed the galleries to the public, composed largely of labor unionists loyal to Wallace, in order to preclude any repeat of the previous day's demonstration. On the first ballot, in which Illinois cast its fifty-eight votes for Lucas, Wallace led Truman by a margin of 429.5 to 319.5. In the midst of the second balloting, after Illinois had already cast its vote again for Lucas, Kelly informed Jackson that his state wanted the opportunity to caucus. This act signaled other delegations to change their votes; in succession, Indiana, Alabama, and New York jumped to Truman, and the stampede was on. Returning from Committeeman John Touhy's headquarters across Madison Street from Chicago Stadium, Kelly announced that Illinois wished to change its vote to fifty-five for Truman and three for Wallace. The end came shortly thereafter, with Truman netting the necessary votes for nomination. The *New York Times* referred to the proceedings as the "second Missouri compromise," and Republican James A. Hagerty called the victory "a triumph of the bosses"; Kelly termed it "good politics."[43]

Having done the president's bidding at the convention, Kelly next resolved to produce impressively at the polls in November. When Roosevelt spoke at Soldier Field a few weeks before election day, he asked Kelly by what margin he might expect to carry Cook County. Kelly predicted a plurality of four hundred thousand—roughly four times that of 1940—and Roosevelt laughed incredulously. That night over one hundred thousand people packed the stadium, while authorities turned away an estimated three hundred thousand more. And, just as Kelly foresaw, Roosevelt won Cook County by almost half a million votes.[44]

The huge vote totals in Chicago, highlighted by an unusually heavy absentee vote for the president, led to accusations that Kelly had manipulated the servicemen's vote. His unsuccessful request that the Chicago Board of Election Commissioners count the votes of soldiers killed in battle, a practice outlawed by the state, did nothing to quell the rumors. Senator Homer Ferguson of New York launched an investigation to determine "whether the activities warrant looking into by the Senate Campaign Expenditures Committee." He found that Kelly sent a "political" letter to every Chicago soldier a day or so after his induction. Furthermore, the mayor sent Roosevelt campaign literature along with absentee ballot applications to, by Kelly's estimate, approximately 150,000 soldiers. The Senate found this practice, though unethical, not in violation of the Soldier Voter Act, and turned up no further evidence to merit the disqualification of Cook County votes. The *Chicago Daily News*, in evaluating the Chicago boss's performance, concluded that "Mayor Kelly emerges as the most successful of the big city machines in delivering the vote."[45]

After the fall 1944 elections, Kelly returned his attention to the more immediate concerns of Chicago and Illinois politics. Dwight H. Green had beaten back the challenge of Democrat Tom Courtney to win another term in the statehouse, but to the general surprise of the electorate, a resumption of the Kelly-Green feud did not ensue. In January 1945 the two antagonists met at the governor's mansion to discuss a program of détente and mutual aid. Sobered by his narrow victory over Courtney and the generally lackluster performance of his statewide political machine, Green perceived the need to broaden his base beyond the scope of "Tribune-McCormickism." Kelly, anxious to break the legislative deadlock in Springfield, sought to force through some much-needed reforms for Chicago. As a result, Kelly and Green announced their joint support of a comprehensive program to provide for better housing and public transportation in Chicago and a new constitution for the state.[46]

For Kelly, the housing shortage remained one of Chicago's most pressing problems. He and Green composed for submission to the General Assembly a program that would permit the city to acquire blighted land for redevelopment purposes, to authorize insurance companies to invest up to 10 percent of their funds in housing projects, and otherwise to fill in the gaps between corporate investment and publicly financed subsidized housing for low-income groups. The mayor and the governor also drew up legislation to set up a metropolitan transit authority for Chicago that would assume public ownership and operation of all transit lines—bus, surface, and elevated. The principal companies had been in federal courts for many years and currently pleaded bankruptcy. By the conclusion of the war the Kelly-Green public transit bill had passed the state legislature, but its constitutionality still required sanction by the federal courts.[47]

Green also promised his support for the calling of a constitutional convention. The Illinois constitution had not been completely revised since 1870 and had seldom been amended since 1900; it remained egregiously anachronistic in its heavy allocation of representation to the state's rural areas. Redistricting would mean more seats in the legislature for Cook County, both Democratic and Republican, and fewer for downstate. Opposition centered around the constitution's revenue clause, which forestalled a state income tax, a reform that both Kelly and Green promised to support. In all, the proposed legislative package, lauded by good-government groups and the press alike, was an ambitious, progressive attempt to solve some long-festering problems in Chicago. Moreover, it was particularly newsworthy because of the genuinely bipartisan enthusiasm expressed at its proposal and the surprise at its genesis in the cooperation of two machine politicians.[48]

The favorable publicity generated by the Kelly-Green entente at the end of World War II capped a four-year period of feverish activity for Chicago's mayor. As chief executive of the United States' second city and civilian defense coordinator for one of the nation's premier industrial areas, Kelly did, by all accounts, a creditable job of administration. If nothing else, he proved his autocratic brand of leadership admirably suited to the exigencies of wartime, where production took precedence over all else. Politically, Kelly survived the war years in good fashion, adding to his national reputation as a dependable vote producer for the Democratic party and maintaining control of the local machine apparatus. By the summer of 1945, however, events in Chicago presaged the critical problems of postwar cities and revealed chinks in the aging armor of the machine over which Kelly now maintained solitary control.

8 End of an Era

 IN THE months following the conclusion of the Second World War, Kelly continued to be as active as he had been during the previous four years. He maintained his position as chief of civilian defense until the program's termination in the summer of 1945. Although the Illinois War Council held its last meeting in June of that year, Kelly prevailed upon federal authorities to keep the Chicago Office of Civilian Defense (OCD) operative for several months thereafter. Kelly argued, with some justification, that continued troop movements required OCD regulation, but he also knew that the extension of OCD operations would keep a great number of city hall supporters on the payroll. Whatever his motivation, Kelly accurately foresaw that the delayed termination of the OCD in Chicago would at last temporarily ease the crisis in unemployment destined to befall cities after the return of the U.S. forces.[1]

Kelly called the postwar employment situation in Chicago "a mixture of hopeful and depressing factors." The city's wartime expansion concentrated mostly in industries offering slight prospects for postwar employment, he observed, particularly the weaponry and aircraft concerns. Between March 1940 and January 1945, Chicago's labor force increased by 438,000, some 200,000 of whom immigrated to take advantage of employment opportunities. When the war ended, 531,000 workers labored in the munitions industry. Moreover, the city would have to find jobs for an estimated 407,000 returning servicemen. On the positive side, the mayor noted, the iron and steel works boasted a backlog of orders sufficient to keep employment high for the next two years, and the farm machinery industry was expanding dramatically. He emphasized the importance of cooperation between government and industry to alleviate the anticipated employment problem.[2]

To aid Chicago-based businesses Kelly extolled the virtues of the city as a site for commerce and industry. He testified before the Senate Subcommittee on Foreign Relations, urging the construction of the St. Lawrence Seaway as a boon to the Chicago shipping trade. He wrote to President Truman, importuning him to designate Chicago as a terminal point on the international air transportation operations of the Pan American Airways Corporation; and to facilitate increased air traffic, Kelly urged expansion of airport accommodations. Although Municipal (renamed Midway) Airport fulfilled contemporary expectations—its 120 landings and departures per hour ranked first among the nation's airports—Kelly argued that for Chicago to maintain its position as the nation's air center, it would have to expand to meet future needs. Therefore, he appointed a committee to choose a site for a second airport on the city's Northwest Side, the first step in the location of O'Hare International Airport.[3]

As hub of the nation's transportation system and, Kelly hoped, a vital link in the rapidly developing international air network, Chicago seemed ably suited for the permanent headquarters of the United Nations. In his arguments for Chicago, the mayor also emphasized its cultural and educational facilities; its cosmopolitan, ethnically diverse population; and its heritage as a model of democratic government. On November 19, 1945, Kelly left Municipal Airport for England aboard the American Airlines flagship for the first transatlantic commercial flight from an inland city. In addition to demonstrating the viability of direct air travel between Chicago and Europe, the mayor sought to advance his city's cause before the United Nations' preparatory commission. Abetted by the acting director of the U.S. delegation, Chicago resident Adlai Stevenson, Kelly lobbied strenuously, though ultimately unsuccessfully, for the selection of Chicago as the United Nations' permanent location.[4]

While engaged in a wide variety of enterprises in late 1945 and early 1946—he was elected to succeed New York City's Fiorello LaGuardia as president of the U.S. Conference of Mayors, for example, and he spoke in favor of the creation of a Jewish nation in Palestine at a mass rally in Chicago Stadium—Kelly came to focus his attention increasingly on Chicago's critical housing shortage. During the war years, construction virtually ceased in Chicago, so that a serious problem from the previous decade was exacerbated: From 1929 to 1939 housing construction in Chicago declined 47.6 percent, a development in keeping with the national phenomenon of reduced building during the depression. From 1940 to June 1945, 35,000 dwelling units were erected in the suburbs, while only 19,800 privately constructed units appeared in Chicago.[5]

Not only had the construction industry lapsed into inactivity, but existent structures suffered from neglect and fell into disrepair. The Chicago Plan Commission concluded that "Chicago's housing supply is inadequate from both a quantitative and a qualitative standpoint," reporting that in 1947 Chicago contained twenty-three square miles of residential areas classified as "blighted" and "near-blighted." Of the city's 1,050,000 family dwelling units, nearly one-fourth (242,000) fell into these classifications. These dwellings housed approximately 840,000 persons, almost one-quarter of the city's population.[6]

Subsequent to passage of the Federal Housing Act of 1937, which provided for the construction of low-rent housing for the poor, the Chicago Housing Authority (CHA), created in 1938, assumed control of eleven public housing projects (seventy-nine hundred dwelling units). The CHA accepted as tenants only people earning no more than sixty-five dollars per month and currently living in substandard housing. In the early years of its existence, the CHA prospered under the benevolent rule of Mayor Kelly, who granted it a great deal of autonomy and protected it from gross political interference. Many aldermen remained hostile toward the agency, because it declined to make appointments on the request of council members and refused to dispense jobs on a patronage basis. CHA executive secretary Elizabeth Wood said of the city council: "They really hate us. They'd love to have that gravy." But Kelly, who took great pride in his role as the "patron saint of public housing," continually supported the liberal Wood in her fight for independence. Alderman John J. Duffy summarized: "Under Kelly, the Housing Authority submitted a proposal and that was it."[7]

Late in 1945 the city frantically began utilizing converted military barracks, trailers, Quonset huts, and prefabricated houses to accommodate returning military personnel. In 1946 the city council authorized the CHA to construct and manage, under the supervision of the federal government, temporary housing for the rapidly increasing number of discharged servicemen. Given vacant land already owned by the Park District, Sanitary District, and Board of Education, the CHA found its prospective sites located in outlying areas of the city, all but one of them in white neighborhoods. The city constructed projects in twenty-one sites in eleven wards, adhering initially to a policy of segregation. But with blacks constituting 20 percent of the veterans in need of housing, the CHA, spurred on by Executive Secretary Wood and Director Robert Taylor, and with the pledged support of Kelly, began selecting tenants solely on the basis of need.[8]

Kelly enthusiastically supported the idea of integration but cautioned that the proportion of blacks admitted to previously all-white housing projects should be limited at first to 10 percent of the total residents, noting that blacks constituted 10 percent of the city's population. Espousing gradualism, the CHA decided to integrate only the largest temporary projects, those of over 150 units. Using carefully selected black families, the agency integrated roughly half of the twenty-one projects without incident. But what one historian called Chicago's last attempt to employ both scattered sites and "at least an apparently nondiscriminatory tenant selection policy" foundered when white resistance flared at a Southwest Side project.[9]

Trouble erupted at Airport Homes, a 185-unit project near Midway Airport in the West Lawn neighborhood. As early as August 1946 white residents began protesting the establishment of the Airport Homes project, which was scheduled to open in November with several black families in residence. A coterie of fifty-nine white "squatters" assumed control of units the CHA had designated for black families, leaving only when the city threatened legal action. On November 16 a black family moved in but met immediate resistance; a mob surrounded the newcomers, and a detail of four hundred police had to intervene to protect them. The intimidation and harassment continued, even though Kelly pledged to defend the new inhabitants and promised that "all law-abiding citizens may be assured of their right to live peaceably anywhere in Chicago." When two black families moved into Airport Homes on December 9, two hundred policemen swinging nightsticks battled an equal number of white demonstrators. After that incident, the black residents left and none would take their place: Kelly and the Chicago police notwithstanding, the white residents of West Lawn won their battle to exclude blacks from the neighborhood.[10]

Kelly's Commission on Human Relations then mobilized to oppose the use of restrictive covenants, a tactic employed at Airport and Sauganash homes. It sponsored the Conference for the Elimination of Restrictive Covenants, at which Bishop Bernard J. Sheil addressed a group of eighty civic, church, labor, and business leaders, and launched an extensive public relations campaign to condemn the practice of forced segregation. But despite the efforts of the administration, black Chicagoans remained confined to the black belt and continued to be the group hit hardest by the housing shortage. In a report issued in 1947, the Commission on Human Relations concluded:

> It can be stated flatly that during 1946 we made no gains on conquering this problem, or even alleviating it. In fact, Chicago was worse off at the end of 1946 than at the end of 1945. The city had actually lost more dwelling units through fire, simple decay and disintegration than it put up during the year. And on top of those already living in unspeakably crowded conditions, more people moved in.[11]

While blacks met stiff resistance to housing desegregation, they confronted equally staunch opposition to efforts at integrating schools. During the war, conditions in South Side schools deteriorated because of crowding induced by heavy immigration of blacks and the inability of authorities to secure materials for building. In 1943 sixteen South Side schools operated on double shifts to accommodate the number of students. Although both black and white pupils had attended several Chicago public schools for years without serious problems, a number of all-white schools remained bulwarks against integration in mid-decade. In September 1945 a rash of anti-black strikes broke out in Chicago area schools. Following a walkout by white students at Froebel High School in Gary, Indiana, whites struck at Englewood, Morgan Park, and Calumet high schools in Chicago. The Mayor's Commission on Human Relations, the president of the Board of Education, and the mayor all issued statements condemning the strikes and guaranteeing blacks access to all public schools. The police gave escorts to black students, broke up demonstrations, and arrested white strikers. The city press heeded Kelly's recommendation to downplay the incidents, relegating their coverage to back pages and forsaking photographs. These combined efforts by Chicago officials resulted in the breaking of the strikes and at least a limited success for the Kelly program of gradual integration.[12]

The problem of segregation was just one of the many crises confronting the beleaguered Chicago public school system in the post–World War II years. Since the passage of the Otis Act in 1917, the Board of Education had been a separate body from the city government; it passed its own budget, selected its own employees, and determined its own policies. The board consisted of eleven members, appointed by the mayor and subject to the approval of the city council, which, in turn, selected the superintendent to direct educational development. Since the mayor chose the board members, its autonomy depended upon the desires of the city's chief executive. With Kelly in the mayor's office, the Board of Education was an independent institution in name only. From the outset of the Kelly years, the school system maintained its position at the center of one controversy after another.[13]

In his first two months in office, Kelly appointed seven new members to the Board of Education, thus assuring himself control of the body. On July 12, 1933, the board instituted a wide-ranging program of reform aimed at rescuing the financially wrecked school system. In the process of economizing, the board came under criticism for trimming important educational programs and firing fourteen hundred teachers, while adding seven hundred political appointees and failing to terminate any of the five hundred politically appointed janitors in the schools. Robert Maynard Hutchins, president of the University of Chicago, declared that the precipitous actions taken by the board in the summer of 1933 were based

> either on a complete misunderstanding of the purpose of public education, a selfish determination that its purpose shall not be fulfilled, or an ignorant belief that a system which has been wrecked can still function. The economic and social condition of Chicago will be worse for twenty-five years because of what the Board of Education has done.[14]

The poorly conceived budget cuts and questionable educational practices of the new Board of Education could be explained largely by the absence of educators among the Kelly appointees. Rather than choosing teachers or others familiar with the workings of the Chicago public school system, the mayor chose laymen whose primary qualification was loyalty to the Democratic machine. A typical appointee was Charles W. Fry, an official of the local machinists' union, who responded to a parent-teacher committee questioning his suitability:

> I ain't got no ax to grind. . . . Let me say to you young ladies and gentlemen educators who are so uncouth . . . if you were members of my union you would get disciplined. There probably is never a year that Chicago University ain't facin' a deficit. . . . When I ask them (students) that has been receivin' this kind of education that you are advocatin' . . . what they want to be . . . as God is my judge, they don't know what they want to be. They receive so much of this kind of education, it shoved them from spot to spot, that they cannot make up their minds what they want to do. That is no kiddin', boys and girls.[15]

Kelly set the tone of anti-intellectualism by his appointment of James B. McCahey as president of the school board. The choice of McCahey, a coal dealer, triggered dissent for several reasons: his founding of the Truckers and Transportation Exchange, a renegade union that had engaged in territorial skirmishes with other locals for control of the Chicago teamster membership; his reputed association with gangsters Red Barker and Jack "Three-Finger" White; and his Catholicism. The fears of many Protestant groups over the appointment of a Catholic to head the public school system seemed well founded when McCahey hired a disproportionately large number of Catholic women to teach in the schools.[16]

Under McCahey's rule, politics crept into the school system. Obtaining a teaching job depended upon political connections rather than qualifications or experience. In the 1934–35 school year, for example, the school board granted 500 temporary teaching certificates to those applicants with political sponsors and assigned 340 of these applicants to positions, while ignoring 842 regularly certified instructors. Moreover, the board required the teachers to perform blatantly political tasks, such as contributing money to the Democratic party, attending political rallies, and selling tickets to the mayor's Christmas charity football game. Questioned about these dubious practices, Kelly utilized the tactic he frequently employed when confronted with wrongdoing in the schools: He reminded his critics that the Board of Education was a totally separate institution over which he exercised no control.[17]

In 1936 Superintendent of Schools William J. Bogan died, and upon the recommendation of Mayor Kelly, the board named William H. Johnson as his successor. Johnson, who had been appointed assistant superintendent by McCahey over the protests of Bogan, suffered from a lack of experience in educational administration and from his indebtedness to the superiors who installed him in the position. Marking no claim to fill his role professionally, he said: "I am no fool. I am willing to go along for what the job pays. I get fifteen thousand dollars a year and that is more than any college professor gets." Before long, stories of Johnson's ineptitude and malfeasance further clouded the record of the school system.[18]

Shortly after Johnson became superintendent, he was singled out for complicity in a new rash of scandals. Three of the largest and most reputable textbook companies (Allyn and Bacon, Ginn and Company, and Harcourt, Brace and Company) announced that they would no longer do business with the Board of Education because of its illegal purchasing practices. The *Chicago Daily News* charged that syndicate kingpin Billy Skidmore had been making collections on textbook sales as well. Further investigation revealed that the school board purchased materials from dummy corporations by splitting orders into units of $300 each, thereby circumventing the mandate that orders in excess of that price be submitted to competitive bidding. In one year, nine dummy corporations sold the schools $786,000 worth of merchandise in orders of less than $300 apiece.[19]

In November 1937 Superintendent Johnson outlined a plan by which 20 percent of Chicago's high school students would be allowed to take "general" courses, while the remaining 80 percent would take "vocational" courses. Basing his proposal on the exigencies of depression America, Johnson argued that the arts and sciences had no value in a society in which employment constituted the universal goal of the citizenry. Kelly and school board president McCahey applauded the plan, but others, most notably Paul Douglas and Illinois

Institute of Technology president Henry Heald, launched a strenuous protest against the proposed "de-intellectualization" of the public school system. When the resultant public clamor clearly demonstrated widespread opposition, Johnson calmly announced that he had never advanced such a plan and the media had made a grievous misinterpretation.[20]

Johnson's biggest gaffe materialized in 1937 with the revelations concerning examinations for school principals. As a result of suits filed against the Board of Education by Hiram B. Loomis and Raymond M. Cook, two teachers passed over for principalships on the basis of questionable examining practices, the true nature of the promotion system came to light. The examination for principals consisted of two parts, a written test given in September 1936 and an oral test given in March 1937. The Board of Education conceded that low written scores were sometimes either elevated or offset by extremely high oral grades and that the superintendent, one of three members of the examining committee, manipulated scores to aid preferred applicants.[21]

One of the other examining committee members, J. J. Zmrhal, testified that the committee never took an actual vote on candidates, as prescribed by law. The superintendent informed the other examiners before the oral test which candidates he favored, which would fail, and which he did not care about. In the case of Raymond M. Cook, Zmrhal recalled, Johnson had said: "This man has high marks on the written and evaluation. I will have to mark him low enough so as to be sure to fail him." On the published list of successful applicants, Zmrhal also related, he found the names of candidates who had scored below the acceptable standard on the written exam. In a telegram to the *Chicago Daily News,* the other member of the examining committee corroborated Zmrhal's testimony.[22]

As a result of the superintendent's conduct of the examinations, scores of deserving applicants failed in order to make room for decidedly inferior candidates. Marie McCahey, sister of the board president, had repeatedly failed the test but passed in her first attempt under the Johnson administration. Of the 155 who passed the exam, 15 received immediate appointments: McCahey, 8 of her friends and relatives, and 6 relatives of local Democratic politicians. Eighty percent of those chosen had failed the written exam but compensated by their performance on the subjectively graded orals. Further, 122 of the 155 newly appointed principals had been pupils of Johnson's in a class he conducted for pay at Loyola University to prepare the teachers for the exam.[23]

With the controversy over the principals' examinations still alive in the months before the 1939 mayoral election, Kelly appointed a committee of distinguished Chicagoans to examine the school system. Professor James Weber Lynn, the driving force on the panel, died during the investigation, and three other members (Hull House's Charlotte Carr, Professor Frank Freeman, and businessman Lester Selig) resigned when Kelly refused to approve the inspection of contracts for supplies signed by the Board of Education. When the remaining four members demonstrated their subservience to the mayor by recommending his handpicked candidate to replace an out-going board member, the Citizens' School Committee requested their resignations; in the following weeks, the investigating panel disintegrated, publishing no findings and indeed leaving no record of ever having existed.[24]

In subsequent years Kelly dismissed the many requests for renewed investigation of the school system, disavowing any responsibility for actions taken by the school board and reaffirming his belief in the quality education provided for Chicago public school students. But the issue resurfaced in full-blown form in 1945 when the National Education Association (NEA) released the findings of an investigation it conducted at the request of the Woman's City Club of Chicago, the Cook County League of Women Voters, and the Chicago Citizens' School Committee. The NEA compiled its data despite the refusal of the Chicago schools to cooperate in the investigation. The report comprehensively criticized Johnson, board president McCahey, Kelly, and the entire Board of Education for practices resulting in a "progressive degeneration of the Chicago schools which will mark and handicap them for many years."[25]

In addition to the aforementioned transgressions, the report detailed a number of other unethical practices. Superintendent Johnson, with the school board's approval, had adopted for classroom use twenty-two books that he had authored or coauthored—largely on school time. Among the financial irregularities uncovered were the rejection of low bids for school supplies, the dispensation of jobs for money, and the awarding of contracts to relatives of school officials and to racketeers. The NEA further reported that the Board of Education, primarily through McCahey's efforts, had created a political machine inside the school system by means of preferential treatment for loyal teachers and principals, favoritism in promotions, indiscriminate transfers of "troublesome" teachers, and the development of an elaborate spy system. Finally, it concluded, the responsibility for the entire sordid mess rested with Kelly, who had appointed all the board members and who, in fact, controlled the board's policies through McCahey.[26]

Johnson glibly dismissed the report, calling the NEA "only a hiking club," but the city council succumbed to public opinion and voted to hold a hearing on the charges. For two days Chicagoans packed the council chambers as speakers from the Citizens' School Committee, the Chicago Teachers Union, the Independent Voters of Illinois, the Parent-Teacher Association, and other organizations testified against the school board. At the conclusion of the hearing, the five aldermen charged with hearing the evidence, having sat in inscrutable silence throughout the proceedings, issued a four-page mimeographed statement exonerating the schools. They based their conclusions on the fact that the North Central Association, the accrediting agency for schools in midwestern states, had kept the Chicago public schools in good standing throughout the controversy. To assuage the fears of the city council, Johnson said, "Don't worry about the North Central. I can control them. They'll do as I say."[27]

The day after the publication of the city council committee's report, however, the North Central Association released its annual evaluation of Chicago high schools, which threatened withdrawal of accreditation pending the creation of a politically independent Board of Education. Faced with the possible reduction of the public school system to a shambles, Kelly appointed another investigating committee of Chicago-based educators and promised to abide by its recommendations. On June 18, 1946, the committee publicly issued its conclusion: that only the resignation of the superintendent and the entire school board could extricate the local educational system from the quagmire into which it had sunk. Johnson and one other board member resigned immediately (Kelly promptly appointed Johnson president of the Chicago Junior College), and three others followed suit by September. To replace them, the investigating committee submitted a list of acceptable candidates to the mayor, from which he chose the new members. McCahey announced that he would step down at the conclusion of his term in May 1947.[28]

The school crisis, festering since the beginning of Kelly's mayoralty, had thus come to a head in 1945–46 as a result of accumulated grievances that could no longer be ignored. Kelly's reluctant action stemmed from the pressure brought to bear by the NEA and the North Central Association, whose threat of sanctions foreboded disaster for the public school system. For years the Democratic machine had utilized the teacher ranks as an adjunct political organization, frequently at the expense of education; but with another municipal election forthcoming in 1947, the NEA disclosures had to be addressed. As *Chicago Sun* political columnist Milburn P. Akers rhetorically asked Mayor Kelly, "Is Jim McCahey worth more [to you] than all the votes of independent Democrats and the many thousands of persons of no party affiliation?"[29]

Another problem of long standing that came to haunt

Kelly in the postwar years was that of the city's antiquated mass transportation system. The traction situation had plagued not only Kelly but
his predecessors as well, hailing back to the first decade of the twentieth century. In 1907 the city's reformers, bent upon securing better
service from the various transit companies in operation, struck a compromise with the financial community by forsaking municipal ownership. The compromise ordinance drafted that year also established a
purchasing price at which the city might someday take over the lines,
combined the twelve existing surface lines into one company, and set
a universal five-cent fare. It became apparent, however, that adequate
service could not be provided without a major change left unmade by
the 1907 settlement: the unification of all local transit concerns, both
surface and elevated lines. In 1925 Mayor William Dever's unification
plan, which called for municipal ownership, passed the city council
but failed to survive a public referendum. Consequently, when the
1907 ordinance expired in 1927, the city council granted day-to-day
extensions of franchises pending a comprehensive settlement.[30]

In 1930 an ordinance providing for unification under
private ownership, actively supported by utilities magnate Samuel In-
sull, passed the city council and a popular referendum. The transit
companies refused to accept the ordinance, however, pleading financial inability to comply, most notably because of the provision calling
for the payment of 3 percent of gross revenue into a city transit fund.
Indeed, the Chicago Surface Lines went into receivership in 1926,
and the elevated lines followed in 1932. When Kelly became mayor in
1933 he faced a disastrous situation: Bankrupt companies had no
capital to make structural improvements; streetcars averaged twenty-
five years old and suffered from disrepair; and elevated trains varied
in age from twelve to forty years. In all, the public transportation
system, once the pride of Chicago, paled in comparison with its counterparts in virtually every other large American city.[31]

Kelly found himself in an anomalous situation: He consistently affirmed his commitment to the city's purchase of a unified
transit facility—in fact, PWA chief Harold L. Ickes had made it a
precondition for the granting of funds for subway construction—but
he felt obliged to restrict capitalization of the existing companies. This
restriction ensured a better deal for the city but retarded the development of transportation services. In his effort to keep property valuation
down, the mayor charged that the companies listed dead horses and
decrepit buildings in their assets to inflate their net worth. While the
surface lines managed to keep their existing equipment in relatively
good condition, the elevated lines suffered from the mayor's opposition
to the purchase of new facilities. As a result of Kelly's intractability,
the transit situation worsened rapidly, and as one student of the prob-

lem noted, "Surface service was more than ever miscast as a substitute for rapid transit, and existing elevated service deteriorated alarmingly." As the years passed, Kelly's unwillingness to compromise the city's bargaining position meant that a lingering problem went unsolved, and Chicago's straphangers chafed at the inaction.[32]

During the time of his stalemate with the transit companies, Kelly fashioned a set of long-range proposals for Chicago's transportation system. Aware of the need for expanded and improved mass transit, he also recognized the importance of the automobile in the city's future. In the plan he presented to the city council, the mayor noted that the number of autos in Chicago increased by 375,000 from 1920 to 1936; in the ten years preceding 1936, however, annual elevated ridership decreased from 228,000,000 to 129,568,000, a 43 percent drop, while the city's population rose 13.6 percent. He therefore urged that mass transit expansion be limited to subway construction and that elevated structures be converted to superhighways.[33]

Kelly's comprehensive plan called for a heavy emphasis upon superhighway construction, featuring an eight-lane highway along Congress Street from Grant Park westward to the city limits, with a rapid transit facility in a tunnel and in the median strip; an extension of the Outer Drive north from Foster Avenue to the city limits; a southwest superhighway along the Illinois and Michigan Canal from Harrison Street to 74th Street; an extension of the Outer Drive southeast from 49th Street to the Indiana state line; a northwest super highway from Orleans Street to the city limits; and a north-south "crosstown" artery connecting the southwest superhighway at 74th Street with its northwest counterpart at the northern edge of the city. But these long-term proposals, some of which came to fruition in later years, offered no solution for the immediate problem of the city's bankrupt and ineffective transit concerns.[34]

A resolution of the traction conundrum finally came with the Kelly-Green détente after the war. In 1942 the city council passed a Kelly unification plan, which the public approved in a popular referendum and a federal court upheld in a test of its constitutionality, but which the Illinois Commerce Commission rejected as "unsound." Kelly then called in a group of engineers to devise a new plan; their recommendation became the crux of the plan Kelly offered to Green in 1945: A Chicago transit authority, financed by private capital, would buy up all facilities and operate them as an independent agency. Authorized to operate in eighty-one municipalities in Cook County, the supporting agency would be empowered to issue bonds, payable solely out of its own revenues, but not to levy taxes.[35]

On February 17, 1945, Green and Kelly issued a joint

statement urging that the Illinois General Assembly pass the Metropolitan Transit Authority Act, which it did on April 12. On April 23 the city council unanimously granted the newly created Chicago Transit Authority (CTA) an exclusive franchise for the next fifty years, and on June 4 the authority cleared the hurdle of public referendum in Chicago. In October 1947, after selling $105 million worth of bonds, the CTA began operation in metropolitan Chicago. The creation of the CTA, a landmark in the city's development and decidedly one of the most notable achievements of the Kelly mayoralty, came at what should have been a politically propitious moment for the Democratic machine, just before the mayoral election of 1947. But the traction settlement was largely overlooked in the preelection atmosphere—unfortunately so for Kelly, who found himself in a bitter struggle to maintain control of a fractious Democratic party and to secure for himself the party's nomination for mayor.[36]

By the middle of Kelly's fourth term, the Democratic party in Chicago had become rife with dissension. Without Pat Nash around to calm the tensions between the rival factions, particularly among the ever-querulous Irish, party discipline faltered as seldom before. The years of Kelly's dictatorial rule of the party were catching up with him as accumulated grievances gained a new immediacy. In the case of the influential Tom Nash, Pat's nephew and a renowned criminal lawyer of shady reputation, whose clients included Al Capone, the animosity could be traced to a 1943 decision: Kelly had selected Mike Mulcahey over Nash's man, John Duffy, to replace Peter Carey as county sheriff. Kelly also failed to accept Jim McDermott, another Tom Nash protégé, as the party's candidate for state's attorney. For the first time, Democratic aldermen dared to criticize Kelly in council sessions, and talk that the mayor did an inadequate job as county chairman became widespread. His prolonged absences from the city, chiefly spent in Palm Beach, Florida, treating his colitis, generated additional criticism. Kelly also faced disapproval of his 1946 slate of candidates, which many party members felt had been haphazardly assembled by an indifferent mayor; they voiced their concern because of the threat of substantial Republican gains in that off-year election. Arguing that doing both jobs demanded too much from the seventy-year-old Kelly, the Irish took the lead in calling for a new party leader.[37]

The man chosen was Jacob M. Arvey. The son of Russian Jewish immigrants, Arvey grew up on Chicago's Near West Side just north of famed Maxwell Street. The young lawyer immersed himself in Democratic politics, becoming 24th Ward alderman in 1923 and party committeeman in 1934. He gained national notoriety in 1936 when President Roosevelt paid homage to Chicago's 24th as "the banner Democratic ward in the United States." (It had produced 26,112 votes for Roosevelt and only 974 for Alf Landon.) As city council finance committee chairman, Arvey was widely recognized as the "third man" in the Kelly-Nash machine by the late thirties. In 1941 he resigned his various offices to enlist in the army, thereby gaining a lengthy hiatus from the increasingly fratricidal machinations within the city's Democratic party—a situation exacerbated by Nash's death in 1943.

When he returned after the war, Arvey emerged as the ideal compromise candidate to supplant Kelly as party chief: His non-involvement in the previous years' jockeying for power made him acceptable to such widely disparate and ambitious Democrats as finance committee chairman John Duffy, 19th Ward committeeman Tom Nash, 44th Ward committeeman Joe Gill, 29th Ward committeeman Al Horan, 27th Ward boss John Touhy, county commissioner Dan Ryan, 14th Ward committeeman Joseph McDermott, and 30th Ward alderman John S. Clark. Because of Arvey's declining power base— the Jewish vote in Chicago had long been dwindling as a result of demographic changes—the anti-Kelly Irish did not consider him a threat. They intended to use him as a wedge to drive Kelly out of power, and he would serve as a custodian until one of the others could muster the power necessary to assume control.[38]

Kelly's position became more tenuous as a result of the 1946 elections. Although the mayor had spoken optimistically about the outcome, even assuring Truman that Cook County Democrats would triumph, his equanimity proved misplaced: Republican successes that year marked the biggest setback for county Democrats since 1930. The Republicans captured several key county offices, including sheriff, treasurer, probate court judge, and president of the Board of Commissioners. The GOP also won five of the county's ten contested seats in Congress. Acknowledging that the Republicans benefited from the national trend away from the Democratic incumbency, local politicos still suspected that the results stemmed largely from a growing public resentment of the abuses of the Kelly machine. Arvey, who disavowed any responsibility for the 1946 debacle, maintaining that he had assumed control of the party after the slate-making process, pledged to evaluate the mayor's electability before sanctioning his renomination in 1947.[39]

Shortly after the 1946 election, Arvey, Joe Gill, and Al Horan began conducting public opinion polls in Chicago movie theaters and commissioned one of Kelly's speech writers to canvass by telephone. They inquired about the popularity of the mayor and unearthed some sobering results. Arvey summarized: "Well, we were still solid with the Jews, we could see, and better than even with the Negroes, but everywhere else—the Poles, the Irish even, the Germans—we were in trouble. 'Him?' they'd say. 'Are you kidding? We'd sooner vote for a Chinaman." The once popular Kelly had seen his esteem crumble under the weight of several damaging scandals and the failure of his administration to deliver services to the citizenry. The schools controversy, official tolerance of organized crime, an ineffective and corrupt police department, haphazard garbage collection and street cleaning, high taxes with no apparent return in municipal services—all of these shortcomings surfaced in Arvey's canvassing.[40]

The voices of Chicago's civic leaders echoed the complaints of the populace. Leo A. Lerner, speaking for the Independent Voters of Illinois, issued a statement condemning the excesses of the Kelly administration—most notably in relation to the schools question—and pledged to oppose his renomination. Marshall Field, whose newspapers supported Kelly in 1943, pledged to oppose his candidacy in 1947. Paul H. Douglas threatened to launch another anti-machine campaign if Kelly received the Democratic nomination. Even Colonel McCormick's *Tribune*, ever a Kelly defender, advised against his seeking another term, saying that "his tenure, the longest in the history of Chicago, has taken its toll not only of him personally but of his reputation and the city's."[41]

The opposition of the city's better government advocates, the reformers, independents, and "goo-goos," had surfaced in each of Kelly's election campaigns. Scandals of every stripe had plagued the Democratic machine over the years, yet it had always managed to survive. In the opinion of Arvey, however, one new issue that arose in the mid-forties crystallized public opinion against Kelly: the open housing controversy. The mayor's repeated pledges to guarantee the availability of housing citywide to blacks galvanized the public and helped to explain the findings of the machine's canvassing: The Germans, Irish, and Poles shared one thing in common—an opposition to Kelly's stand on open housing.[42]

Certainly, among the most concerned by Kelly's unpopular stand on desegregated housing were his Irish opponents within the Democratic party; their opposition to the mayor, in fact, reflected not only their own ambitions but also the attitudes of their constituents. Ultimately, the opposition within the party, not just public indignation, which had been transcended repeatedly in the past, persuaded Arvey to dump Kelly. Supporting the incumbent mayor, hazardous enough on the basis of his record, would have been disastrous without the united support of the party's central committee, and Arvey, vulnerable in his new post at the head of the machine, was in no position to alienate the other party dignitaries while possibly losing his first election. Despite his feelings of loyalty toward Kelly, Arvey had to bow to the weight of the mayor's opposition. [43]

Unfortunately for Arvey, who foresaw a blowup in the event of a Kelly candidacy, the mayor had every intention of running again. The county chairman therefore had to convince him of the futility of such an enterprise. Accompanied by Joe Gill and Al Horan, Arvey met with the mayor in his office and disclosed the results of the party's public opinion polls. Kelly refused to accept the negative findings as accurate until Arvey told him that Spike Hennessey, one of Kelly's speech writers and closest friends, had conducted the telephone inquiries. The crestfallen mayor listened as Arvey appealed to his party loyalty: "If he wanted to go, we'd be with him, even if we were the last three votes he'd ever get in the city of Chicago—even so, we'd still be with you, we said, and it was the truth. It'd be all uphill, though, we told him, a tough one. It would be an awful lot easier if we ran somebody else. 'It'd be a lot less of a strain for the Organization,' we said." [44]

At the conclusion of the meeting, the forlorn Kelly agreed not to seek reelection. Arvey and the other party leaders began to consider alternative candidates: State's Attorney William J. Touhy emerged as the early favorite, while Chief Justice of the Circuit Court Robert Jerome Dunne, son of former governor Edward F. Dunne, commanded a considerable amount of support within the party as well. But before the speculation went too far, Kelly informed Arvey that he had reconsidered. The Republicans had announced that their candidate would be Russell W. Root, Governor Green's choice as Republican county chairman; the selection of Root, an obscure party hack, led the Chicago press to conclude that the Republicans failed to offer an alternative superior to the incumbent. Rejuvenated by the prospect of opposing Root, Kelly asked Arvey for his support, but the Democratic chairman, by then firmly convinced of the necessity of a new city administration, refused to change. [45]

On December 19, 1946, the Democratic Central Committee met at Morrison Hotel headquarters for its slate-making session. Arvey told the assembled committeemen that, pursuant to Kelly's decision to retire, he urged the selection of Martin H. Kennelly as the party's candidate for mayor. The selection of Kennelly, a nonpartisan, civic-minded reformer, confounded the party members, the press, and Chicago's citizens. It also led many to question how Arvey had come to select this heretofore outspoken critic of Chicago Democracy. Arvey claimed that the idea came from Kelly, who insisted upon the selection of an outsider and a genuine reformer. But several factors cast doubt on Arvey's contention: According to eyewitnesses, Kelly seemed taken

Outgoing mayor Kelly swears in his successor, Martin Kennelly. (Chicago Historical Society, *ICHi-10933*.)

aback by the mention of Kennelly's name in the slate-making session; his "endorsement" of Kennelly at the session—"let's nominate Kennelly and get through with it"—did not suggest unrestrained enthusiasm; and he made no mention in his memoirs of suggesting Kennelly. A likelier explanation would be that Arvey simply chose the former moving van magnate as an attractive candidate who met his criteria of freedom from scandal, political independence, and un-questioned credibility.[46]

Whatever the genesis of Kennelly's selection, Arvey es-tablished himself as Kennelly's champion in the Democratic party, arguing persuasively for the selection of the political neophyte. The Democratic politicos blanched when Kennelly lectured them that they would have to abandon the notions that "government belongs to a party" and "to the victor belong the spoils," but they went along with his candidacy—because they realized that no party faction loomed powerful enough to dictate a successor to Kelly; because they felt certain that the naive Kennelly could be easily manipulated from the

Morrison Hotel; and because he, like Arvey, was seen as a temporary nuisance to be endured during a time of transition. As for Kelly, he sat out most of the campaign in Palm Springs, California. In his infrequent appearances on the campaign trail, the mayor assured the Democratic faithful, "Martin is OK." He told party regulars: "I have no doubt he knows you can't make a church out of this city. He's no blue nose and I know him well enough to say that." Finally, the outgoing mayor underwent the ritual of party orthodoxy and praised Kennelly as he swore him in at the latter's inauguration.[47]

Stripped of the mayoralty and the county committee chairmanship, Kelly quickly found himself the forgotten man of the Chicago Democrats. Ignored by old friends in public, not consulted about local politics—a pariah who, without change in a hotel men's room only months after his departure from city hall, was not even recognized by the attendant—Kelly clung tenaciously to what little influence he had as Democratic national committeeman for Illinois. He heartily endorsed Arvey's selection of political unknown Adlai E. Stevenson for governor, in part to thwart the ambitions of his old nemesis, Tom Courtney. As for Arvey's other surprise choice in 1948, Paul H. Douglas for U.S. senator, Kelly was not as openly enthusiastic. Nevertheless, Douglas believed that Kelly used his influence to ensure that Democratic ward organizations made an honest effort for all members of the ticket—including the longtime Kelly foe.[48]

When Harry Truman's reluctance to declare for another term in 1948 led to speculation that the incumbent would step down, Kelly leaned toward the man he had trumpeted for vice-president four years earlier, William O. Douglas. Kelly suggested that Douglas be the main speaker for the memorial dinner commemorating the one-hundredth anniversary of the birth of former Illinois governor John P. Altgeld; he hoped that Douglas would make a great speech and catapult himself into the forefront of the presidential race. The push for Douglas, fueled largely by the Americans for Democratic Action, died out when Truman finally decided to seek reelection, and Kelly fell into step behind the incumbent.[49]

At the 1948 Democratic National Convention, Kelly assumed the role of elder statesman in the Illinois delegation, which stood firmly behind Truman from the outset. When Hubert Humphrey's stirring speech in favor of a strong civil rights plank threatened to precipitate a rebellion by the southern wing of the party, Kelly ordered the Illinois delegation to demonstrate its support for Humphrey, placing the state standard in the hands of Paul Douglas and motioning the delegates to follow him in an impromptu parade. As delegations from South Carolina, Louisiana, Alabama, Mississippi, and Georgia marched out of the convention hall, Kelly remarked to Douglas: "Paul, those fellows look just like the APA'ers who used to stone us Catholic kids when I was a boy. We can do without them." His comment proved prophetic, as the Democrats carried Illinois for Truman, a vital victory for the president in his successful reelection.[50]

After the 1948 campaign Kelly settled into a life of semiretirement, occasionally going to the downtown office of his engineering consulting firm but mostly vacationing in Wisconsin and California. His last years were plagued by a series of physical ailments, including a mysterious leg ailment that he took to be cancer and for which he carried in his trousers pocket a golden spike supposedly blessed with curative powers. He became very ill while traveling in an automobile on May 26, 1950, and subsequently spent seven weeks in a hospital for what doctors diagnosed as "acute indigestion." They found no evidence of heart trouble. On October 20, 1950, he visited the office of Dr. Vincent J. O'Connor, a urologist, for a routine examination; afterward he told the doctor, "I've never felt better in my life." Minutes later, while standing at the secretary's desk making an appointment, he suffered a massive heart seizure and died almost immediately. Several political dignitaries, including Frank Hague, Governor Stevenson, Senator Douglas, and U.S. attorney general J. Howard McGrath, an emissary from President Truman, attended his funeral, and Cardinal Stritch gave the eulogy; he was buried at the family mausoleum in Calvary Cemetery, Chicago.[51]

Even in death, Ed Kelly could not escape the controversy that characterized his years as boss of Chicago Democracy. In December 1950, the executor of the Kelly estate, Michael Mulcahey, announced that Kelly had left approximately $600,000, consisting primarily of stocks, bonds, and real estate holdings. Though this was a sizable amount, the Kelly estate had been thought to be much larger. Mulcahey's estimate proved particularly surprising to Kelly's widow, who swore that the executor failed to mention over $1 million in cash that she had recently seen in the Kelly bank vault. She refused to sign the inventory of the estate and directed her lawyer, Stephen A. Mitchell, to start court proceedings to uncover the missing fortune. Mulcahey and his tax adviser, Ed Gorman, disputed Mrs. Kelly's claim, arguing that no such cache had ever existed. On November 9, 1951, Mrs. Kelly finally signed the inventory, valued at $686,799, while Mitchell opined that the lavish manner in which the late mayor had lived gave her "ample grounds" for expecting a larger estate; he added that the search for additional assets would continue. No further money appeared, however; Mrs. Kelly was cast as a victim of either foul play or inflated expectations, and the mystery remained unsolved.[52]

9 "You've Gotta Be a Boss!"

 A FEW hours after Ed Kelly died, Illinois governor Adlai E. Stevenson delivered a eulogy to the mayor on a state-wide radio broadcast. Stevenson, who had always kept a wary distance from his fellow Democrat, rendered a balanced assessment of Kelly's political career. He finished with these words:

> Like so many public figures who must take positions, who have responsibility and must exercise it, who must manage men to attain ends, who must do, not talk, he was and he will be a center of controversy for a long time. We would be bold and foolish to assign his place in the history of Chicago and of our troubled times. But of one thing we may be sure: Here was a leader! Strong, adroit and tireless, he guided the destiny of Chicago as its Mayor longer than anyone in history. . . . And he will be studied by students of American politics as a leader who was never afraid to lead. We will miss Ed Kelly.[1]

Kelly was without question an aggressive, self-confident leader. He boasted to a reporter, "I tell a million people what to think, and they listen to me because they vote for me." He exercised nearly complete control over the city council, so much so that until the last year of his mayoralty, never more than ten of the fifty alderman ever dared to oppose a measure he favored. Kelly argued that the extraordinary times in which he served necessitated the usurpation of executive powers: "During that period, unless the mayor was the leader of the city council and unless he had the full support and confidence of his lieutenants the city would have suffered because of the urgent need for emergency action as against the usual legislative delays. The city suffers when its mayor and council are at odds." To those who railed against the Kelly autocracy, he replied: "These people look to me for leadership. To be a real mayor you've got to have control of the party. You've got to be a potent political factor. You've gotta be a boss!"[2]

In his classic study of twenty city bosses, political scientist Harold Zink concluded that there was no such thing as a "typical boss." Nonetheless, acknowledging the diversity of his randomly selected politicos, Zink sketched this composite portrait: The boss was probably a longtime resident of his city, with parents who had been born in a foreign country. He hailed from modest circumstances and went to work at an early age, usually abandoning school before completion. He professed an abiding interest in religion and, while countenancing a considerable amount of moral laxity in his organization, was personally of upright character. Surprisingly perhaps, he was abstemious, hardworking, devoted to his family, and trustworthy. With but a few modifications, this description fits Ed Kelly well; except for his late entry into electoral politics—Zink found that the elevation to boss status culminated a lifelong commitment to office seeking—Kelly's rise from poor ethnic to municipal satrap was unexceptional.[3]

Among his peers, infamous bosses like Frank Hague, Ed Crump, Tom Pendergast, and James Michael Curley, Kelly seemed at first blush at home. Indeed, the press lumped the group together, assuming a commonality of origin (in fact, all but Crump were Irish) and purpose. True enough, they often worked together for common goals, and they collectively supported Franklin Roosevelt's policies. And, owing to a need for funds to "grease the machine," all permitted vice a free hand in their communities. Yet in many ways Kelly's Chicago machine differed signficantly from those in other cities: Unlike Hague and especially Curley, Kelly did not blatantly exploit the issue of religion; while garnering the support of Chicago's heavily Roman Catholic ethnic population, Kelly never waged war on Protestants or Jews at election time. Nor did his dictatorial domination of the Democratic party impinge on the lives of most Chicagoans. Crump personally persecuted his Memphis critics, often driving them out of town. Hague made a mockery of civil liberties and stubbornly refused even to allow CIO representatives to speak in Hudson County. (He blustered, "I am the law. I decide. I do. Me.") And unlike Hague, who railed against the Communist menace, Kelly seldom resorted to such blatant demagoguery. The Chicago Democratic machine required no stalking-horses, no ideological bogeymen, no personality cults. It ran on patronage, ethnic loyalty, and partisanship.[4]

Under Kelly-Nash leadership, the Chicago machine commanded the loyalty of its members because it produced at the polls and rewarded the faithful with a share of the spoils. By the admission of one of its own leaders the Republican party was all but nonexistent in Chicago—at least until the mid-forties, when scandal and complacency combined to threaten the suzerainty of the Democrats. At that time, the Democratic leadership, wrested away from an aging and increasingly unpopular Kelly, chose reformer Martin Kennelly to defuse the Republicans' use of corruption as an issue. The centrifugal forces unleashed within the Democratic party had long been kept in check by the success of the Kelly-Nash organization. The patronage and money guaranteed to loyalists of all ethnic groups smoothed over the areas of potential conflict among the heterogeneous factions making up the coalition, especially among the ambitious individuals chafing under the dictatorial Kelly yoke.

Similarly, the Democratic organization benefited from the acceptance, if not the wholehearted endorsement, of Chicago's business community. While many of the city's wealthiest and most influential families shared a generations-old affiliation with the Republican party and abhorred the politics of Franklin D. Roosevelt and the national Democratic party, they reached a comfortable arrangement with the Kelly-Nash organization. This situation often resulted in a kind of political schizophrenia in which Chicago's well-to-do actively opposed the New Deal while concurrently contributing to the Kelly-Nash coffers. For that reason, the friendship between Kelly and the *Tribune*'s Colonel McCormick, arguably the most powerful Democrat and Republican in the state, respectively, not only flourished but often worked to the advantage of both.[5]

The goodwill within the business community accumulated by the Kelly administration hailed from the relative order and healthy economic climate maintained in the city. Seen against the backdrop of the Big Bill Thompson era, the Chicago of the thirties shone in comparison: Gangland violence diminished significantly, and while the ubiquitous gambling parlors bothered some merchants, they offered little threat to public safety. Bankers tolerated Kelly because he kept the city finances in order, guaranteeing a profitable market for city bonds and tax anticipation warrants. Moreover, Kelly's dramatic success in keeping Chicago solvent between 1933 and 1935 earned him the gratitude of the LaSalle Street bankers. The mayor courted the Loop merchants by providing services for the downtown area. First-rate police and fire protection, along with prompt maintenance work on streets and sidewalks, constituted everyday reminders of city hall's beneficence. Most noteworthy, however, was the construction of the State Street subway, a boon to the Loop merchants and one link in a revised transportation network designed to provide consumers with easy access to the city center. And finally, Kelly earned the plaudits of the business community through his sustained opposition to personal property and state income taxes.[6]

To a great degree the ability of the Kelly-Nash organization to command the allegiance of the various Democratic factions and the goodwill of the businessmen constituted a continuance of Anton

Cermak's policies. If these had been the only accomplishments of the fourteen-year Kelly stewardship, his sole claim would have been that he preserved the status quo for his successor. But the machine not only survived but expanded during the Kelly years, as a result of three new resources tapped by his machine. The additional revenue and votes supplied by blacks, organized crime, and the New Deal enabled Chicago Democracy to survive the 1930s and 1940s, two decades that saw the collapse of the nation's other great urban political machines.

Contrary to the belief that urban blacks switched to the Democratic party solely because of Roosevelt's New Deal, Kelly's success in recruiting black voter support suggests a more complex phenomenon. As Harold F. Gosnell and Elmer W. Henderson detailed, many factors coalesced to cause black renunciation of the Republican party in Chicago, and Kelly's popularity in the black community existed independently of, and indeed preceded, Roosevelt's. Kelly set out to capture the Bronzeville vote and did so by appointing blacks to an increasing number of municipal posts, by selecting them as candidates for elective offices, and by distributing government largess—first municipal and later, in much larger quantities, federal—to the depression-stricken South Side. Moreover, the mayor intervened on several occasions to defend the principles of desegregated housing and education. As a result of these concerted efforts, blacks supported the Democratic tickets in all elections, consistently giving Kelly a greater percentage of the vote than he received in the city at large.[7]

Kelly's securing of the black vote proved to be a monumental contribution to the Democratic machine in Chicago. Political scientist James Q. Wilson correctly dated the birth of the Democratic black submachine to 1939, when William L. Dawson switched parties and became Kelly's 2nd Ward committeeman. From that time on, with the black population of Chicago increasing and whites fleeing to the suburbs, the black vote became a precious commodity to the white politicians seeking to maintain political control of the city. The importance of Kelly's feat became evident years later, during the Daley era; in 1963, for instance, Daley lost the white vote in the city—Benjamin Adamowski got 51 percent of the votes cast in the white wards—but carried the black vote by such an overwhelming margin that he managed to secure reelection.[8]

While the black community provided votes in substantial quantities for the machine, its modest economic resources precluded contribution of another essential need, money. For that factor, the Kelly-Nash organization turned to organized crime. Kelly deplored the publicity that attended gangland killings, and to a great degree his administration restrained the rampant lawlessness of preceding years, but the gambling revenue was so important to the ward organizations that no genuine effort was launched to enforce the anti-gambling statutes. In 1934 the *Chicago Daily News* reported that the machine raked in $1 million per month from illicit vice operations. The involvement of the Democratic machine with the Nitti-Guzik syndicate was solidly entrenched at virtually every level of government: Many machine precinct captains operated gambling houses, and frequently their partners occupied prominent positions in the syndicate hierarchy. While involvement pervaded all wards of the city, some, like the 1st and the 24th, blatantly flaunted standards of propriety. Moreover, the police, controlled by the ward committeemen, and the judiciary shared culpability with the politicians. As for Kelly himself, the lack of evidence of personal involvement belied his tacit approval—indeed, his defense—of vice and gambling.[9]

The New Deal contributed to the growth and sustenance of the Chicago Democratic machine in the thirties both financial resources and ensuing electoral support from thousands of beholden relief recipients. Clearly, the intrusion of the federal government into areas previously thought to be in the purview of private enterprise or local governments did not threaten the existence of the political machine in depression Chicago. But to say that the New Deal became an arm of the Kelly-Nash machine would be equally inaccurate: Chicago Democrats exercised virtually no control over the relief and public works certification process, although they certainly claimed this power while politicking among the needy. Charges of voter coercion, principally based upon the loss of jobs or relief checks, seem equally inflated; again, the threat of retribution was the machine's chief weapon. The primary contribution of the New Deal lay in the financial bellwether it provided for the Kelly administration during the debilitating depression era. Armed with federal money, the city avoided the payment of great sums for the support of the indigent and unemployed. With this working capital, patronage and city services did not have to be cut. At a time when the greatest threat to the Democratic machine came from financial disaster, rather than from a robust opposition party, the New Deal largess assured Chicago's solvency.

Kelly became a master at reaping political capital from the machine's New Deal alliance. As a historian of the New Deal in Chicago noted, "Kelly and his organization clung so tightly to the New Deal that the two seemed to be one." For federally financed work projects the mayor chose items of a highly visible and enduring nature, usually with no special assessments required. The mayor made much of his association with Roosevelt, Hopkins, and Hunter, and insofar as the Democratic machine in Chicago produced satisfactory vote totals for the national ticket, he could rely on support from Washington. As Lyle W. Dorsett pointed out in *Franklin D. Roosevelt and the City Bosses,* Kelly and the president achieved a quid pro quo relationship based upon political self-interest. Roosevelt's New Deal provided Chicago Democracy with prestige, the stamp of legitimacy, and, most important, the financial resources it desperately required to ensure the loyalty of the voters.[10]

While Kelly's leadership clearly resulted in growth and stability for the Democratic organization, his years as the city's mayor are more difficult to evaluate. Chicago continued to be characterized as a modern-day Gomorrah, a city that took its head from the morally bankrupt political machine that guided its fortunes. Secretary of the Interior Harold L. Ickes lamented the influence of the Kelly-Nash government on his native city: "They have brought Chicago to the lowest ebb in its history. There probably isn't any community in the whole United States that is so abjectly rotten, so dominated by a corrupt and stinking political machine." While frequently guilty of hyperbole, Ickes and other reformers correctly condemned the machine for its lack of ethics; Chicago during the Kelly years suffered from an expedient brand of moral relativism proffered by a corrupt political machine reaping the benefits of lax law enforcement.[11]

Kelly lamely defended his administration by saying, "There will always be a measure of larceny in our state and urban politics, just as there is in business. Show me an administration that is one hundred per cent pure and I will show you a new species of human being." But the "measure of larceny" to which the mayor referred took on awesome proportions in Chicago: Graft and favoritism permeated all levels of government, penetrating even the public school system. By the end of Kelly's fourth term in office, not only had the schools deteriorated, but the police department reeled from a series of scandals. And, much to the chagrin of the Chicago taxpayers, other city services suffered as well. An unpleasant but tolerable situation worsened to the degree at which an aroused citizenry cast serious doubts on the "automatic" election of the machine candidates in 1947.[12]

But despite the scandals and political degeneracy, some notable achievements came out of the Kelly years. Chicago survived the depression in better condition than many cities, and though, as Gene Delon Jones pointed out, Kelly's reputation as a fiscal savior rested solely upon his performance in the first two years in office, his successes during those crisis-filled days seemed like a godsend to Chicagoans. Undoubtedly the wealth of federal largess made available to Kelly enabled him to provide jobs and a modicum of relief for the city's destitute; it also made possible a number of long-overdue physical improvements in Chicago. As a result of WPA and PWA funds, the city's transportation network came to maturity with the completion of Lake Shore Drive from Foster Avenue to Jackson Park and the opening of the State Street subway. Thanks to PWA funds, thirty new schools opened in the years 1933 to 1940, and three housing projects—Jane Addams, Julia Lathrop, and Trumbull Park homes—were constructed. (Later in Kelly's mayoralty, federal funding resulted in the construction of several other housing projects, including the Ida B. Wells Homes, Altgeld Gardens, Frances Cabrini Homes, Bridgeport Homes, Lawndale Homes, and Brooks Homes.) The partnership between Kelly and the New Deal indeed resulted in a major facelift for Chicago.[13]

Perhaps Kelly's supreme achievement in office was the resolution of the public transportation question. The creation of a unified transit authority, privately financed and operated, resolved a decades-old problem that had made the Chicago mass transit system an unworkable anachronism. Kelly also deserved praise for his zealous mustering of Chicago resources and energies during the Second World War; at a time when Chicago prospered greatly from the war-induced industrial boom, the mayor won plaudits for insisting that much of the profit be funneled back into support programs for the nation's military.

Kelly's paternalistic protection of U.S. fighting men paralleled his feeling for blacks in Chicago. Though admittedly gradualistic, the mayor's programs for integration exceeded the conventional mores of contemporary white society, and he punctuated his rhetoric with action supportive of black aspirations. He provided the executive secretary of the Chicago Housing Authority, Elizabeth Wood, with the freedom to institute new policies aimed at open housing in Chicago, and he kept the CHA, unlike the school system, free of political interference. On several occasions Kelly committed both the prestige and the power of his administration to the cause of peaceful integration of the races.

Yet even when supporting the aspirations of an oppressed minority or championing a humanitarian cause, Ed Kelly was no democrat. He alone made decisions, then commanded that the city council, the members of his party, and the citizens of Chicago carry out his orders. At the time of his death the *Chicago Sun-Times* noted, "He remained a big city boss to the end," adding that the mayor was "first of all a practical politician in every sense of the word, good and bad. . . . Kelly had the instincts of a dictator."[14] Unwavering in the face of public criticism, Kelly confidently pointed to electoral victories as public approval of his actions; convinced that his opposition to the good-government advocates and naysayers who threatened to turn Chicago into a puritanical town reflected the feelings of his constituency, he wielded power without hesitation. With the sheer force of his personality, the additions he made to the political machine he inherited, and the effects, both salutary and regrettable, that resulted from his fourteen-year mayoralty, Ed Kelly made a formidable impact on the history of Chicago.

Notes

Introduction

1. Among the recent works offering a more balanced assessment of bossism are Lyle Dorsett, *The Pendergast Machine* (New York: Oxford University Press, 1968); Mark Foster, "Frank Hague of New Jersey: The Boss as Reformer," *New Jersey History* 86 (Summer 1968): 106–17; Zane Miller, *Boss Cox's Cincinnati: Urban Politics in the Progressive Era* (New York: Oxford University Press, 1968); and Jerome Mushkat, *Tammany: The Evolution of a Political Machine* (Syracuse, N.Y.: Syracuse University Press, 1971).

2. Adlai E. Stevenson, *The Papers of Adlai E. Stevenson*, ed. Walter Johnson, vol. 3 (Boston: Little, Brown and Co., 1973), p. 311; Mike Royko, *Boss: Richard J. Daley of Chicago* (New York: E. P. Dutton and Co., 1971), p. 54; Len O'Connor, *Clout: Mayor Daley and His City* (New York: Avon Books, 1975), pp. 53–54; Harold F. Gosnell, *Machine Politics: Chicago Model* (Chicago: University of Chicago Press, 1937), p. 25; Thomas B. Littlewood, *Horner of Illinois* (Evanston, Ill.: Northwestern University Press, 1969), pp. 240–41.

1 From Axman to City Hall

1. "Mayor Kelly's Own Story," *Chicago Herald-American*, May 5, 1947; Barbara C. Schaaf, *Mr. Dooley's Chicago* (Garden City, N.Y.: Doubleday and Co., 1977), pp. 72, 82, 98.

2. "Mayor Kelly's Own Story"; Charles N. Wheeler, "Kelly's Life Full of Drama, Peril, Conflict, Fame," n.d., Chicago Historical Society, typescript; Charles B. Cleveland, "Biography of Edward J. Kelly," n.d., typescript in the possession of the author, p. 58.

3. "Mayor Kelly's Own Story," May 5, 6, 1947; John T. Flynn, "These Our Rulers," *Collier's* 105 (June 29, 1940): 14–15; Cleveland, "Biography of Kelly," p. 59. Kelly was employed by the Sanitary District from 1895 until his selection as mayor in 1933. Donald S. Bradley and Mayer N. Zald, "From Commercial Elite to Political Administrator: The Recruitment of the Mayors of Chicago," *American Journal of Sociology* 71 (September 1965): 153–67.

4. Wheeler, "Kelly's Life"; Cleveland, "Biography of Kelly," p. 60.

5. *Lightnin'*, May 1932, p. 4; Cleveland, "Biography of Kelly," p. 62; "Elected to Fill Former Mayor Cermak's Unexpired Term,"

Newsweek 1 (April 22, 1933): 19. The Brighton Park Athletic Club was one of many such "athletic clubs," which flourished in Chicago during that era. Others included Ragen's Colts, Aylwards, Our Flag, and the Hamburgs (the club to which Richard J. Daley belonged). Though nominally acting as social organizations, they actually were extremely partisan; many, in fact, became extensions of their parent party organizations. Royko, *Boss*, pp. 37–38; O'Connor, *Clout*, pp. 18–20. At this tender age, Kelly learned the rough-and-tumble ways of Chicago politics. On one occasion, the young precinct worker found himself in the center of a melee that catapulted him through the window of the polling booth directly on top of the ballot boxes; he held on tenaciously until the belated arrival of the police. Victor Rubin, "You've Gotta Be a Boss," *Collier's* 116 (September 25, 1945): 33.

    6. "Mayor Kelly's Own Story," May 6; Cleveland, "Biography of Kelly," pp. 62, 65.

    7. "Mayor Kelly's Own Story," May 6; Cleveland, "Biography of Kelly," p. 65.

    8. Kelly was severely shaken by his son's tragic death. He previously had been a heavy drinker, but, he asserted, he never took a drink thereafter. While some doubted his claim, it was universally acknowledged that he became markedly more abstemious. Cleveland, "Biography of Kelly," p. 69; Abraham Lincoln Marovitz, interview with author, Chicago, Ill., November 14, 1979; Robert E. Kennedy, interview with author, Marco Island, Fla., December 1, 1979; Flynn, "These Our Rulers," p. 15.

    9. "Funeral of a Boss," *Life* 29 (November 6, 1950): 40.

    10. "Funeral of a Boss," p. 40; *Lightnin'*, February 1932, p. 4.

    11. "The Kelly-Nash Political Machine," *Fortune* 14 (August 1936): 117; Virgil W. Peterson, *Barbarians in Our Midst: A History of Chicago Crime and Politics* (Boston: Little, Brown, and Co., 1952), p. 163.

    12. Flynn, "These Our Rulers," p. 42; "The Kelly-Nash Political Machine," p. 117.

    13. Elmer Lynn Williams, *The Fix-It Boys: The Inside Story of the Kelly-Nash Machine* (Chicago: Elmer Lynn Williams, 1940), pp. 16–20.

    14. Two consistent beneficiaries of Kelly's contract awards were Nash Brothers and Dowdle Brothers construction companies. The Nash Brothers, headed by Pat Nash, received an estimated $8 million worth of contracts. The Dowdles, nephews of the Nash brothers, received yet another $4 million in contracts. *Lightnin'*, April 1934, pp. 14–15; Williams, *The Fix-It Boys*, p. 16; "The Kelly-Nash Political Machine," p. 114.

    15. Flynn, "These Our Rulers," p. 42.

    16. Ibid.; Alex Gottfried, *Boss Cermak of Chicago: A Study of Political Leadership* (Seattle: University of Washington Press, 1962), pp. 185–86; "The Kelly-Nash Political Machine," p. 117; Williams, *The Fix-It Boys*, pp. 24–25.

    17. V. K. Brown, "Chicago Makes Her Preparations for the Recreation Congress," *Recreation* 29 (July 1935): 204; *Lightnin'*, September 1933, p. 4; *Who's Who in Chicago and Vicinity, 1936* (Chicago: A. M. Marquis Co., 1937), p. 542.

    18. "Chicago's Record of Accomplishment under Mayor Edward J. Kelly: The Remarkable Regeneration of America's Second City under Its Democratic Mayor," 1940, Chicago Historical Society, manuscript, pp. 1, 3 (quoted); Walter A. Townsend, *Illinois Democracy* (Springfield, Ill.:

Democratic Historical Association, 1935), pp. 34–37; Brown, "Chicago Makes Her Preparations," p. 204; "The "Kelly-Nash Political Machine," p. 117; *Lightnin'*, February 1934, p. 10.

19. John M. Allswang, *A House for All Peoples: Ethnic Politics in Chicago, 1890–1936* (Lexington: University Press of Kentucky, 1971), pp. 19, 42, 54, 205, 206; John M. Allswang, *Bosses, Machines, and Urban Voters: An American Symbiosis* (Port Washington, N. Y.: Kennikat Press, 1977), pp. 92–96.

20. Gottfried, *Boss Cermak of Chicago*, pp. 347, 350; Edward R. Kantowicz, *Polish-American Politics in Chicago, 1888–1940* (Chicago: University of Chicago Press, 1975), p. 209.

21. Allswang, *A House for All Peoples*, pp. 156–60. For additional information on Cermak's election in 1931, see "Chicago Swaps Bosses," *New Republic* 66 (April 22, 1931): 260–62.

22. *Chicago Sun*, October 7, 1943; *Chicago Tribune*, April 12, 1933.

23. "Old Pat," *Newsweek* 22 (October 18, 1943): 62; *Chicago Sun*, October 7, 1943; Gottfried, *Boss Cermak of Chicago*, p. 179.

24. Gottfried, *Boss Cermak of Chicago*, p. 184. For more on the Cermak mayoralty, see Lester Freeman, "Behind the Cermak Closet Door," *Real America* 2 (September 1933): 8–17; and Lester Freeman, "Tony Cermak, the Political Attila—None Ever Wielded Such Power—None Misused Power More," *Real America* 2 (October 1933): 46–49.

25. Aaron Smith, "The Administration of Mayor Anton J. Cermak, 1931–1933" (master's thesis, University of Illinois, 1955), pp. 471–73; Gottfried, *Boss Cermak of Chicago*, pp. 305, 316–18. The years following Cermak's death saw the development of a conspiracy theory, which asserted that Zangara had intended to kill Cermak from the outset and that the attempt on Roosevelt's life had been a diversion. According to this scenario, Chicago gangsters sought to eliminate Cermak, who had been making threatening signs of breaking the syndicate's hold on Chicago. Specifically, the attempt on Cermak's life had been precipitated by a similar attack on gangland chief Frank Nitti—an attack carried out by Chicago police and authorized by Cermak. But both Gottfried and Smith convincingly argue that Zangara acted as a free agent with designs on no one but Roosevelt. No evidence has surfaced to substantiate any of the other claims. For more on the 1932 election see Harold F. Gosnell and Norman Gill, "An Analysis of the 1932 Presidential Vote in Chicago," *American Political Science Review* 29 (December 1935): 967–84; and Duncan MacRae, Jr., and James A. Meldrum, "Critical Elections in Illinois: 1888–1958," *American Political Science Review* 54 (September 1960): 669–83.

26. Marovitz interview; Cleveland, "Biography of Kelly," p. 22; Lester Freeman, "The End of 'Boss' Cermak," *Real America* 2 (November 1933): 19–27.

27. Cleveland, "Biography of Kelly," p. 26; O'Connor, *Clout*, p. 50.

28. Quoted in Milton Rakove, *We Don't Want Nobody Nobody Sent: An Oral History of the Daley Years* (Bloomington: Indiana University Press, 1979), p. 9.

29. *Chicago Tribune*, March and April 1933; *Chicago American*, March and April 1933; Cleveland, "Biography of Kelly," pp. 31–32; Arthur G. Lindell, *City Hall: Chicago's Corporate History*, 1966, Municipal Reference Library, Chicago, p. 246.

30. *Chicago Tribune*, March 13, 1933; Cleveland, "Biography of Kelly," p. 30.

31. Apparently Nash had already broached the subject with Corr, for he carried a letter of resignation signed by Corr. Cleveland, "Biography of Kelly," pp. 37–42; City Council of the City of Chicago, *Journal of the Proceedings of the City Council of the City of Chicago, Illinois* (1932–33), 10 A.M. Special Meeting, March 14, 1933, pp. 3377–80.

32. Cleveland, "Biography of Kelly," p. 43.

33. *Chicago Tribune,* March 15, 1933 (quoted); City Council of the City of Chicago, *Journal of the Proceedings,* (1932–33), 5 P.M. Special Meeting, March 14, 1933, pp. 3381–84; John Hoellen, interview with author, Chicago, Ill., October 27, 1979.

34. *Chicago Tribune*, March 15, 31, 1933; Cleveland, "Biography of Kelly," pp. 46–47 (quoting Nash). Governor Horner's willingness to go along with Nash can be attributed largely to the long-standing friendship between the two men. But another factor may have been Horner's gratitude for Nash's support in an intraparty row the previous year. It was rumored that Cermak initially chose Horner to run for governor in 1932 on the assumption that he would lose; when preelection sentiment indicated a favorable climate for a Democratic candidate, Cermak planned to dump Horner and run himself. Nash heard of the plot and marshaled support for Horner among the Chicago Democrats, forcing Cermak to back down. Cleveland, "Biography of Kelly," p. 48; Littlewood, *Horner of Illinois,* pp. 67–69; Gottfried, *Boss Cermak of Chicago,* p. 292.

35. *Chicago Tribune*, April 12, 1933; "The Kelly-Nash Political Machine," p. 114.

36. Cleveland, "Biography of Kelly," p. 50.

37. Others present were Moe Rosenberg, Joe McDonough, M. S. Szymczak, and Dick Nash (Pat Nash's brother). Arvey was the only alderman. Littlewood, *Horner of Illinois,* p. 103; Williams, *The Fix-It Boys,* pp. 47–48.

38. Benjamin S. Adamowski, interview with author, Chicago, Ill., November 1, 1979 (quoted); Littlewood, *Horner of Illinois,* p. 103.

39. City Council of the City of Chicago, *Journal of the Proceedings* (1932–33), April 13, 1933, pp. 3–6.

40. Gottfried, *Boss Cermak of Chicago,* p. 425n. Ralph Berkowitz was the Republican. Rakove, *We Don't Want Nobody Nobody Sent,* pp. 21–22; Marovitz interview; Gene Delon Jones, "The Local Political Significance of New Deal Relief Legislation in Chicago: 1933–1940" (Ph.D. diss., Northwestern University, 1970), pp. 41–42.

41. *Chicago Tribune,* April 14, 1933.

42. Rubin, "You've Gotta Be a Boss," p. 33.

43. "Mayor Kelly's Own Story," May 8, 1947.

2 "Out of the Red, Into the Black"

1. Broadus Mitchell, *Depression Decade* (New York: Rinehart and Co., 1947), p. 105; Irving Bernstein, *The Lean Years: A History of the American Worker, 1920–1933* (Boston: Houghton Mifflin Co., 1966), pp. 297, 298. For an overview of American cities during the depression, see Mark I. Gelfand, *A Nation of Cities: The Federal Government and Urban America, 1933–1965* (New York: Oxford University Press, 1975); and

George E. Mowry, *The Urban Nation, 1920–1960* (New York: Hill and Wang, 1965). For an examination of the depression in one city, see Charles H. Trout, *Boston, The Great Depression, and the New Deal* (New York: Oxford University Press, 1977).

2. Mitchell, *Depression Decade*, p. 105; Paul Douglas, "Chicago's Financial Muddle," *New Republic* 61 (February 12, 1930): 324–26.

3. Arthur D. Gayer, *Public Works in Prosperity and Depression* (New York: National Bureau of Economic Research, 1935), p. 317; Lyman B. Burbank, "Chicago Public Schools and the Depression Years of 1928–1937," *Journal of the Illinois State Historical Society* 64 (Winter 1971): 365–81; Jones, "Local Political Significance of New Deal Relief Legislation," pp. 17–18; Smith, "Administration of Mayor Anton J. Cermak," pp. 115–26.

4. Bernstein, *The Lean Years*, p. 297; Burbank, "Chicago's Public Schools," p. 366; Jones, "Local Political Significance of New Deal Relief Legislation," pp. 18–19; Smith, "Administration of Mayor Anton J. Cermak," 188–96; Douglas Sutherland, *Fifty Years on the Civic Front* (Chicago: Civic Federation, 1943), pp. 62–67. Chicago never totally eliminated this backlog in the 1930s. As late as 1939, Alderman Paul Douglas was calling for a drive to collect unpaid real estate taxes, which he estimated at $146 million. Jones, "Local Political Significance of New Deal Relief Legislation," p. 19.

5. Burbank, "Chicago Public Schools," pp. 367–69; Smith, "Administration of Mayor Anton J. Cermak," pp. 288–94; *New York Times*, November 27, 1932; Bernstein, *The Lean Years*, p. 297; Jones, "Local Political Significance of New Deal Relief Legislation," pp. 20–21.

6. Smith, "The Administration of Mayor Anton J. Cermak," pp. 234, 241; Burbank, "Chicago Public Schools," pp. 369–70; Gottfried, *Boss Cermak of Chicago*, p. 254; *Chicago Tribune*, April 10, 1932, March 7, 1933; Leo M. Lyons, "Illinois Investigates the Relief Situation," *National Municipal Review* 27 (January 1938): 24.

7. Bernstein, *The Lean Years*, p. 467. Among the delegates representing Chicago were the chief executives of Armour, International Harvester, Santa Fe Railroad, Marshall Field's, Inland Steel, Bendix, Colgate-Palmolive-Peet, U.S. Gypsum, A. B. Dick, Illinois Bell Telephone, First National Bank of Chicago, Chicago Daily News, and Chicago American. Ibid.

8. Gelfand, *A Nation of Cities*, p. 41; Bernstein, *The Lean Years*, p. 467; *Chicago Tribune*, June 22, 1932; *New York Times*, June 22, 1932.

9. Jones, "Local Political Significance of New Deal Relief Legislation," pp. 32–33; Bernstein, *The Lean Years*, p. 471; Gelfand, *A Nation of Cities*, p. 41; Gottfried, *Boss Cermak of Chicago*, p. 241; *New York Times*, September 23, 1932.

10. *Newsweek* 5 (April 13, 1935), p. 7; Littlewood, *Horner of Illinois*, p. 4; Charles T. Holman, "Chicago Elects a New Mayor," *Christian Century* 50 (April 26, 1933): 567–68; *New York Times*, April 16, 1933; Arthur F. Miles, *Federal Aid and Public Assistance in Illinois* (Chicago: University of Chicago Press, 1941), pp. 16–20.

11. *Chicago Tribune*, April 26, 1933; Burbank, "Chicago Public Schools," p. 371; *Chicago Daily News*, April 6, 1933; *New York Times*, April 16, 1933; John T. Flynn, "These Our Rulers," *Collier's* 106

(July 20, 1940): 18; Lindell, *City Hall: Chicago's Corporate History,* p. 247; Townsend, *Illinois Democracy,* p. 38.

12. *Chicago Tribune,* April 26, 1933; *Public Service Leader,* December 20, 1933 (quoted). As of 1940, Chicago had been able to collect 12 percent of the 1928 taxes, 18 percent of the 1929 taxes, 20 percent of the 1930 assessment, 37 percent of the 1931 levy, and 37 percent of the 1932 bill. Flynn, "These Our Rulers," July 20, p. 19.

13. *Public Service Leader,* December 20, 1933; Burbank, "Chicago Public Schools," pp. 373–75; *Chicago Tribune,* April 27, 28 (quoted), 1933.

14. *Lightnin',* July 1933, p. 10; Burbank, "Chicago Public Schools," p. 375.

15. *Chicago Tribune,* April 28, 1933; *Chicago Daily News,* April 28, 30, 1933.

16. Littlewood, *Horner of Illinois,* p. 110.

17. Burbank, "Chicago Public Schools," p. 376; *Chicago Tribune,* May 15, 1934.

18. Jones, "Local Political Significance of New Deal Relief Legislation," pp. 48–50.

19. *Chicago Tribune,* September 11, 12, 1933; Littlewood, *Horner of Illinois.* p. 111; Harry Hopkins to Henry Horner, telegram, October 7, 1933, Records of the FERA, Record Group 69, Illinois State File, Box 69, National Archives; Jones, "Local Political Significance of New Deal Relief Legislation," pp. 51–52.

20. *Chicago Herald and Examiner,* August 12, 1933.

21. Cleveland, "Biography of Kelly," p. 99. In 1952, a *Chicago Tribune* reporter uncovered this information under a new government policy opening compromise settlements, upon request, to public inspection. Ibid., pp. 95, 96; Williams, *The Fix-It Boys,* p. 27; Ted Leitzell, "Chicago, City of Corruption," *American Mercury* 49 (February 1940): 146; *Chicago Herald-American,* September 10, 1952. The Hearst papers had been tipped about Kelly's involvement by Dwight H. Green, U.S. attorney in Chicago, who had been chief counsel in the Chicago revenue office at the time of the investigation and thus was privy to the details of the case. Cleveland, "Biography of Kelly," p. 91; Littlewood, *Horner of Illinois,* p. 104; *Chicago Herald-American,* September 10, 1952.

22. *Chicago Herald and Examiner,* August 18, 1933; John T. Flynn, "These Our Rulers," *Collier's* 106 (July 6, 1940): 58.

23. *Chicago Tribune,* August 17, 19, 1933.

24. Flynn, "These Our Rulers," July 6, p. 58.

25. "Radio Talk of Mayor Edward J. Kelly of Chicago over Radio Station WENR, Chicago, Illinois," Franklin D. Roosevelt Papers, President's Personal File, Container 3166, Franklin D. Roosevelt Library, Hyde Park, N.Y.

26. Charles E. Blake to Franklin D. Roosevelt, September 5, 1933, Roosevelt Papers, President's Personal File, Container 3166; Homer S. Cummings to Franklin D. Roosevelt, September 19, 1933, ibid.; Franklin D. Roosevelt to Charles E. Blake, n.d., ibid. It was rumored at the time that Roosevelt had protected Kelly from indictment by the Justice Department in the spring of 1933. While that matter remains only speculation, Kelly did have some influential friends helping him: Governor Horner traveled to Washington on March 24, 1933, to plead Kelly's case; when he paid the

$100,000 settlement, Kelly used a check from William D. Kenny, Al Smith's protégé and a wealthy Tammany contractor. O'Connor, *Clout*, p. 54; Littlewood, *Horner of Illinois*, p. 104; Flynn, "These Our Rulers," July 6, 1940, p. 56.

27. *Chicago Tribune*, August 24, 1933; Flynn, "These Our Rulers," July 6, 1940, p. 58; Charles T. Holman, "Chicago Heads in Tax Trouble," *Christian Century* 50 (September 6, 1933): 1122.

28. *Chicago Tribune*, August 26, 1933 (quoted); *Chicago American*, August 29, 1933; *Chicago Herald and Examiner*, August 28, 1933.

29. *New York Times*, August 26, 1933; *Chicago American*, August–October, 1933; *Chicago Herald and Examiner*, August–October, 1933.

30. "Elected to Fill Former Mayor Cermak's Unexpired Term," p. 19 (quoted); *New York Times*, April 16, 1933.

31. Emmett Dedmon, *Fabulous Chicago* (New York: Random House, 1953), pp. 336–37.

32. Harold M. Mayer and Richard C. Wade, *Chicago: Growth of a Metropolis* (Chicago: University of Chicago Press, 1969), pp. 362–64; Arthur G. Lindell, *City Hall Chronology,* 1966, Municipal Reference Library of Chicago, vol. 2.

33. Littlewood, *Horner of Illinois*, pp. 135–36; Jones, "Local Political Significance of New Deal Relief Legislation," p. 78; Edward H. Mazur, "Minyans for a Prairie City: The Politics of Chicago Jewry, 1850–1940" (Ph.D. diss., University of Chicago, 1974), p. 368; Walter S. G. Kohn, "Illinois Ratifies the Twenty-first Amendment," *Journal of the Illinois State Historical Society* 56 (Winter 1963): 692–95.

34. *Chicago Daily News*, December 23, 1933; *Chicago Herald and Examiner*, December 23, 1933; Littlewood, *Horner of Illinois*, p. 137 (quoted).

35. *Chicago Tribune*, December 9 (quoted), 19, 24, 1933, January 5, 12, 26, 1934; Littlewood, *Horner of Illinois*, p. 138.

36. William E. Leuchtenburg, *Franklin D. Roosevelt and the New Deal* (New York: Harper and Row, 1963), p. 121; Howard O. Hunter to Harry Hopkins, memo, December 4, 1933, Harry Hopkins Papers, Hunter General Correspondence, 1933–1940, Container 90, Franklin D. Roosevelt Library, Hyde Park, N.Y.

37. *Chicago American*, December 7–10, 1933; *Chicago Daily News*, December 18, 22, 1933.

38. Howard O. Hunter to Harry Hopkins, memo, December 4, 1933, Hopkins Papers, Hunter General Correspondence, 1933–1940, Container 90.

39. *Chicago Daily News*, January 3, 4, 1934; *Chicago American*, January 11, 1934.

40. *Chicago Daily News*, January 23, 1934; *Chicago American*, January 25, 26, 1934; Forrest A. Walker, "Graft and the CWA," *Southwestern Social Science Quarterly* 46 (September 1965): 169; Jones, "Local Political Significance of New Deal Relief Legislation," p. 61.

41. Searle F. Charles, "Harry L. Hopkins: New Deal Administrator, 1933–1938," (Ph.D. diss., University of Illinois, 1953), p. 99; Howard O. Hunter to Harry Hopkins, December 19, 1933, Hopkins Papers, Hunter General Correspondence, 1933–1940, Container 90.

42. By and large, McCormick's *Tribune* centered its criticism

on Roosevelt and the New Deal while treating Kelly with kid gloves. The Republican *Daily News* was equally critical of the New Deal, if not as solicitous of the mayor. The Hearst papers, the *American* and the *Herald and Examiner,* consistently attacked Kelly and local New Deal programs, though they generally stopped short of attacking the president.

43. Howard O. Hunter to Harry Hopkins, memo, January 7, 1934, Records of the FERA, Illinois 1933–1936, Box 81; Harold Ickes to Robert Dunham, March 1934, Hopkins Papers, Harold L. Ickes Correspondence, No. 91; Walker, "Graft and the CWA," p. 170; "Report of the Federal Civil Works Administration for Illinois," March 31, 1934, Records of the CWA, Record Group 69, National Archives.

44. Leuchtenburg, *Roosevelt and the New Deal,* pp. 122–24; Florence Petersen, "CWA: A Candid Appraisal," *Atlantic Monthly* 153 (May 1934): 587–90.

45. Jones, "Local Political Significance of New Deal Relief Legislation," pp. 74–75. A number of possible candidates opposing Kelly had been mentioned, including Newton Jenkins and University of Chicago professors Paul Douglas and Charles Merriam. Paul Douglas to Charles Merriam, January 23, 1934, Charles E. Merriam Papers, Correspondence, Box 36, University of Chicago Library.

46. *Chicago Herald and Examiner,* March 28, 1934; Howard E. Flanigan to Franklin D. Roosevelt, February 1, 1934, Democratic National Committee Papers, Official File 300, Box 26, Franklin D. Roosevelt Library, Hyde Park, N.Y.; *Chicago Tribune,* April 11, 1934; *Chicago American,* April 11, 1934 (quoted).

47. Gene Delon Jones, "The Origin of the Alliance between the New Deal and the Chicago Machine," *Journal of the Illinois State Historical Society* 67 (June 1974): 261; Gosnell, *Machine Politics,* p. 116. The Democrats polled a 270,000-vote plurality in Cook County, capturing every statewide and Cook County office contested and increasing their margins in both houses of the state legislature. Philip G. Bean, "Illinois Politics during the New Deal" (Ph.D. diss., University of Illinois, 1976.)

48. Harold L. Ickes, *The Secret Diary of Harold L. Ickes: The First Thousand Days, 1933–1936* (New York: Simon and Schuster, 1954), pp. 246, 275; Frank Knox to Harold Ickes, December 11, 1934, Records of the FERA, Illinois 1933–1936, Box 87. The card read: "I am unable to mark my ballot and in accordance with Section 25 of the Ballot Law, Approved June 22, 1891, in force July 1st, 1891, and so amended.—1. I desire to vote the Democratic ticket straight. 2. I desire to vote the Municipal Court ballot straight Democratic. 3. I desire to vote 'yes' for the Relief Bond Issue. 4. I desire to vote 'yes' on the Constitution Amendment."

49. Harold Ickes, Diary, p. 732, Ickes Papers, Library of Congress; James A. Farley, *Jim Farley's Story: The Roosevelt Years* (New York: McGraw-Hill, 1948), pp. 49–50. Ickes suspected that Farley had secretly been in Kelly's corner. "There is no doubt in my mind," he wrote in his diary, "that he is for Kelly and that instead of trying to get Kelly out of the race, he has encouraged him to stay in." Ickes, *Secret Diary: First Thousand Days,* p. 272.

50. *Chicago Tribune,* January 2, 3, 1935; *Chicago Daily News,* January 2, 1935.

51. *New York Times,* February 24, 1935; *Chicago Tribune,* January 18, February 24 (quoted), 1935. In the primary Wetten received 69,600 votes out of 116,529 cast, while Kelly garnered 479,826 out of

539,596. These vote totals represented the smallest Republican turnout since 1911 and the largest Democratic vote ever. *Chicago Tribune,* February 27, 1935.

52. *Chicago Tribune,* February 27 (quoted), 28, 1935; Gosnell, *Machine Politics,* p. 19; Cleveland, "Biography of Kelly," p. 129; James F. "Spike" Hennessey, interview with author, Chicago, Ill., January 9, 1980; Kennedy interview.

53. Cleveland, "Biography of Kelly," p. 127; *Newsweek* 5 (April 13, 1935): 7; *Chicago Tribune,* April 1, 1935 (quoted).

54. *Chicago Daily News,* March 20–27, 1935; *Chicago Tribune,* March 7, 1935; *New York Times,* March 7, 1935; *Chicago American,* March 28, 29 (quoted), 1935.

55. *Chicago Tribune,* March 28, 1935.

56. *Papers of Adlai E. Stevenson,* vol. 1 (1972), p. 294; *Chicago Herald and Examiner,* March 30, 1935; *Chicago Tribune,* March 31, 1935.

57. "The Kelly-Nash Political Machine," p. 117; *Newsweek* 5 (April 13, 1935): 7; *Chicago American,* April 3, 1935 (quoted); *Chicago Tribune,* April 3, 1935; "Old Pat," p. 62.

58. "The Kelly-Nash Political Machine," p. 117; Cleveland, "Biography of Kelly," p. 130.

59. *Newsweek* 5 (April 13, 1935): 7; Howard O. Hunter to Harry Hopkins, memo of telephone conversation, April 5, 1935, Hopkins Papers, Box 73.

60. *Chicago Herald and Examiner,* April 3, 1935; *Chicago Tribune,* April 7, 1935; Harry Hopkins to Howard O. Hunter, memo of telephone conversation, August 9, 1935, Hopkins Papers, Box 73. Neither the permanent fair nor the lakefront airport was ever approved by Roosevelt, but Hopkins did argue Kelly's case to the president. Over the next several years, Hopkins and Ickes debated the two proposals, trying to sway Roosevelt, whose inaction ultimately favored Ickes. Franklin D. Roosevelt to Harry Hopkins, memo, November 25, 1938, Roosevelt Papers, President's Secretary's File, Box 52; Ickes, Diary, pp. 3080–81, Library of Congress; Harold L. Ickes to Franklin D. Roosevelt, July 7, 1934, Roosevelt Papers, President's Official File no. 6, Box 1.

61. *Chicago Tribune,* May 1, 2, 1935; *Chicago Herald and Examiner,* March 1, 1935; *New York Times,* April 14, 1935; Jones, "Local Political Significance of New Deal Relief Legislation," pp. 87–98.

62. Howard O. Hunter to Harry Hopkins, memo of second telephone conversation, May 15, 1935, Hopkins Papers, Box 93; Howard O. Hunter to Harry Hopkins, memo of first telephone conversation, May 15, 1935, Hopkins Papers, Box 93; *Chicago Tribune,* May 23, 24, 1935.

63. Howard O. Hunter to Harry Hopkins, Field Report, May 29, 1935, Records of the FERA, Illinois Files, Box 81.

64. *New York Times,* October 20, 1936; "Chicago's Record of Accomplishment"; *New York Times,* March 4, 1935; "The Financial Troubles of Our Cities," *Saturday Evening Post* 206 (June 9, 1934): 26.

3 Hegemony Denied

1. Wheeler, "Kelly's Life"; Cleveland "Biography of Kelly," p. 119; Warren H. Pierce, "Chicago: Unfinished Anomaly," in *Our Fair City,* ed. Robert S. Allen (New York: Vanguard Press, 1947), p. 179; Edward J.

Kelly, with Walter Davenport, "Politics Is People," *Collier's* 117 (April 13, 1946): 74 (quoted). Kelly always maintained that his organization never told precinct captains to steal votes. That claim may have been true, but by placing such demanding requirements for favorable returns on party workers, the machine put them in a position where they may have had to use extralegal methods in order to stay in good graces.

2. Lloyd Wendt and Herman Kogan, *Bosses in Lusty Chicago: The Story of Bathouse John and Hinky Dink* (Bloomington: Indiana University Press, 1974), pp. 352–53. For more on the importance of the precinct-level worker in the Kelly-Nash machine, see Gosnell, *Machine Politics,* and Sonya Forthal, *Cogwheels of Democracy: A Study of the Precinct Captain* (New York: William Frederick Press, 1946).

3. Gottfried, *Boss Cermak of Chicago;* p. 207; Allswang, *A House for All Peoples,* p. 42.

4. Edward R. Kantowicz, "American Politics in Polonia's Capital: 1888–1940" (Ph.D. diss., University of Chicago, 1972), pp. 429–30, 466 (quoted), 506. In the 1936 primary, Kelly received 72.5 percent of the Polish vote to Horner's 27.5 percent. In the 1939 mayoral primary, Kelly netted 60.5 percent to Courtney's 39.5 percent. Ibid., p. 506.

5. Allswang, *A House for All Peoples,* p. 42.

6. For brief accounts of Kelly's uneasy relations with the Irish, see Royko, *Boss;* and O'Connor, *Clout.*

7. "The Kelly-Nash Political Machine," p. 130.

8. Marshall Korshak, interview with author, Chicago, Ill., January 7, 1980; John Dreiske, interview with author, Oak Park, Ill., January 16, 1980.

9. Jacob Arvey, interview with Milton Rakove, Chicago, Ill., August 1976, transcript in the possession of Rakove, University of Illinois at Chicago (quoted); *We Don't Want Nobody Nobody Sent,* p. 276. My interviews with Chicago politicans revealed a unanimity of reverence for Nash. In general, they also suggested that Kelly evoked much the opposite reaction.

10. Cleveland, "Biography of Kelly," p. 100; Harry Barnard, interview with author, Wilmette, Ill., January 26, 1980; Adamowski interview (quoted).

11. Dreiske interview (quoted); Wheeler, "Kelly's Life."

12. Bill Gleason, *Daley of Chicago* (New York: Simon and Schuster, 1970), p. 196 (quoting Adamowski); Korshak interview; Wheeler, "Kelly's Life"; John Leonard East, interview with author, Chicago, Ill., November 13, 1979; Rubin, "You've Gotta Be a Boss," p. 36 (quoting Kelly). Kelly was so confident in his control of the city council that he urged one of his greatest critics, Paul Douglas, to run for the alderman's seat of the 5th Ward. He even offered Douglas the Democratic organization's endorsement, saying that the council was too one-sided and needed some new blood to spark debate. Paul H. Douglas, *In the Fullness of Time* (New York: Harcourt Brace Jovanovich, 1971), pp. 87–88.

13. Littlewood, *Horner of Illinois;* Barnard interview; *Public Service Leader,* June 5, 20, 1935; *Chicago Tribune,* May 29, 1935; *Chicago Daily News,* June 14, 1935; *Chicago Herald and Examiner,* June 21, 1935.

14. *Chicago Tribune,* May 29, 1935 (quoted); *Chicago Daily News,* June 14, 1935; *Chicago Herald and Examiner,* June 21, 1935.

15. *Chicago Tribune,* June 26, July 12, 14, 1935; Littlewood,

Horner of Illinois, pp. 151–52; *Chicago Daily News,* July 12, 1935; *Chicago American,* June 27, July 10, 12, 1935 (quoted).

16. Littlewood, *Horner of Illinois,* pp. 150–51; Marovitz interview.

17. Gottfried, *Boss Cermak of Chicago,* p. 313; Cleveland, "Biography of Kelly," p. 146.

18. Littlewood, *Horner of Illinois,* p. 158; *Chicago Daily News,* August 22, 1935.

19. Adamowski interview; *Chicago Daily News,* October 7, 1935; Arvarh E. Strickland, "The New Deal Comes to Illinois," *Journal of the Illinois State Historical Society* 63 (Spring 1970): 55, 68.

20. Scott Lucas to Franklin D. Roosevelt, telegram, August 20, 1935, Roosevelt Papers, President's Personal File 2422; Ickes, *Secret Diary: First Thousand Days,* p. 493; Bean, "Illinois Politics during the New Deal," p. 149 (quoting Farley); *Chicago American,* November 27, 1935; *New York Times,* November 28, 1935.

21. Present at Kelly's home were Bruce Campbell, state committee chairman; John Stelle, state treasurer; William Dieterich, U.S. senator; John Devine, speaker of the Illinois House; Howard Doyle, U. S. district attorney; V. Y. Dallman, collector of customs; Chester Thompson, congressman; Warren Orr, state supreme court justice; Kelly; and Nash. *Chicago Daily News,* December 8, 9, 1935; *Chicago Tribune,* December 8, 9, 1935.

22. Littlewood, *Horner of Illinois,* p. 159.

23. Jones, "Local Political Significance of New Deal Relief Legislation," p. 105; Littlewood, *Horner of Illinois,* p. 159; Ickes, Diary, p. 1311, Library of Congress; *Chicago Daily News,* December 24, 1935.

24. *Chicago Tribune,* January 4, 1936; "The Kelly-Nash Political Machine," p. 118; Littlewood, *Horner of Illinois,* p. 166; *Chicago American,* January 13, 1936.

25. *Chicago American,* January 14, 1936.

26. Jones, "Local Political Significance of New Deal Relief Legislation," pp. 108–12; *New York Times,* January 4, 1936; *Chicago Tribune,* February 26, 1936.

27. Cleveland, "Biography of Kelly," pp. 150–52.

28. Ibid., pp. 150–53; Littlewood, *Horner of Illinois,* p. 157.

29. An alternative explanation suggested that Kelly chose a weak candidate because he really wanted the Republican, Curly Brooks, to win—a motive explained by the close association between Kelly and McCormick, Brooks's political patron. With Horner slowed down by Bundesen in the primary and derailed by Brooks in the general election, Kelly would be left the unquestioned leader of the Illinois Democrats. Moreover, the mayor could expect more amicable relations with a McCormick Republican than he had enjoyed with the obstinate Horner. This scenario, though unconfirmed, gained widespread popularity after Bundesen's defeat, particularly among disgruntled Democrats.

30. *Chicago Herald and Examiner,* April 2, 1936; Littlewood, *Horner of Illinois,* p. 178.

31. *Chicago Tribune,* March 5, 1936; *Chicago American,* February 25, 1936.

32. *Chicago Tribune,* February 28, March 5, 1936.

33. Bean, "Illinois Politics during the New Deal," p. 182; Cleveland, "Biography of Kelly," p. 177; Gosnell, *Machine Politics,* p. 23;

Thomas L. Marshall to Henry Horner, February 22, 1936, Henry Horner Papers, Box 307, Illinois State Historical Library, Springfield.

34. *Chicago Daily News*, April 4, 1936.

35. *Chicago Tribune*, March 14, 1936.

36. *Chicago American,* March 13, 1936; *Chicago Tribune,* March 27, 1936; Edward J. Kelly Speeches of 1936, Horner Papers, Box 7.

37. Franklin D. Roosevelt to James A. Farley, memo, January 24, 1936, Roosevelt Papers, President's Personal File 309; Ickes, Diary, p. 1364, Library of Congress.

38. Jones, "Local Political Significance of New Deal Relief Legislation," pp. 113–14; Records of the WPA, Record Group 69, Illinois State Files, National Archives; *New York Times,* March 10, 1936; Lorena Hickok to Harry Hopkins, August 21, 1936, Hopkins Papers, FERA-WPA Narrative Field Reports, Box 89.

39. *Chicago Tribune*, March 12, 29, 1936.

40. Mazur, "Minyans for a Prairie City," p. 378; Harry Fisher to Henry Horner, February 25, 1936, Horner Papers, Case 56, Drawer 2; James T. Patterson, *The New Deal and the States: Federalism in Transition* (Princeton, N.J.: Princeton University Press, 1969), p. 184.

41. See Littlewood, *Horner of Illinois*, pp. 184, 186–87. The final totals were Horner 788,762, Bundesen, 649,937. Horner carried the 5th, 6th, 7th, 29th, 39th, 40th, 48th, and 49th wards. He narrowly lost his own, the 4th. *Chicago Daily News*, April 15, 1936; *Chicago Tribune*, April 15, 1936.

42. "The Kelly-Nash Political Machine," p. 47; Charles W. VanDevander, *The Big Bosses* (New York: Howell-Soskin, 1944), p. 280 (quoted); Douglas Bukowski, "Judge Edmund K. Jarecki: A Rather Regular Independent," *Chicago History* 8 (Winter 1979–80): 214.

43. Cleveland, "Biography of Kelly," pp. 185–86 (quoted); *Chicago Tribune*, April 9, 1936; VanDevander, *The Big Bosses*, p. 280.

44. Littlewood, *Horner of Illinois*, pp. 173 (quoted), 184–85; Mazur, "Minyans for a Prairie City," pp. 374, 377.

45. Stanley Frankel and Holmes Alexander, "Arvey of Illinois: New Style Political Boss," *Collier's* 123 (July 23, 1949): 66.

46. Bean, "Illinois Politics during the New Deal," p. 191.

47. *Chicago Daily News*, April 27, 1936; *Chicago Herald and Examiner,* May 1, 1936; Littlewood, *Horner of Illinois*, p. 190 (quoted).

48. *Chicago Herald and Examiner*, May 2, 1936.

49. Permanent registration became mandatory in the ten largest Illinois cities—Chicago, Aurora, Bloomington, Cairo, Danville, East St. Louis, Galesburg, Peoria, Rockford, and Springfield. Cleveland, "Biography of Kelly," p. 198; Littlewood, *Horner of Illinois*, p. 189.

50. *Chicago Tribune*, June 23, 24, 1936; Cleveland, "Biography of Kelly," p. 199.

51. Edward J. Kelly to James A. Farley, July 24, 1936, Democratic National Committee Papers, Container 1093, Farley Correspondence; Ickes, Diary, pp. 1755–56, Library of Congress; *Chicago Tribune,* August 26, 1936; *New York Times,* August 27, 1936.

52. Littlewood, *Horner of Illinois*, p. 190; Lorena Hickok to Harry Hopkins, July 18, 1936, Lorena Hickok Papers, Box 11, FERA Reports, Franklin D. Roosevelt Library, Hyde Park, N.Y.; Edward J. Kelly to James A. Farley, September 12, 1936, Democratic National Committee Papers, Container 1094, Farley Correspondence.

53. Littlewood, *Horner of Illinois*, pp. 192–93.

54. Donald G. Sofchalk, "The Chicago Memorial Day Incident: An Episode of Mass Action," *Labor History* 6 (Winter 1965): 17; *Chicago Tribune*, July 23, 1937 (quoted); Guenther Baumgart, "Strikes Are Not a Chicago Custom," *Commerce* 37 (November 1940): 16.

55. Barnard interview; Irving Bernstein, *Turbulent Years: History of the American Worker, 1920–1933* (Boston: Houghton Mifflin Co., 1969), p. 486; *Report of Citizens' Joint Commission of Inquiry on South Chicago Memorial Day Incident*, August 31, 1937, Municipal Reference Library of Chicago, p. 3.

56. U.S. Congress, Senate Committee on Education and Labor, *The Chicago Memorial Day Incident: Hearings before a Subcommittee of the Senate Committee on Education and Labor*, 75th Cong., 1st sess., 1937, p. 2.

57. Bernstein, *Turbulent Years*, pp. 825–26; *Chicago Tribune*, May 31, 1937.

58. *Report of Citizens' Joint Commission of Inquiry*, pp. 2, 12–14.

59. U.S. Senate Committee on Education and Labor, *The Chicago Memorial Day Incident*, pp. 37, 39, 40. The members of the subcommittee were Chairman LaFollette; Elbert D. Thomas of Utah; John J. Abt, counsel; and Robert Wohlforth, secretary. The Paramount newsreel was released in several cities, but not in Chicago; upon Mayor Kelly's urging, the Police Movie Censor Bureau banned the film. Sofchalk, "The Chicago Memorial Day Incident," p. 38; Douglas, *In the Fullness of Time*, p. 102.

60. Barbara Newell, *Chicago and the Labor Movement: Metropolitan Unionism in the 1930's* (Urbana: University of Illinois Press, 1961), pp. 178–79, 224–25, 250; Barnard interview; E. Pendleton Herring, *The Politics of Democracy: American Parties in Action* (New York: Rinehart and Co., 1940), p. 149; Louis L. Friedland, "Organized Labor and the City Boss," *Annals of the American Academy of Political and Social Science* 353 (May 1964): 40–51. Much to the consternation of CIO leaders, President Roosevelt refused to chastise Kelly for the Memorial Day affair. Roosevelt, unsympathetic to the "Little Steel" strikes, including the one against Republic Steel in Chicago, finally broke his silence with the famous "a plague on both your houses" remark. Sofchalk, "The Chicago Memorial Day Incident," p. 36; *New York Times*, June 30, 1977; Bernstein, *Turbulent Years*, p. 494.

61. Newell, *Chicago and the Labor Movement*, pp. 224–25; Mary F. Watters, *Illinois in the Second World War*, 2 vols. (Springfield: Illinois State Historical Library, 1952), 2:214–15; Art Preis, *Labor's Giant Step: Twenty Years of the CIO* (New York: Pioneer Press, 1964), pp. 77, 222.

62. *Chicago Daily News*, December 11, 1937, January 8, 1938; *Chicago Herald and Examiner*, December 23, 25, 1937; *New York Times*, December 26, 1937.

63. *Chicago Daily News*, May 18, 21, 1938; *New York Times*, September 19, 1937; Howard Hunter to Aubrey Williams, memo of telephone conversation, May 13, 1938, Aubrey Williams Papers, Box 28, WPA Field Reports, Franklin D. Roosevelt Library, Hyde Park, N.Y.

64. Kantowicz, *Polish-American Politics*, pp. 201–4; Adamowski interview; *Chicago Tribune*, February 1, 1938.

65. Bean, "Illinois Politics During the New Deal," pp. 249–50; *Chicago Tribune*, February 2, 1938.

66. *Public Service Leader*, March 31, 1938; *Chicago Tribune*, February 2, 1938; Cleveland, "Biography of Kelly," pp. 218–20.

67. U.S. Senate Committee to Investigate Senatorial Campaign Expenditures and Use of Governmental Funds in 1938, *Report of the Committee to Investigate Senatorial Campaign Expenditures and Use of Governmental Funds in 1938*, 76th Cong., 1st sess., 1939, pt. 1, pp. 30, 42–44.

68. *Chicago Tribune*, April 5, 11, 1938; *Chicago Herald and Examiner*, February 19, 1938; *Chicago Daily News*, April 11, 1938.

69. While he received only 50.48 percent of the votes cast in the city, Jarecki garnered 67.50 percent of the Polish vote. Kantowicz, "American Politics in Polonia's Capital," p. 506.

70. *Chicago Herald and American*, April 3, 1938; *Chicago Tribune*, April 11, 13, 1938; Kantowicz, *Polish-American Politics*, p. 205.

71. In the primary, Lucas won by 75,284 votes, beating Igoe 418,530 to 163,999 downstate while losing by 179,247 in Cook County. Littlewood, *Horner of Illinois*, pp. 204, 207. In the general election, Lucas lost downstate by 108,193 and lost Cook County suburbs by 51,492 but won Chicago by 255,277. Bean, "Illinois Politics during the New Deal," pp. 276–78; Leuchtenburg, *Roosevelt and the New Deal*, p. 271.

72. Cleveland, "Biography of Kelly," pp. 155–61; *New York Times*, December 22, 1935; *Chicago Tribune*, January 17, 1936.

73. In addition to serving as state senator, Courtney was also assistant attorney for Kelly's Sanitary District, secretary of the Chicago City Council Building and Zoning Committee, and sergeant-at-arms for the city council. Milton S. Mayer, "Chicago Doesn't Care," *Nation* 146 (February 5, 1938): 151; Williams, *The Fix-It Boys*, pp. 67–68; *Beacon*, November 1937, p. 16.

74. Mayer, "Chicago Doesn't Care," p. 151; Milton S. Mayer, "It's Hell to Be a Chicago Liberal," *Nation* 148 (February 25, 1939): 223; Kennedy interview; *Chicago Tribune*, February 5, 1939. Several exposés pointed out Courtney's questionable ethics, for example, Labor's Non-Partisan League of Cook County, *Now It Must Be Told! Mayoralty Election. The Truth About Courtney. The Real Facts About the Phoney Reformer and New Deal Enemy, Courtney*, 1939, Chicago Historical Society; and Elmer Lynn Williams, *The Curious Career of Thomas Courtney Unveiled: A Documented Report of the Little Known Political History of a Payroll Patriot*, 1944, Chicago Historical Society.

75. Harold L. Ickes, *The Secret Diary of Harold L. Ickes: The Inside Struggle, 1936–1939* (New York: Simon and Schuster, 1954), pp. 512–15; Douglas, *In the Fullness of Time*, p. 86; Ickes, Diary, pp. 3087–88, Library of Congress (quoting Kelly); *Chicago Daily News*, December 5, 15, 1938 (quoting Ickes).

76. *Chicago Tribune*, August 18, October 5, 1938; John T. Flynn, "Too Much Fun," *Collier's* 104 (October 7, 1939): 36; Leitzell, "Chicago, City of Corruption," p. 149; John T. Flynn, "These Our Rulers," *Collier's* 106 (July 13, 1940): 47 (quoted).

77. *Chicago Tribune*, February 6, 1939; Cleveland, "Biography of Kelly," p. 230; Kantowicz, *Polish-American Politics*, p. 206.

78. Littlewood, *Horner of Illinois*, pp. 208–11 (quoting Courtney); *Chicago Tribune*, February 10, 1939; *Chicago Daily News*, Jan-

uary 13, 1939; Edward J. Kelly to Henry Horner, telegram, March 1, 1939, Horner Papers, Box 191, Mayor Edward J. Kelly Correspondence; *Chicago Herald and Examiner,* March 7, 1939.

79. Cleveland, "Biography of Edward J. Kelly," p. 236; *Chicago Tribune,* March 1, 1939; Ickes, *Secret Diary: Inside Struggle,* p. 586.

80. *New York Times,* March 1, 1939; VanDevander, *The Big Bosses,* p. 283; *Chicago Tribune,* February 15, March 1, 1939. The only biography of Dwight Green is Robert J. Casey and W. A. S. Douglas, *The Midwesterner: The Story of Dwight H. Green* (Chicago: Wilcox and Follett, 1948). It was thrown together for the 1948 gubernatorial campaign and does not constitute a critical treatment of Green's public life to that time.

81. *Chicago Daily News,* March 22, 1939; *Chicago Tribune,* March 21, 22, 1939.

82. *Chicago Tribune,* March 21, 1939; *Chicago Daily News,* March 13, 1939.

83. *Chicago Daily News,* May 11, 1939; Citizens' Committee on Public Information, *Out of the Red, Into the Black: The Truth about Chicago's Municipal Government. A Frank Statement Reviewing the Years 1933 to 1938,* 1938, pp. 11–12; Better Government Association, "An Issue for the Mayoralty and Aldermanic Elections, 1939," Chicago Historical Society, Records of the Citizens' Association of Chicago, Box 2, 1930–1940.

84. Jones, "Local Political Significance of New Deal Relief Legislation," pp. 172–75; Ickes, Diary, pp. 2875–77, Library of Congress; *New York Times,* March 5, 1939; Franklin D. Roosevelt to Edward J. Kelly, telegram, October 20, 1938, Roosevelt Papers, President's Personal File 3166.

85. *Chicago Herald and Examiner,* March 2, 1939; *Chicago American,* March 1, 1939; Jones, "Local Political Significance of New Deal Relief Legislation," pp. 177–79; *New York Times,* April 5, 1939. The fifteen wards carried by Green were the 6th, 7th, 8th, 9th, 12th, 17th, 19th, 36th, 37th, 38th, 39th, 41st, 45th, 49th, and 50th. Fred W. Blaisdell, "The Republican Party in Chicago," Better Government Assocation, 1939, Chicago Historical Society, typescript, pp. 32–60.

86. Blaisdell, "The Republican Party in Chicago," pp. 32–60.

87. *Chicago Tribune,* April 6, 1939.

88. *Chicago Tribune,* April 5, 1939 (quoted); Ickes, Diary, p. 3350, Library of Congress.

89. Littlewood, *Horner of Illinois,* pp. 218–20.

4   Kelly, Roosevelt, and the New Deal

1. Leuchtenburg, *Roosevelt and the New Deal,* p. 270; *New York Times,* January 8, 9, 1939; Arthur W. MacMahon, John D. Millett, and Gladys Ogden, *The Administration of Federal Work Relief* (New York: De Capo Press, 1971), pp. 285–86. Many contemporary articles charged politicization of the WPA. See Stanley High, "WPA: Politician's Playground," *Current History* 50 (May 1939): 23–25; Sidney Hollander, "The Public Holds Its Nose," *Survey Midmonthly* 74 (May 1938): 173–76; William H. Matthews, "These Past Five Years," *Survey Midmonthly* 84 (March 1938): 70–72; Albert J. Nock, "WPA—The Modern Tammany," *American Mercury* 45 (October 1938): 215–19; and "Politics and Relief," *Social Science Review* 12 (September 1938): 495–99. Harry Hopkins defended the WPA, calling

it a political liability. Awarding funds makes enemies of those overlooked, he argued, in "They'd Rather Work," *Collier's* 96 (November 16, 1935): 41.

2. U.S. Senate Committee on Appropriations, *Work Relief and Relief, Fiscal Year 1939: Hearings before a Subcommittee of the Senate Committee on Appropriations*, 76th Cong., 1st sess., May 8, 1939, pp. 404, 405.

3. Jones, "Local Political Significance of New Deal Relief Legislation," p. 148 (quoted ["I have been . . ."]); Walter Davenport, "From Whom All Blessings Flow," *Collier's* 96 (July 20, 1935): 7, 8, 34–36; Lorena Hickok to Harry Hopkins, July 18, 1936, Hickok Papers, FERA Reports, Box 11.

4. Lawrence Sullivan, "The Negro Vote," *Atlantic Monthly* 166 (October 1940): 480.

5. John M. Allswang, *The New Deal and American Politics* (New York: John Wiley and Sons, 1978), p. 86; Gosnell, *Machine Politics*, pp. 1, 65–66.

6. Gosnell, *Machine Politics*, p. 78; *Chicago Tribune*, April 26, 1937; Speech of Wayne McMillen, January 25, 1938, Records of the National Association of Social Workers, Chicago Chapter, Box 5, Chicago Historical Society; Leo M. Lyons, "Illinois Investigates the Relief Situation," *National Municipal Review* 27 (January 1938): 26.

7. *Chicago Daily News*, March 20, 1939 (quoting Douglas); Jones, "Local Political Significance of New Deal Relief Legislation," p. 144; Gosnell, *Machine Politics*, p. 78.

8. Blaisdell, "The Republican Party in Chicago," p. 4.

9. Frank Knox to Harold L. Ickes, December 11, 1934, Records of the FERA, Illinois 1933–1936, Box 87; Jones, "Local Political Significance of New Deal Relief Legislation," pp. 151–52; Records of the WPA, Illinois State Files; Harriet M. Robertson, ed., *Dishonest Elections and Why We Have Them: The Records Tell the Story* (Chicago: Women's Civic Council of the Chicago Area, n.d.), 2:8 (quoted).

10. *Chicago Daily News*, March 4, 23, 1939; Jones, "Local Political Significance of New Deal Relief Legislation," p. 176.

11. Gosnell, *Machine Politics;* p. 175; Harold F. Gosnell, "The Negro Vote in Northern Cities," *National Municipal Review* 30 (May 1941): 265; Jones, "Local Political Significance of New Deal Relief Legislation," p. 241; Norman A. Graebner, "Depression and Urban Votes," *Current History* 23 (October 1952): 234–38. On the developing Democratic strength in the late 1920s and early 1930s, see Samuel Lubell, *The Future of American Politics* (New York: Harper and Row, 1952); Carl Degler, "American Political Parties and the Rise of the City: An Interpretation," *Journal of American History* 51 (June 1964): 50–59; V. O. Key, Jr., "A Theory of Critical Elections," *Journal of Politics* 17 (February 1955): 3–18; and Angus Campbell, *Elections and the Political Order* (New York: Harper and Row, 1966).

12. Jones, "Local Political Significance of New Deal Relief Legislation," pp. 187–90.

13. Arthur E. Burns, "Federal Emergency Relief Administration," *Municipal Year Book, 1937*, p. 413; Frank Z. Glick, *The Illinois Emergency Relief Commission* (Chicago: University of Chicago Press, 1940), p. 188; Wayne McMillen, "Statement on Report: Relief Administration," Records of the National Association of Social Workers, Chicago Chap-

ter, Box 5; "Data on Relief Situation in Chicago and Cook County, Illinois," January 27, 1937, ibid., Box 4.

14. Edward C. Banfield, "The Dilemma of a Metropolitan Machine," in *Urban Government: A Reader in Administration and Politics*, ed. Edward C. Banfield (New York: Free Press of Glencoe, 1961), pp. 322–23; Charles Casey, *Final Report, 1935–1943, of the Works Project Administration of Illinois* (Chicago, April 20, 1943), p. 100.

15. Harry Hopkins to Franklin D. Roosevelt, July 11, 1938, Records of the WPA, Illinois Files, Box 1216; "Chicago Street Projects," September 1937, ibid.

16. City of Chicago, *Chicago's Report to the People, 1933–1946* (March 1947), pp. 8–9; *Lightnin'*, March 1, 1935; Citizen's Committee on Public Information, *Out of the Red, Into the Black*, p. 11; Flynn, "These Our Rulers," July 20, p. 19.

17. Casey, *Final Report, 1935–1943*, pp. 98–103; Martin H. Bickham, *Achievements of WPA Workers in Illinois, July 1st, 1935, to June 30th, 1938* (Information Service of WPA, n.d.), pp. 3–4; City of Chicago, *Chicago's Report to the People*, p. 9 (quoted); Chicago Plan Commission, *S.O.S. Chicago! Ten Radio Broadcasts over Station WJJD* (1939).

18. MacMahon, Millett, and Ogden, *Administration of Federal Work Relief*, p. 199; Howard O. Hunter to Harry Hopkins, June 22, 1935, Records of the FERA, Box 129 (quoted); *New York Times*, November 17, 1935; Jones, "Local Political Significance of New Deal Relief Legislation," p. 137.

19. Ickes, *Secret Diary: First Thousand Days*, pp. 494, 557; Arthur M. Schlesinger, Jr., *The Age of Roosevelt: The Politics of Upheaval* (Boston: Houghton Mifflin Co., 1960), pp. 442–43; Edward J. Kelly to Harry Hopkins, memo of telephone conversation, September 10, 1935, Hopkins Papers, Box 93.

20. Ickes, *Secret Diary: First Thousand Days*, pp. 579, 586 (quoted); Ickes, *Secret Diary: Inside Struggle*, pp. 484–86; Searle F. Charles, *Minister of Relief: Harry Hopkins and the Depression* (Syracuse, N.Y.: Syracuse University Press, 1963), pp. 206–19; Howard O. Hunter to Harry Hopkins, November 21, 1938, Hopkins Papers, Box 91.

21. Farley, *Jim Farley's Story*, p. 92; Ickes, *Secret Diary: First Thousand Days*, p. 463; James A. Farley to Edward J. Kelly, September 17, 1936, Democratic National Committee Papers, Illinois File.

22. Edward J. Kelly to Franklin D. Roosevelt, received August 30, 1932, Roosevelt Papers, Personal File 3166; Franklin D. Roosevelt to Edward J. Kelly, September 12, 1932, ibid.; Samuel I. Rosenman, *Working with Roosevelt* (New York: Harper and Row, 1952), p. 123. The Chicago machine polled Loop and neighborhood theater patrons to determine voter attitudes, believing that "neighborhood theaters offered the best cross-section of both racial and community background as represented in the fifty wards and seventy-five communities of Chicago." Edward J. Kelly to Franklin D. Roosevelt, September 13, 1940, Roosevelt Papers, President's Personal File 3166.

23. *Chicago Daily News*, April 13, 1937; Leuchtenburg, *Roosevelt and the New Deal*, p. 234; James MacGregor Burns, *Roosevelt: The Lion and the Fox* (New York: Harcourt, Brace and World, 1956), p. 309; Jones, "Local Political Significance of New Deal Relief Legislation," p. 126; Bean, "Illinois Politics during the New Deal," p. 246; Farley, *Jim Farley's Story*, p. 92.

24. Lyle W. Dorsett, *Franklin D. Roosevelt and the City Bosses* (Port Washington, N.Y.: Kennikat Press, 1977), p. 93; Ralph Madison, "Letter from Chicago," *New Republic* 112 (April 23, 1945): 549–51. In *Roosevelt and the City Bosses,* Dorsett argues that the president's relations with the city bosses were of an ad hoc nature, dependent upon political considerations, and largely self-serving. Consequently, FDR turned against Tom Pendergast, Frank Hague, and James Michael Curley, while maintaining good relations with Ed Flynn, Ed Crump, Fiorello LaGuardia, and Kelly. This argument, which calls into question many of the assumptions of the "Last Hurrah" thesis, seems valid with regard to Kelly's mayoralty. (For an elaboration of the thesis, see n. 34 to this chapter and the accompanying text.)

25. Dorsett, *Roosevelt and the City Bosses,* p. 93; Barnard interview; Kennedy interview; Hennessey interview.

26. Kelly, with Davenport, "Politics Is People," p. 13; Jones, "Local Political Significance of New Deal Relief Legislation," pp. 197–98 (quoting Adamowski); Kennedy interview.

27. News clipping, *Washington Times-Herald,* April 15, 1939, Roosevelt Papers, President's Personal File 3166; "Mayor Kelly's Own Story," May 12, 1947 (quoted).

28. *Chicago Herald-American,* February 7, 1940; "Mayor Kelly's Own Story," May 13, 1947. Kelly got the bulk of the money for the convention from the Chicago Park District, which loaned the city $125,000. The loan was repaid from the revenue generated by the convention. *New York Times,* February 11, 1940. Kelly also entered Chicago in the Republican convention competition but lost when Philadelphia bid a whopping $250,000. *Chicago Herald-American,* February 17, 1940. Roosevelt let it be known that he favored Chicago as the convention site, an indication that he had no objection to Kelly's machinations in his behalf. He told Harold Ickes: "I am not overlooking the fact that Kelly could pack the galleries for us." Burns, *Roosevelt,* p. 412; Ickes, *The Secret Diary of Harold L. Ickes: The Lowering Clouds, 1939–1941* (New York: Simon and Schuster, 1954), p. 122.

29. Edward J. Flynn, *You're the Boss* (New York: Viking Press, 1947), p. 156; Dorsett, *Roosevelt and the City Bosses,* pp. 94–96; Thomas J. Fleming, "I Am the Law," *American Heritage* 20 (June 1969): 32–48; "Mister Farley's Successor," *New Republic* 102 (April 8, 1940): 471.

30. Farley, *Jim Farley's Story,* p. 274; *New York Times,* July 16, 1940; *Chicago Tribune,* July 16, 1940; *Chicago Herald-American,* July 20, 1940; Burns, *Roosevelt,* p. 428.

31. Rosenman, *Working with Roosevelt,* pp. 206, 210, 212 (quoted ["almost by acclamation"]); Burns, *Roosevelt,* p. 427 (quoting Barkley); *New York Times,* July 17, 1940.

32. *Time* 56 (October 30, 1950): 89; "Mayor Kelly's Own Story," May 13; *Time* 36 (July 29, 1940): 14; Leuchtenburg, *Roosevelt and the New Deal,* pp. 315–16.

33. Farley, *Jim Farley's Story,* p. 309; "Mayor Kelly's Own Story," May 13; Franklin D. Roosevelt to Edward J. Kelly, July 31, 1940, Roosevelt Papers, President's Personal File 3166.

34. See Edward O'Connor, *The Last Hurrah* (Boston: Little, Brown and Co., 1956); the best explanation of the "Last Hurrah" thesis appears on pp. 101, 329–31. In *The Brains Trust* (New York: Viking Press, 1968), Rexford G. Tugwell defends O'Connor's thesis but offers little sub-

stantiation; moreover, he mistakenly refers to Boss Kelly's handling of the 1932 Democratic Convention in Chicago, when in fact Anton Cermak was mayor then. C. C. Ludwig ("Cities and the National Government under the New Deal," *American Political Science Review* 29 [August 1935]: 640–48) supports the contention that the federal government supplanted many traditional functions of local government but fails to explain the political ramifications. Using New Orleans as a case study, William C. Havard ("From Bossism to Cosmopolitanism: Changes in the Relationship of Urban Leadership to State Politics," *Annals of the American Academy of Political and Social Sciences* 353 [May 1964]: 84–94) affirms the "Last Hurrah" thesis and further asserts that Roosevelt's influence forced bossism to give way to professionalism in politics.

35. Jones, "Local Political Significance of New Deal Relief Legislation," pp. 207–8; *Public Service Leader*, December 20, 1935; Van-Devander, *The Big Bosses*, pp. 277–78; Gosnell, *Machine Politics*, pp. 70–73.

36. This study's conclusions about the compatability of the New Deal and the Chicago machine agree with those of three other studies, all of which question the "Last Hurrah" thesis: Bruce M. Stave, *The New Deal and the Last Hurrah: Pittsburgh Machine Politics* (Pittsburgh: University of Pittsburgh Press, 1970); Dorsett, *The Pendergast Machine;* and Jones, "Local Political Significance of New Deal Relief Legislation."

5 "Big Red" in Bronzeville

1. St. Clare Drake and Horace R. Cayton, *Black Metropolis: A Study of Negro Life in a Northern City* (New York: Harcourt, Brace and Co., 1945), p. 353; William M. Tuttle, Jr., *Race Riot: Chicago in the Red Summer of 1919* (New York: Atheneum Publishers, 1978), pp. 186–203; Lloyd Wendt and Herman Kogan, *Big Bill of Chicago* (Indianapolis: Bobbs-Merrill Co., 1953), pp. 167–69; John M. Allswang, "The Chicago Negro Voter and the Democratic Consensus: A Case Study, 1918–1936," *Journal of the Illinois State Historical Society* 60 (Summer 1967): 167.

2. *Chicago Defender*, April 11 (quoted), August 15, October 10, November 14, 22, December 5, 1931.

3. Ovid Demaris, *Captive City: Chicago in Chains* (New York: Lyle Stuart, 1969), p. 171 (quoting Cermak); Charles Branham, "The Transformation of Black Political Leadership in Chicago, 1865–1942" (Ph.D. diss., University of Chicago, 1981), chap. 7, p. 29 (quoting the *Defender*); East interview.

4. Allswang, *A House for All Peoples*, p. 162; Rita W. Gordon, "The Change in the Political Alignment of Chicago's Negroes during the New Deal," *Journal of American History* 56 (December 1969): 597; Elmer W. Henderson, "A Study of the Basic Factors Involved in the Change in the Party Alignment of Negroes in Chicago, 1932–1938" (master's thesis, University of Chicago, 1939), p. 23; Harry W. Morris, "The Chicago Negro and the Major Political Parties, 1940–1948" (master's thesis, University of Chicago, 1950) p. 37.

5. Irene McCoy Gaines to Edward J. Kelly, September 22, 1937, Irene McCoy Gaines Papers, Chicago Historical Society; Edward J. Kelly to Irene McCoy Gaines, October 4, 1937, ibid.; Sullivan, "The Negro Vote," p. 479; Henderson, "Change in the Party Alignment of Negroes," pp. 79–80. According to James Q. Wilson ("Negro Leaders in Chicago"

[Ph.D. diss., University of Chicago, 1959], p. 56n), "There is no doubt that at one time gambling, particularly the policy racket, flourished on the South Side, with evident police and political protection." Gambling was so open in Bronzeville that many establishments prominently displayed large signs over their entrances proclaiming "Open All Night." *Chicago Daily News,* June 14, 1939.

6. *Chicago Daily News,* August 11, July 25, 1931, March 6, 1928; *Chicago Defender,* May 23, 1931, November 26, 1932; Gosnell, "The Negro Vote," p. 267.

7. Henderson, "Change in the Party Alignment of Negroes," p. 78.

8. Drake and Cayton, *Black Metropolis,* p. 353; Henderson, "Change in the Party Alignment of Negroes in Chicago," pp. 23–24; Branham, "Transformation of Black Political Leadership," chap. 7, p. 29.

9. *Chicago Defender,* October 5, 1935; Perry R. Duis, "Arthur W. Mitchell, New Deal Negro in Congress" (master's thesis, University of Chicago, 1966), p. 72; Branham, "Transformation of Black Political Leadership," chap. 7, p. 29 (quoted). Kelly had an exceptional rapport with blacks. He could joke with them about race as no other white politician could, noted newspaperman John Dreiske. Sporting a tan from his recent vacation, Kelly told an audience of blacks that he was trying to look like them; they roared with approval. Dreiske interview.

10. *Chicago Defender,* February 9, 1935 (quoted ["that the public . . ."]); Branham, "Transformation of Black Political Leadership," chap. 7, p. 30; Edison Love, interview with author, Chicago, November 15, 1979.

11. *Chicago Defender,* October 6, 1934.

12. *Chicago Defender,* October 13, 20 (quoted), 1934; Mayor's Commission on Human Relations, *Race Relations in Chicago* (1945), pp. 15–17; Newell, *Chicago and the Labor Movement,* p. 238.

13. Duis, "Arthur W. Mitchell," pp. 26–38; Gordon, "Political Alignment of Chicago's Negroes," p. 597; Allswang, "The Chicago Negro Voter," p. 172; *Chicago Tribune,* October 27, November 7, 1934; Arthur W. Mitchell to Edward J. Kelly, March 11, April 15, 1933, March 22, October 18, 1934, Arthur W. Mitchell Papers, Chicago Historical Society. Mitchell's margin of victory over DePriest, a slim 3,134 votes out of a total of 52,792 cast, was fashioned largely in the white, machine-controlled 4th and 11th wards: DePriest carried the black vote in a losing cause. Branham, "Transformation of Black Political Leadership," chap. 7, p. 10.

14. *Chicago Defender,* March 16, 23 (quoted), 1935; Allswang, "The Chicago Negro Voter," pp. 167–75; Gordon, "Political Alignment of Chicago's Negroes," p. 598.

15. *Chicago Defender,* March 23, 30 (quoted), 1935.

16. Ibid., April 18, 1936; Henderson, "Change in the Party Alignment of Negroes," p. 36.

17. Duis, "Arthur W. Mitchell," p. 95; *Chicago Defender,* December 3, 1938, February 4, April 1 (quoted), 1939; Gosnell, "The Negro Vote," p. 265; Morris, "The Chicago Negro," pp. 15–16.

18. Drake and Cayton, *Black Metropolis,* p. 354. In "The Negro Vote," Lawrence Sullivan suggested that President Roosevelt's support was based upon relief and was therefore very tenuous. He also noted a growing disenchantment with the New Deal among blacks, which would, he predicted, lead to a diminished support for Roosevelt in 1940. Both

Gosnell ("The Negro Vote," pp. 264–67) and Henderson ("Change in the Party Alignment of Negroes," pp. 95–97) disagreed with Sullivan's analysis, explaining Roosevelt's increased vote totals in the thirties as a reflection of the multifaceted appeal to blacks generated by the Democratic party.

19. Drake and Cayton, *Black Metropolis*, p. 354 (quoted ["Let Jesus . . ."]); Allswang, "The Chicago Negro Voter," p. 175; *Chicago Defender*, October 12, October 19, November 2, 1940 (quoted); Sullivan, "The Negro Vote," p. 478 (quoted ["Harry Hopkins . . ."]).

20. Gosnell, "The Negro Vote," pp. 264–65; Henderson, "Change in the Party Alignment of Negroes," pp. 95–97. Rita W. Gordon, for example, ("Political Alignment of Chicago's Negroes," pp. 592–93) attributed the altered loyalties of Chicago blacks to New Deal policies alone. She wrote: "The changes resulting from the takeover in Chicago by a Democratic machine were largely caused by the Democratic landslide on the national level. Local Democratic politicians cashed in on the popularity of the New Deal."

21. Jones, "Local Political Significance of New Deal Relief Legislation," pp. 204–5.

22. Wilson, "Negro Leaders in Chicago," p. 102.

23. David Halberstam, "Daley of Chicago," *Harper's* 237 (August 1968): 25–36; Harold F. Gosnell, *Negro Politicians: The Rise of Negro Politics in Chicago* (Chicago: University of Chicago Press, 1935), p. 190; William L. Dawson, interview with James Q. Wilson, Chicago Ill., September 24, 1958, transcript in the possession of the author; *Chicago Daily News*, February 23, 1933; *Chicago Defender*, February 2, 1935.

24. Dawson-Wilson interview, October 24, 1958; Duis, "Arthur W. Mitchell," pp. 85, 94n; *Chicago Defender*, November 6, 1937. In explaining his decision to forsake the Republicans, Dawson emphasized his conversion to the philosophy of Rooseveltian Democracy and the importance of the New Deal for black Chicagoans. Dawson-Wilson interview, September 19, 1958.

25. *Chicago Defender*, April 6, 1935, January 4, 1936, June 24, July 15 (quoted), 1939.

26. Ibid., July 15, 1939; Branham, "Transformation of Black Political Leadership," chap. 8, pp. 29–32.

27. *Chicago Defender*, January 14, March 6, 1939, February 10, 1940, January 28, March 26, October 22, August 6, 1938.

28. Duis, "Arthur W. Mitchell," p. 96; *Chicago Defender*, April 8, 1939; Branham, "Transformation of Black Political Leadership," chap. 8, pp. 21–22, 28–29; Dawson interview, September 19, 1958. Dawson later maintained that he lost the 1939 aldermanic election on purpose to facilitate his jump to the Democrats. He said: "I had decided to switch parties, but I didn't want to do it in office." Dawson-Wilson interview, September 19, 1958.

29. Love interview; Dawson-Wilson interview, September 19, 1958.

30. Dawson-Wilson interview, September 19, 1958.

31. *Chicago Defender*, February 10, March 15, 23, 1940; Dawson-Wilson interview, September 19, 1958.

32. *Chicago Defender*, October 28, November 25, 30, December 7, 1939; Branham, "Transformation of Black Political Leadership," chap. 8, pp. 32–33. Dawson explained his support of Mitchell by saying that the word had come down from Roosevelt to reelect all incumbent con-

gressmen. Whether or not this was true, Dawson acted in accordance with the Democratic Central Committee. Dawson-Wilson interview, September 24, 1958.

33. *Chicago Defender,* July 22, December 9, 1939, January 20, 27, May 11, 1940; Studs Terkel, *Hard Times* (New York: Avon Books, 1970), p. 452; *Chicago Herald-American,* January 9, 1941; Dawson-Wilson interview, September 24, 1958.

34. Duis, "Arthur W. Mitchell," p. 113; *Chicago Times,* January 26, 28, 1942; Branham, "Transformation of Black Political Leadership," chap. 8, pp. 42–46 (quoted); *Chicago Tribune,* April 15, 1942.

35. Henderson, "Change in the Party Alignment of Negroes," pp. 23–24; James Q. Wilson, *Negro Politics: The Search for Leadership* (Glencoe, Ill.: Free Press of Glencoe, 1960), p. 50; Branham, "Transformation of Black Political Leadership," chap. 8, pp. 52–55.

36. Joel Weisman and Ralph Whitehead, Jr., "Untangling Black Politics," *Chicagoan* 1 (July 1974): 74; Wilson, *Negro Politics,* pp. 50–51.

37. Wilson, *Negro Politics,* p. 80. While Kelly willingly allowed such a submachine, later Democrats bridled at the power wielded by Dawson. Where Kelly had allowed a great deal of autonomy, Mayor Richard Daley demanded centralization: Saying, "There can be no organization within The Organization," he successfully merged the Dawson machine into his own. See Weisman and Whitehead, "Untangling Black Politics"; and Halberstam, "Daley of Chicago," pp. 307–9.

38. Terkel, *Hard Times,* p. 452.

6 An Imperfect World

1. Douglas Bukowski, "William Dever and Prohibition: The Mayoral Elections of 1923 and 1927," *Chicago History* 7 (Summer 1978): 113–16; Wendt and Kogan, *Big Bill of Chicago,* pp. 242–44; John Bright, *Hizzoner Big Bill Thompson* (New York: Jonathan Cape and Harrison Smith, 1930), pp. 282–85. Alex Gottfried, Cermak's biographer, cites in *Boss Cermak of Chicago,* pp. 212–13, the speculation that Cermak had underworld ties prior to his election as mayor, but Gottfried remains noncommittal on the accuracy of those charges. He does believe it "unlikely" that Cermak enjoyed "widespread" underworld support in the 1931 mayoral campaign.

2. Chicago Crime Commission, "Report of Operating Director" (Henry Barrett Chamberlain), Annual Meeting, January 19, 1933, Chicago Historical Society; *Chicago Herald and Examiner,* October 31, 1932; Gottfried, *Boss Cermak of Chicago;* pp. 281–82 (quoted ["There has been . . ."]).

3. East interview; Leitzell, "Chicago, City of Corruption," p. 144; Humbert S. Nelli, *The Business of Crime* (New York: Oxford University Press, 1976), p. 178; Wendt and Kogan, *Bosses in Lusty Chicago,* p. 351.

4. *Chicago Daily News,* December 19, 1933; Demaris, *Captive City;* p. 187 (quoted).

5. *Public Service Leader,* September 9, 1943; Rubin, "You've Gotta Be a Boss," p. 36 (quoted).

6. Kelly, with Davenport, "Politics Is People," p. 73. On his 1935 and 1936 federal income tax returns, Kelly listed as income "gam-

bling, $50,000." This information was leaked to Frank Knox by Carter H. Harrison, collector of internal revenue in Chicago; Harold Ickes thought that although Kelly would probably claim this income as racetrack winnings, it more likely represented his take from the gambling interests in Chicago. Ickes, Diary, pp. 3179–80, Library of Congress.

7. *Chicago Daily News*, October 30, 1934; Flynn, "Too Much Fun," p. 15; Virgil W. Peterson, interview with author, Riverside, Ill., December 5, 1979; East interview.

8. Irene McCoy Gaines to Edward J. Kelly, September 22, 1937, Gaines Papers; Branham, "Transformation of Black Political Leadership"; Dawson-Wilson interview, September 19, 1958. For other examples of Dawson's defense of gambling see Wilson, "Negro Leaders in Chicago," p. 56n; and John Madigan, "The Durable Mr. Dawson of Cook County, Illinois," *Reporter* 15 (August 9, 1956): 39–40.

9. *Chicago Daily News*, December 7, 1950; Chicago Crime Commission, "A Report on Chicago Crime for 1954," February 2, 1955, Chicago Historical Society, typescript, p. 10; Peterson, *Barbarians in Our Midst*, p. 180. In the mid-fifties, Chicago newspapers confirmed Dawson's connections with the gambling interests in a series of articles: *Chicago Tribune*, March 10, 1955; *Chicago Sun-Times*, March 10, 11, 1955.

10. In 1935 then-Congressman O'Brien was arrested in a raid of a handbook in the downtown Saratoga Hotel. In 1939 a federal grand jury summoned Sheriff O'Brien to explain his department's inability to curtail gambling in the county. "Blind Tom" pleaded ignorance of the existence of widespread gambling and was not indicted. *Chicago Tribune*, September 28, 1939.

11. Leitzell, "Chicago, City of Corruption," p. 149; *Chicago Daily News*, September 9, 1939; Peterson, *Barbarians in Our Midst*, pp. 187–88 (quoted).

12. *Chicago Tribune*, September 9, 1937 (quoted); *Chicago Daily News*, September 10, 1937; *Chicago Herald and Examiner*, September 9, 1937.

13. William H. Stuart, *The Twenty Incredible Years* (Chicago: M. A. Donahue and Co., 1935), p. 536; Peterson, *Barbarians in Our Midst*, p. 165; Pierce, "Chicago: Unfinished Anomaly," p. 177; *Chicago Daily News*, October 30, 1934; John Bartlow Martin, "Al Capone's Successors," *American Mercury* 68 (June 1949): 733; Hennessey interview; Peterson interview.

14. *Chicago Daily News*, October 30, 1934; Douglas, *In the Fullness of Time*, p. 90; Pierce, "Chicago: Unfinished Anomaly," p. 177; Flynn, "Too Much Fun," pp. 35–36; Martin, "Al Capone's Successors," p. 733; Peterson, *Barbarians in Our Midst*, p. 165; Kennedy interview.

15. *Chicago Daily News*, October 30, 1934.

16. Kennedy interview; Pierce, "Chicago: Unfinished Anomaly," p. 177; Douglas, *In the Fullness of Time*, p. 91; Eugene Kennedy, *Himself! The Life and Times of Mayor Richard J. Daley* (New York: Viking Press, 1978), p. 62 (quoted).

17. Nelli, *The Business of Crime*, pp. 168–72; Flynn, "Too Much Fun," p. 34; Peterson interview.

18. Wendt and Kogan, *Bosses in Lusty Chicago*, pp. 352–53; Peterson, *Barbarians in Our Midst*, p. 165; Demaris, *Captive City*, p. 138. In the Loop area alone, gambling establishments run by such noted mobsters as Paul Ricca, Jake Guzik, Hymie Levin, Frank Nitti, Louis Cam-

pagna, Charles Fischetti, and Dago Lawrence Mangano operated openly with total impunity. Peterson interview.

19. *Chicago Daily News,* February 13, 1939; Peterson, *Barbarians in Our Midst,* p. 176.

20. Barnard interview; Flynn, "These Our Rulers," (July 6), pp. 24, 56; Chicago Crime Commission, *Criminal Justice* 71 (April 1944): 3. Rosenberg became ill on the train coming back to Chicago from Washington, D.C., and died a week later under very suspicious circumstances. At his funeral Kelly said, "Moe was a father to me." Flynn, "These Our Rulers," (July 6), p. 56.

21. Peterson interview; Flynn "Too Much Fun," p. 34; Virgil W. Peterson, "Gambling: Should It Be Legalized?" Chicago Crime Commission, 1945, Chicago Historical Society, typescript, pp. 17–18.

22. *Chicago Daily News,* September 1, 1939, February 28, March 9, 1941; *Chicago Tribune,* March 1, 1940, February 27, March 9, 1941; Peterson, "Gambling," pp. 18–19; Demaris, *Captive City,* p. 115; Ickes, Diary, p. 3236, Library of Congress. According to black civic leader George Wellington Lambert, South Side policy kings also paid protection money to Skidmore. Every Friday Illy Kelly visited Skidmore's junkyard, accompanied by two gunmen, and presented the syndicate bagman a sum of $9,500. *Chicago Daily News,* February 13, June 14, 1939.

23. *Chicago Daily News,* February 24, 1939; Ickes, Diary, p. 6298, Library of Congress; Franklin D. Roosevelt Memorandum, January 9, 1941, Roosevelt Papers, President's Personal File 3166; *Chicago Daily News,* October 30, 1934, September 7, 8, 1937.

24. *Chicago Daily News,* February 21, 1939; Adamowski interview; Leitzell, "Chicago, City of Corruption," p. 143.

25. *Chicago Tribune,* October 25–29, 1941.

26. Peterson, *Barbarians in Our Midst,* p. 196; Chicago Crime Commission, *Criminal Justice* 68 (November 1942): 3, 4.

27. Peterson, *Barbarians in Our Midst,* pp. 197–98; Peterson interview.

28. *Chicago Sun,* July 17, September 5, December 11 (quoted), 12, 1942; *Chicago Tribune,* December 11, 1942; Chicago Crime Commission, *Criminal Justice,* November 1942, p. 4.

29. *Public Service Leader,* September 9, 1943; *Chicago Sun,* September 5, 1942; Peterson interview.

30. *Chicago Tribune,* March 18, 20, 1943; Nelli, *The Business of Crime,* p. 251; U.S. Senate Special Committee to Investigate Organized Crime in Interstate Commerce, *The Kefauver Committee Report on Organized Crime* (New York: Didier, 1951), p. 31.

31. *Chicago Tribune,* March 22 (quoted), 1943.

32. *Chicago Sun,* October 20, 1943.

33. Ibid., October 28, 1943; Martin, "Al Capone's Successors," p. 732.

34. Pierce, "Chicago: Unfinished Anomaly," p. 178; Chicago Crime Commission, "Chicago Crime for 1954," p. 9; Martin, "Al Capone's Successors," p. 732; Chicago Crime Commission, *Criminal Justice* 74 (May 1947): 1–9. It was during Kelly's administration that the legatees of the Capone mob—Paul Ricca, Frank Nitti, Louis Campagna, and Jake Guzik—organized the nationwide racing wire service that Estes Kefauver concluded was the heart of the national crime syndicate. See U.S. Senate Special Committee to Investigate Organized Crime in Interstate Com-

merce, *The Kefauver Committee Report;* Chicago Crime Commission, *Criminal Justice* 75 (July 1947): 21; O'Connor, *Clout*, pp. 54–56.

7 War and Politics

1. *Chicago Herald-American,* February 5, 1940; *Chicago Daily News,* January 9, 1940; Burns, *Roosevelt*, pp. 317–19; *Chicago Tribune,* October 6, 7, 1937.

2. "Advice from Chicago," *Time* 38 (September 29, 1941): 11 (quoted ["You're going . . ."]); Edward J. Kelly to Franklin D. Roosevelt, September 13, 1940, Roosevelt Papers, President's Personal File 3166 (quoted ["assure the working people . . ."]); Eliot Janeway, The *Struggle for Survival* (New Haven: Yale University Press, 1951), pp. 280–81.

3. City of Chicago, *Chicago's Report to the People*, pp. 37–38; Watters, *Illinois in the Second World War*, 1:37–38, 50. The Civilian Defense Office defined the Chicago metropolitan area as the land bounded by Waukegan on the north; Gary, Indiana, township on the east; Chicago Heights on the south; and Naperville on the west. This area comprised most of Cook County, parts of Lake and DuPage counties, a small section of Will County, and Lake County, Ind. It covered 1,171 square miles and contained over 4.5 million people. Watters, *Illinois in the Second World War,* 1:37.

4. Watters, *Illinois in the Second World War,* 1:69–71 (quoted); *Chicago Herald-American,* March 6, 1941.

5. Watters, *Illinois in the Second World War*, 2:244–45; *Chicago Sun,* February 22, 1944; *Chicago Daily News,* February 21, 1944 (quoted); Donald M. Nelson, *Arsenal of Democracy: The Story of American War Production* (New York: Harcourt, Brace and Co., 1946), p. 270.

6. John Morton Blum, *V Was for Victory* (New York: Harcourt Brace Jovanovich, 1976), pp. 124–31; City of Chicago, *Chicago's Report to the People,* p. 24; U.S. Senate Committee on Naval Affairs, *Hearings before the Senate Committee on Naval Affairs,* 76th Cong., 1st sess., 1941, S. 1847, p. 88.

7. U.S. Senate Committee on Naval Affairs, *Hearings,* 76th Cong., 1st sess., 1941, S. 1847, pp. 89–91; *New York Times,* December 3, 1941, January 14, 1942; Blum, *V Was for Victory,* pp. 126–28; Nelson, *Arsenal for Democracy,* pp. 275–83.

8. *New York Times,* March 27, 28, 1941, January 7, 1942; *Commerce* (November 1940): 16–17; City of Chicago, *Chicago's Report to the People,* p. 35; *Chicago Tribune,* December 2, 1944. Some labor disputes arose in Chicago during the war years, most notably involving the "Little Steel" plants of Inland and Republic Steel in 1942 and Montgomery Ward in 1944, but Kelly could rightfully claim that all such disagreements were handled with minimal damage. Watters, *Illinois in the Second World War,* 2:340.

9. City of Chicago, *Chicago's Report to the People,* pp. 33–46.

10. Edward J. Kelly to Franklin D. Roosevelt, September 24, 1941, Roosevelt Papers, Official File 189, Box 2; Stephen Early to Director of the Budget, memo, September 30, 1941, ibid.; John M. Carmody to Edward J. Kelly, telegram, September 30, 1941, ibid.; Franklin D. Roosevelt to Edward J. Kelly, October 24, 1941, ibid.; *Chicago Tribune,* September

16, 1942; Robert M. Yoder, "Chicago Throws a Party," *Saturday Evening Post* 215 (July 18, 1942): 63.

11. *Chicago Tribune*, September 16, 1942; Yoder, "Chicago Throws a Party," p. 62; Kennedy interview.

12. *Chicago Tribune*, February 4, 1942; *Chicago Sun*, February 6, 1942; Ickes, Diary, p. 6233, Library of Congress.

13. Ickes, Diary, pp. 6233, 6297–98, Library of Congress.

14. Ibid., p. 6298; *Chicago Sun*, February 6, 1942; Edward J. Kelly to Franklin D. Roosevelt, February 2, 1942, Roosevelt Papers, President's Personal File 3166. *Time*, reporting an early 1942 Kelly-Roosevelt White House meeting on the subject of the Illinois senatorial nomination from which Kelly emerged clearly crestfallen, intimated that Roosevelt had spurned Kelly's request to run for the office. There is no other evidence to support this story, but neither is there any indication that Roosevelt ever encouraged Kelly in any way. "What about That Toga?" *Time* 39 (February 9, 1942): 16–17.

15. *Chicago Tribune*, February 4, 6, 21, 1942; *Chicago Sun*, April 12, 1942. Douglas lost by a two-to-one margin. While carrying downstate handily, he won only his own ward, the 5th, in Chicago. Douglas, *In the Fullness of Time*, pp. 102–3.

16. *Chicago Daily News*, April 16, 1942; *Chicago Sun*, August 14, October 24 (quoted), 1942; *Public Service Leader*, February 17, 1942.

17. *Chicago Tribune*, November 2, 3, 1942; *Chicago Daily News*, September 10, 1942; Watters, *Illinois in the Second World War*, 2: 486–87; Edward J. Kelly to Franklin D. Roosevelt, October 10, 1942, Roosevelt Papers, President's Personal File 3166.

18. *Chicago Tribune*, November 5, 1942; *Chicago Sun*, November 4, 1942.

19. According to Adamowski, Kelly never mentioned the offer again. Pat Nash, when informed of the mayor's proposal, promised Adamowski that he would make Kelly honor it. Apparently Nash, who by that time was feuding with Kelly, agreed with Adamowski that the mayor had no intention of replacing Barnet Hodes as corporation counsel. Adamowski interview.

20. *Chicago Tribune*, December 22, 1942; *Chicago Sun*, December 22, 1942, January 13, 1943; VanDevander, *The Big Bosses*, p. 289; Irving Dillard, "Chicago as a Sign for 1944," *New Republic* 108 (April 26, 1943): 564 (quoted); "A Candidate Is Picked," *Time* 41 (January 4, 1943): 19; East interview. Coming into McKibbin's campaign headquarters on the night of the primary, Faherty said, "The returns only show that the governor's judgement was right in the selection of a candidate." A reporter asked, "What do you mean by 'the governor's judgement'?" Faherty replied: "Did I say 'governor's judgement'? I meant to say the party's judgement was right." *Chicago Sun*, February 24, 1943.

21. Kennedy interview (quoted); VanDevander, *The Big Bosses*, p. 289; *Public Service Leader*, January 23, 1943.

22. *Chicago Tribune*, February 3, 17, 1943; *Chicago Sun*, January 6, 8, 1943. McKibbin charged that the campaign of his opponent in the Republic primary (former alderman Arthur F. Albert) was being financed by Kelly. The mayor dismissed the allegation, and the issue died quickly. *Chicago Tribune*, February 19, 1943.

23. *Chicago Tribune*, February 23 (quoted ["Pendergast

. . ."]), March 21 (quoted ["The bullet . . ."]), 1943; *Chicago Sun,* March 17, 24, 1943.

24. *Chicago Sun,* March 12, 13 (quoted), 1943; Dillard, "Chicago as a Sign for 1944," p. 564.

25. *Chicago Tribune,* March 20, 1943 (quoted); Dillard, "Chicago as a Sign for 1944," p. 564; Carl W. Condit, *Chicago, 1930–1970: Building, Planning, and Urban Technology* (Chicago: University of Chicago Press, 1974), p. 34; *Public Service Leader,* October 21, 1943; *Official Opening of Chicago Subway, October 16, 1943* (1943). The subway opened for public use on October 17, 1943; the only reason for the "trial run" in April was to reinforce Kelly's role in securing the funds for the project, a gambit that *Life* termed a "political masterstroke with the subtlety of a sledgehammer." "New Chicago Subway Opens," *Life* 14 (April 19, 1943): 32–33.

26. *Chicago Defender,* April 3, 1943; Drake and Cayton, *Black Metropolis,* p. 358.

27. Drake and Cayton, *Black Metropolis,* p. 358 (quoted); Morris, "The Chicago Negro," pp. 40–41. In the 1943 election, Kelly received 61.1 percent of the black vote, up from 59.5 percent in 1939. As evidence for its claim that the restrictive covenant incident aided the incumbent, the *Defender* (April 10, 1943) cited these facts: Kelly beat McKibbin by 2,958 votes (12,307 to 9,349) in the 3rd Ward, although Republican DePriest bested Democrat Benjamin Grant for alderman, 10,176 to 9,715. In the 2nd Ward, Kelly beat McKibbin 12,307 to 9,349, while Democrat William H. Harvey beat Republican Mack Atkins in the alderman race by 14,058 to 13,439. The *Defender* may have been correct, but these vote differentials may also just have reflected the mayor's overall popularity among blacks. Certainly, the Republicans did not prosper from the restrictive covenant debacle.

28. Board of Election Commissioners of the City of Chicago, *Canvass* (April 6, 1943); *Chicago Tribune,* April 7, 1943; Dillard, "Chicago as a Sign for 1944," pp. 563–64; Morris, "The Chicago Negro," p. 103.

29. *Chicago Sun,* April 8, 1943.

30. Blum, *V Was for Victory,* pp. 199–207; Harvard Sitkoff, "Racial Militancy and Interracial Violence in the Second World War," *Journal of American History* 58 (December 1971): 671–81; *New York Times,* July 7, 1943.

31. Arnold R. Hirsch, "Making the Second Ghetto: Race and Housing in Chicago, 1940–1960" (Ph.D. diss., University of Illinois at Chicago Circle, 1978), pp. 62–63; *New York Times,* July 6, 1943; Robert Shogan and Tom Craig, *The Detroit Race Riot: A Study in Violence* (Philadelphia: J. B. Lippincott Co., 1964), p. 90. Throughout the war certain areas in Chicago's South Side were off limits to white sailors. A verbal order forbade entry into the area bordered by 37th, 70th, Cottage Grove, and State streets, and often the Shore Patrol would post guards outside black nightclubs to keep sailors out. Hirsch, "Making the Second Ghetto," p. 71.

32. John Bartlow Martin, "Incident at Fernwood," *Harper's* 199 (October 1949): 87; *Chicago Defender,* July 3, 10, 1943; *New York Times,* July 6, 1943; Mayor's Committee on Race Relations, *Statement of Aims and Purposes* (1943). On the causes of the Detroit race riot, see Alan Clive, *State of War: Michigan in World War Two* (Ann Arbor: University of Michigan Press, 1979); and Alfred McClung Lee and Norman Daymond

Humphrey, *Race Riot* (New York: Dryden Press, 1943). For a comparison of the Detroit and Harlem riots, see Dominic J. Capeci, Jr., *The Harlem Riot of 1943* (Philadelphia: Temple University Press, 1977).

33. Martin, "Incident at Fernwood," p. 87; Hirsch, "Making the Second Ghetto," pp. 63–73; Watters, *Illinois in the Second World War,* 2:180; Clive, *State of War,* pp. 161–64; Shogan and Craig, *The Detroit Race Riot,* p. 116; Capeci, *The Harlem Riot of 1943,* pp. 175–83.

34. *Chicago Sun,* October 7, November 12, 1943.

35. Dreiske interview; *Chicago Tribune,* July 1, 1944.

36. To political editor John Dreiske, the biggest difference for Kelly was his introduction to the role of bureaucrat. Nash had always taken care of the red tape through his subordinates, leaving Kelly free to concentrate upon pressing municipal business; the mayor was not a "detail man." Dreiske interview.

37. *New York Times,* June 16, 1944 (quoted); Dillard, "Chicago as a Sign for 1944," p. 564; *Chicago Tribune,* July 13, 14, 1944.

38. Rubin, "You've Gotta Be a Boss," p. 20; *Public Service Leader,* August 15, 1944; John Morton Blum, ed., *The Price of Vision: The Diary of Henry A. Wallace, 1942–1946* (Boston: Houghton Mifflin Co., 1973), p. 375.

39. Norman Markowitz, *The Rise and Fall of the People's Century* (New York: Free Press, 1973), p. 102; Ickes, Diary, p. 9086, Library of Congress; Barnard interview; "Mayor Kelly's Own Story," May 14, 1947; Blum, *The Price of Vision,* p. 368n (quoted). Grace Tully, Roosevelt's private secretary, maintained that the original letter read "Bill Douglas and Harry Truman"; Hannegan convinced Roosevelt to change the order to give Truman's name greater impact. A copy of the "Truman-Douglas" letter still exists, but no other version survives to substantiate Tully's claim. Grace Tully, *FDR, My Boss* (New York: Charles Scribner's Sons, 1949), pp. 275–76; Norman D. Markowitz, *Rise and Fall,* p. 103; Franklin D. Roosevelt to Bob Hannegan, July 19, 1944, Frank Walker Papers, Box 601, University of Notre Dame Library, South Bend, Ind.

40. Markowitz, *Rise and Fall,* p. 106; *Chicago Tribune,* July 17, 1944 (quoting Kelly); James F. Byrnes, *All in One Lifetime* (New York: Harper and Row, 1958), pp. 221, 227–28 (quoting Hannegan); Blum, *The Price of Vision,* p. 368; Henry A. Wallace to Tex McCrary and Jinx Falkenburg, March 12, 1951, Henry A. Wallace Papers, University of Iowa, Iowa City; Frank Walker, "The Note to Bob Hannegan," July 12, 1951, Frank Walker Papers, Box 652. While there is little doubt of organized labor's aversion to Byrnes, the position of blacks is disputed. In "The Day Dawson Saved America from a Racist President" (*Ebony* 17 [July 1972]: 42–45, 48–50), Doris E. Saunders argues that Dawson refused to support Byrnes, a refusal that influenced Kelly to tell Roosevelt he could not guarantee carrying Illinois. This move, in turn, led to the dumping of Byrnes. In "Roosevelt, Byrnes, and the 1944 Vice-Presidential Nomination" (*Historian* 42 [November 1979]: 85–100), John W. Partin contends that Dawson offered no objection to a Roosevelt-Byrnes ticket.

41. *Chicago Tribune,* July 20, 1944; Ickes, Diary, pp. 9099–9101, Library of Congress; "Mayor Kelly's Own Story," May 15, 1947; *New York Times,* July 21, 1944; Rosenman, *Working with Roosevelt,* p. 451 (quoted); Harry S Truman, *Memoirs: Year of Decisions* (Garden City, N.Y.: Doubleday and Co., 1955), pp. 192–93.

42. Edward L. Schapsmeier and Frederick H. Schapsmeier,

Prophet in Politics: Henry A. Wallace and the War Years, 1940–1945 (Ames: Iowa State University Press, 1970), p. 107; Farley, *Jim Farley's Story*, p. 367; *Chicago Tribune*, July 22, 1944; Kelly referred to those who booed him as "mostly leather-lunged students and professional shouters," but Ickes noted that the noise came from the delegates as much as from the gallery. "Mayor Kelly's Own Story," May 15; Ickes, Diary, p. 9114, Library of Congress.

43. *Chicago Daily News*, July 24, 1944; Markowitz, *Rise and Fall*, p. 111; "Mayor Kelly's Own Story," May 15; Ickes, Diary, pp. 9112–13, Library of Congress; Rubin, "You've Gotta Be a Boss," p. 20; *Chicago Tribune*, July 22, 1944; *New York Times*, July 22, 1944 (quoted).

44. Kelly, with Davenport, "Politics Is People," p. 74; Edward J. Kelly to Harry Hopkins, September 13, 1944, Roosevelt Papers, President's Personal File 3166. Kelly had cautiously predicted in the papers only a two-hundred-thousand-vote victory for Roosevelt. *New York Times*, August 24, 1944. For the importance of the Chicago vote on the 1944 election, see Samuel J. Eldersveld, "The Influence of Metropolitan Party Pluralities in Presidential Elections since 1920: A Study of Twelve Key Cities," *American Political Science Review* 43 (December 1949): 1189–1206.

45. *New York Times*, September 21, 1944 (quoted ["whether the activities . . ."]); *Chicago Daily News*, August 19, 1941; Watters, *Illinois in the Second World War*, 1:183, 230; *Chicago Tribune*, September 21, 1944; *Congressional Record*, 78th Cong., 2d sess., 1944, vol. 90, pt. 2, pp. 2065–66; *Chicago Daily News*, November 9, 1944.

46. Madison, "Letter from Chicago," p. 549; Watters, *Illinois in the Second World War*, 2:511; "Political Deal," *Life* 18 (February 19, 1945): 32. In the 1944 gubernatorial contest, Kelly served as Tom Courtney's campaign manager. Peter O'Malley, in "Mayor Martin H. Kennelly of Chicago: A Political Biography" (Ph.D. diss., University of Illinois at Chicago Circle, 1980, pp. 18–19) suggests that he did so because of his appreciation for Courtney's indifferent pursuit of known Kelly-Nash gambling figures in 1943.

47. Madison, "Letter from Chicago," pp. 550–51; *Public Service Leader*, February 21, 1945; Paul F. Barrett, "Public Policy and Private Choice: Mass Transit and the Automobile in Chicago between the Wars," *Business History Review* 49 (Winter 1975): 473–97; Ralph G. Burton, "Mass Transportation in the Chicago Region: A Study in Metropolitan Government" (Ph.D. diss., University of Chicago, 1939), pp. 175–92.

48. Madison, "Letter from Chicago," pp. 550–51; *Chicago Tribune*, February 13, 1945; *New York Times*, February 14, 1945; Herring, *The Politics of Democracy*, p. 149.

8 End of an Era

1. *Chicago Daily News*, May 9, 1945; *Chicago Sun*, May 7, 1945; Watters, *Illinois in the Second World War*, 1:86.

2. *New York Times*, September 12, 1945. In order to encourage compliance with Executive Order 8802, which banned discriminatory hiring in defense-related industries, Kelly proclaimed June 25, 1945, Fair Employment Day in Chicago. *Congressional Record: Appendix*, 79th Cong., 1st sess., 1945, vol. 91, pt. 12, p. A3023.

3. *New York Times*, February 22, 1946; William D. Hassett

to Edward J. Kelly, June 12, 1945, Harry S Truman Papers, Official File 3-I, Harry S Truman Library, Independence, Mo.; *Public Service Leader,* October 30, 1945; *Congressional Record: Appendix,* 79th Cong., 2d sess., 1946, vol. 92, pt. 9, p. A1016.

4. *New York Times,* November 20, 1945; Edward J. Kelly to James F. Byrnes, August 28, 1945, Truman Papers, Official File 85; Edward J. Kelly to City Council of Chicago, memo, July 17, 1945, ibid.; "Resolution by Chicago City Council Extending Chicago's Official Invitation to the United Nations Organization to Establish Its Permanent Headquarters in Chicago, July 17, 1945," ibid.; Thomas E. Hachey, ed., "A Confidential Account of Mayor Kelly's Visit to London, November 1945," *Journal of the Illinois State Historical Society* 70 (November 1977): 276–82; *Chicago Tribune,* November 21, 1945. While in London, Kelly considered visiting Ireland; when asked if he had relatives there, he responded, "No, but there are some tens of thousands of Irish in Chicago and they all have votes." Hachey, "Mayor Kelly's Visit to London," p. 281.

5. *New York Times,* October 16, December 13, 1945; Chicago Plan Commission, *Housing Goals for Chicago* (1946), pp. 75, 95; Albert Lepawsky, "Chicago, Metropolis in the Making," *National Municipal Review* 30 (April 1941): 212–13.

6. Chicago Plan Commission, *Housing Goals for Chicago,* pp. 74, 75 (quoted); City of Chicago, *Chicago's Report to the People,* pp. 155–59; Chicago Plan Commission, *Building New Neighborhoods* (June 1943), pp. 2–9.

7. O'Malley, "Mayor Martin H. Kennelly," p. 101; City of Chicago, *Chicago's Report to the People,* p. 160; Devereux Bowly, Jr., *The Poorhouse: Subsidized Housing in Chicago, 1895–1976* (Carbondale: Southern Illinois University Press, 1978), p. 77; *Chicago Sun-Times,* June 28, 1950 (quoting Wood); Martin Meyerson and Edward C. Banfield, *Politics, Planning, and the Public Interest* (Glencoe, Ill.: Free Press, 1955), pp. 61, 85, 173 (quoting Duffy). Meyerson and Banfield suggest that Kelly supported the CHA so that he could point to it as his contribution to good government when speaking before blacks, labor, civic reformers and other liberal groups. Jake Arvey explained it as a reflection of Kelly's conversion to New Deal principles, saying: "Franklin Delano Roosevelt made a liberal out of Ed Kelly. An inflamed liberal." Ibid., p. 83; Gleason, *Daley of Chicago* p. 90.

8. Martin, "Incident at Fernwood," p. 88; Meyerson and Banfield, *Politics, Planning, and the Public Interest,* p. 124; Hirsch, "Making the Second Ghetto," p. 443; Otis D. Duncan and Beverly Duncan, *The Negro Population of Chicago* (Chicago: University of Chicago Press, 1957).

9. Bowly, *The Poorhouse,* p. 50; Watters, *Illinois in the Second World War,* 2:313–14; Hirsch, "Making the Second Ghetto," p. 443 (quoted).

10. Martin, "Incident at Fernwood," p. 88; Bowly, *The Poorhouse,* p. 50; *New York Times,* December 8, 10, 1946; Meyerson and Banfield, *Politics, Planning, and the Public Interest,* p. 128; "Statement by Mayor Edward J. Kelly regarding Airport Homes Housing Project," November 20, 1946, Gaines Papers (quoted); Mayor's Commission on Human Relations, *Human Relations in Chicago, 1946 Annual Report,* pp. 119–50.

11. Mayor's Commission on Human Relations, *Human Relations in Chicago,* pp. 81–82.

12. Watters, *Illinois in the Second World War*, 2:282–83; *Chicago Sun*, September 27, 1945; Mayor's Commission on Human Relations, *Race Relations in Chicago*, pp. 15, 17; Martin, "Incident at Fernwood," p. 97.

13. City of Chicago, *Chicago's Report to the People*, p. 319.

14. Mary J. Herrick, *The Chicago Schools: A Social and Political History* (Beverly Hills, Calif.: Sage Publications, 1971), pp. 207, 209–12; Burbank, "Chicago Public Schools," pp. 371–75; *Chicago Tribune*, July 13, 22, 1933; *Chicago Herald-Examiner*, July 16 (quoted), 22, 1933.

15. Flynn, "These Our Rulers," July 6, p. 60.

16. Ibid.; Pierce, "Chicago: Unfinished Anomaly," p. 183; Barnard interview.

17. Herrick, *The Chicago Schools*, pp. 221–22; Lepawsky, "Chicago, Metropolis in the Making," pp. 215–16.

18. Flynn, "These Our Rulers," July 6, p. 61; National Commission for the Defense of Democracy through Education of the National Education Association of the United States, *Certain Personnel Practices in the Chicago Public Schools*, May 1945, Chicago Historical Society, p. 57.

19. *Chicago Daily News*, June 5, 9, 1936; Leitzell, "Chicago, City of Corruption," p. 147.

20. Herrick, *The Chicago Schools*, p. 230.

21. National Commission for the Defense of Democracy through Education, *Certain Personnel Practices*, pp. 37–40; Leitzell, "Chicago, City of Corruption," p. 147; Unitarian Fellowship for Social Justice, *Matters Now of Public Record concerning the Conduct of William H. Johnson, Superintendent of the Chicago Public Schools*, 1939, Chicago Historical Society, pp. 3–7.

22. Unitarian Fellowship for Social Justice, *Conduct of William H. Johnson*, pp. 10–12 (quoted); Flynn, "These Our Rulers," July 6, p. 61; *Chicago Daily News*, April 4, 1938.

23. Flynn, "These Our Rulers," July 6, p. 61.

24. Herrick, *The Chicago Schools*, p. 231; Kennedy interview; *Chicago Tribune*, June 15, 1939.

25. *Chicago Sun*, December 14, 1942; *Chicago Tribune*, February 3, 4, 1943; Peterson, *Barbarians in Our Midst*, p. 214; "The NEA's Investigation of Certain Conditions in the Chicago Public Schools," *School and Society* 61 (June 2, 1945): 356 (quoted). In refusing to cooperate with the NEA, the Chicago Board of Education said: "It would be more fitting if this organization devoted its energies to making some contribution to the war and defense effort instead of trying to make this unwarranted inquiry and thereby hamper a patriotic institution which is making a vital contribution to every phase of the war effort." Peterson, *Barbarians in Our Midst*, p. 214.

26. National Commission for the Defense of Democracy through Education, *Certain Personnel Practices*, pp. 35, 41, 45, 46, 54, 55, 61–63; "The NEA's Investigation," p. 356; Milburn P. Akers, "Twilight of Boss Kelly," *Nation* 162 (April 13, 1946): 425; "A Grand Jury Investigation of Chicago Public Schools Asked by a Civic Group," *School and Society* 63 (March 2, 1946): 147; *Chicago Sun*, February 23, 1946.

27. *Chicago Tribune*, January 19, 1946; Herrick, *The Chicago Schools*, p. 273 (quoted ["only a hiking club"]); National Commission for the Defense of Democracy through Education, *Certain Personnel Prac-*

tices, p. 13; *The Bellringer,* April 1946, p. 1, Independent Voters of Illinois Papers, Chicago Historical Society (quoted ["Don't worry . . ."]).

28. *Chicago Sun,* March 3, 1946; *Chicago Tribune,* March 3, 1946; Peterson, *Barbarians in Our Midst,* p. 216; Herrick, *The Chicago Schools,* pp. 274–75; *New York Times,* June 18, 23, 1946; Akers, "Twilight of Boss Kelly," p. 426.

29. *Chicago Sun,* March 31, 1946.

30. Paul F. Barrett, "Mass Transit, The Automobile, and Public Policy in Chicago, 1900–1930" (Ph.D. diss., University of Illinois at Chicago Circle, 1976), pp. 72, 95, 108, 230; *Chicago Sun,* March 1, 1942.

31. Lindell, *City Hall: Chicago's Corporate History,* p. 248; *Chicago Sun,* March 1, 1942.

32. Barrett, "Mass Transit, The Automobile, and Public Policy," pp. 638, 646 (quoted); *Chicago Sun,* March 1, 1942; *Mayor Kelly's Plan for a Comprehensive Transportation System for the City of Chicago,* (January 1937), pp. 4, 5; *Mayor Kelly's Suggested Plan For Settlement of Chicago's Traction Problem* (November 22, 1939).

33. *Mayor Kelly's Plan for a Comprehensive Transportation System* (January 1937), pp. 20–21. Kelly also called for the removal of the Wabash Avenue and Lake Street sections of the Union Loop elevated after the subway opened. *Mayor Kelly's Plan for a Comprehensive Transportation System for the City of Chicago* (October 1937), pp. 9, 10.

34. Chicago Plan Commission, *Chicago Looks Ahead* (March 1945), pp. 65–69; Department of Superhighways, "A Comprehensive Superhighway Plan for the City of Chicago," October 30, 1939, Merriam Papers, Box 91, Folder 7; Barrett, "Mass Transit, The Automobile, and Public Policy," p. 646.

35. "Millenium for Straphangers," *Time* 50 (September 8, 1947): 24, 25; *Chicago Sun,* June 2, 1942; City of Chicago, *Chicago's Report to the People,* p. 192; "Political Deal," p. 32.

36. Lindell, *City Hall: Chicago's Corporate History,* p. 275a; City of Chicago, *Chicago's Report to the People,* p. 196; "Millenium for Straphangers," p. 25; Barrett, "Public Policy and Private Choice," pp. 473–97.

37. O'Connor, *Clout,* pp. 56–58; Arvey-Rakove interview; Kennedy, *Himself!* pp. 61, 79–80; *Chicago Sun,* April 17, 1947.

38. "Call Me Jack," *Time* 48 (July 22, 1946): 19–20; Rakove, *We Don't Want Nobody Nobody Sent,* p. 10; Kennedy, *Himself!* pp. 79, 80; Arthur Hepner, "Call Me Jake," *New Republic* 116 (March 24, 1947): 20–23.

39. Edward J. Kelly to Harry S Truman, telegram, April 10, 1946, Truman Papers; *New York Times,* November 7, 1946; Peterson, *Barbarians in Our Midst,* p. 227; "Anybody Seen Kelly?" *Newsweek* 28 (December 30, 1946): 17; Frankel and Alexander, "Arvey of Illinois," p. 67. One of the prime casualties of the 1946 elections was Richard J. Daley, who ran unsuccessfully for county sheriff. There is a difference of opinion among Daley's biographers about the reasons for his selection as a candidate that year. Eugene Kennedy (*Himself!* pp. 78, 79) contends that Kelly nominated Daley but withdrew the support of the Democratic organization as a means of satisfying the meat-packing interests, who bridled at Daley's siding with the Office of Price Administration against them during World War II. Len O'Connor (*Clout,* p. 57) and Mike Royko (*Boss,* pp. 54–55)

argue that Kelly's selection of Daley was intended as a reward for the loyalty of the rising young politician who had served the machine faithfully in Springfield.

40. Ralph Whitehead, Jr., "The Ward Boss Who Saved the New Deal," *Chicago* 26 (May 1977): 179 (quoted); Akers, "Twilight of Boss Kelly," pp. 425–26; "Protected Gambling in Chicago," *Criminal Justice* 74 (May 1947): 20–23.

41. *The Bellringer*, Independent Voters of Illinois Papers; Mary J. Herrick, *The Chicago Schools*, p. 276; Douglas, *In the Fullness of Time*, p. 128; *Chicago Tribune*, December 2, 1946.

42. Arvey-Rakove interview. Many Chicago blacks shared Arvey's conclusion, feeling that much of the opposition to Kelly from white ethnic groups hailed from the mayor's long-standing defense of black rights. Love interview.

43. Kennedy interview; Korshak interview; O'Connor, *Clout*, pp. 58–59. The dumping of Kelly has been misinterpreted by some scholars as a revolt against the Irish by other ethnic groups within the Democratic party. In *The Irish and Irish Politicians* (Notre Dame, Ind.: University of Notre Dame Press, 1966, p. 155, 167), Edward M. Levine argues that Arvey and Dawson led the non-Irish in a revolt; he fails to mention the critical role of the anti-Kelly Irish. In *The Future of American Politics* (New York: Harper and Row, 1952, p. 66), Samuel Lubell makes essentially the same mistake: He lists the Kelly-Nash machine among the Irish-American big-city machines toppled in the 1940s by other ethnic groups and erroneously implies that Arvey's succession of Kelly as party leader constituted a Jewish conquest of an Irish machine.

44. Hennessey interview; John Bartlow Martin, *Adlai Stevenson of Illinois* (Garden City, N.Y.: Doubleday and Co., 1976), p. 266; Whitehead, "The Ward Boss Who Saved the New Deal," p. 179 (quoted); Frankel and Alexander, "Arvey of Illinois," p. 67; Rakove, *We Don't Want Nobody Nobody Sent*, p. 12; Kennedy, *Himself!* p. 81. A popular story suggested that to convince Kelly of his lack of esteem, Arvey conducted a telephone poll in the mayor's office, and no respondents indicated a desire to reelect the incumbent. In *Boss* (p. 55), for example, Mike Royko alludes to this story as the method by which Kelly was convinced not to run. It seems likely, however, that the tale is apocryphal: Neither Arvey nor Kelly mentions such a poll in his recollections of the meeting, and Spike Hennessey, the conductor of the pre-meeting polls to which Arvey referred, doubts that such a ploy was used. Arvey-Rakove interview; "Mayor Kelly's Own Story," May 5; Hennessey interview.

45. *Chicago Tribune*, March 27, 1960; Milburn P. Akers, "Chicago Dumps Kelly," *Nation* 164 (January 4, 1947): 8; *Chicago Sun*, November 9, December 12, 1946; Arvey-Rakove interview. According to Marshall Korshak, Dunne's candidacy was scotched because he resigned his commission in the National Guard; the Democrats felt that his act might alienate the voters, particularly in the Cold War atmosphere prevalent at the time. Korshak interview.

46. *Chicago Tribune*, December 20, 1946, March 27, 1960; O'Malley, "Mayor Martin H. Kennelly," p. 36; "Anybody Seen Kelly?" p. 18; Arvey-Rakove interview; "No Dog in the Manager," *Time* 48 (December 30, 1946): 17; "Mayor Kelly's Own Story," May 5. The *Chicago Tribune* (March 27, 1960) reported that Arvey was influenced to choose Kennelly by Richard Finnegan, editor of the *Chicago Times* and noted civic reformer. In his

memoirs, ("Mayor Kelly's Own Story," May 5), Kelly minimized the opposition to his renomination and claimed that his decision was based solely on age and the threat of declining health.

47. Akers, "Chicago Dumps Kelly," p. 8; "Anybody Seen Kelly?" p. 18 (quoted ["Martin is OK."]); *Chicago Tribune,* January 25, March 7, 14 (quoted ["I have no doubt . . ."]), April 16, 1947.

48. Martin, *Adlai Stevenson of Illinois,* p. 277; Douglas, *In the Fullness of Time,* p. 137; Kennedy, *Himself!* p. 59; Hennesey interview.

49. Barnard interview; Irwin Ross, *The Loneliest Campaign: The Truman Victory of 1948* (New York: New American Library, 1968), pp. 114–15; *New York Times,* July 10, 11, 1948.

50. Douglas, *In the Fullness of Time,* pp. 133–35 (quoted); Ross, *The Loneliest Campaign,* pp. 124–25; Edward J. Kelly to Harry S Truman, telegram, November 3, 1948, Truman Papers, President's Personal File. Arvey, who took a prominent position in the "Draft Eisenhower" movement earlier that year, was fully behind Truman at the convention and shared Kelly's antipathy for the southerners opposed to a strong civil rights plank. Arvey-Rakove interview.

51. Barnard interview; *Chicago Tribune,* October 21, 24 (quoted), 1950; Peterson, *Barbarians in Our Midst,* p. 267; "Funeral of a Boss," p. 40; Dorsett, *Roosevelt and the City Bosses,* p. 83.

52. *Chicago Daily News,* December 12, 1950 (quoted); *Chicago Herald-American,* May 14, 1951; "The Widow's Mite," *Newsweek* 45 (May 9, 1955): 30; "Treasure Hunt," *Time* 57 (May 28, 1951): 26. Jacob Arvey believed that Kelly had little money when he left office; he reported that the former mayor approached him for help in securing employment. Arvey-Rakove interview.

9 "You've Gotta Be a Boss"

1. *Papers of Adlai E. Stevenson,* 3:311.

2. Alfred Steinberg, *The Bosses* (New York: Macmillan Co., 1972), p. 8 (quoted ["I tell . . ."]); Wheeler, "Kelly's Life;" "Mayor Kelly's Own Story," May 5 (quoted ["During that period . . ."]); Rubin, "You've Gotta Be a Boss," p. 36 (quoted ["These people . . ."]).

3. Harold Zink, *City Bosses in the United States* (New York: Macmillan Co., 1939), pp. 62–65.

4. Dorsett, *Roosevelt and the City Bosses;* Steinberg, *The Bosses,* p. 10 (quoted).

5. "Mayor Kelly's Chicago," *Life* 17 (July 17, 1944): 75. The tendency of businessmen to ally themselves with successful political machines is examined in James A. Riedel, "Boss and Faction," *Annals of the American Academy of Political and Social Science* 353 (May 1964): 14.

6. "The Kelly-Nash Political Machine," pp. 126–30.

7. Gosnell, "The Negro Vote," pp. 264–68; Henderson, "Change in the Party Alignment of Negroes," pp. 95–97.

8. Wilson, "Negro Leaders in Chicago," p. 35; Royko, *Boss,* p. 132; O'Connor, *Clout,* pp. 178, 179.

9. *Chicago Daily News,* October 30, 1934; Peterson, *Barbarians in Our Midst,* p. 169; Peterson, "Gambling," p. 15.

10. Jones, "Local Political Significance of New Deal Relief Legislation," p. 206.

11. Ickes, *Secret Diary: Inside Struggle,* pp. 431–32.

12. "Mayor Kelly's Own Story," May 17, 1947.

13. Jones, "Local Political Significance of New Deal Relief Legislation," p. 244; City of Chicago, *Chicago's Report to the People*, pp. 7, 9; Condit, *Chicago, 1930–1970*, pp. 24, 30, 34, 48n.

14. *Chicago Sun-Times*, October 21, 1950.

Bibliography

Books and Articles

Adams, Grace. *Workers on Relief.* New Haven: Yale University Press, 1939.

"Advice from Chicago." *Time* 38 (September 29, 1941): 11.

Akers, Milburn P. "Chicago Dumps Kelly." *Nation* 164 (January 4, 1947): 7–9.

———. "Twilight of Boss Kelly." *Nation* 162 (April 13, 1946): 425–26.

Allswang, John M. *Bosses, Machines, and Urban Voters: An American Symbiosis.* Port Washington, N.Y.: Kennikat Press, 1977.

———. "The Chicago Negro Voter and the Democratic Consensus: A Case Study, 1918–1936." *Journal of the Illinois State Historical Society* 60 (Summer 1967): 145–75.

———. *A House for All Peoples: Ethnic Politics in Chicago, 1890–1936.* Lexington: University Press of Kentucky, 1971.

———. *The New Deal and American Politics.* New York: John Wiley and Sons, 1978.

Andrews, H. Wayne. *The Battle for Chicago.* New York: Harcourt, Brace and Co., 1946.

"Anybody Seen Kelly?" *Newsweek* 28 (December 30, 1946): 17–18.

Banfield, Edward C. "The Dilemma of a Metropolitan Machine." In *Urban Government: A Reader in Administration and Politics,* edited by Edward C. Banfield. New York: Free Press of Glencoe, 1961.

———. *Political Influence.* New York: Free Press of Glencoe, 1961.

Barrett, Paul. "Public Policy and Private Choice: Mass Transit and the Automobile in Chicago between the Wars." *Business History Review* 49 (Winter 1975) : 473–97.

Baumgart, Guenther. "Strikes Are Not a Chicago Custom." *Commerce* 37 (November 1940): 16–17, 50–51.

Berkow, Ira. *Maxwell Street: Survival in a Bazaar.* New York: Doubleday and Co., 1977.

Bernstein, Irving. *The Lean Years: A History of the American Worker, 1920–1933.* Boston: Houghton Mifflin Co., 1966.

———. *Turbulent Years: A History of the American Worker, 1933–1941.* Boston: Houghton Mifflin Co., 1969.

Betters, Paul V. *Cities and the 1936 Congress.* Washington, D.C.: U.S. Conference of Mayors, 1936.

———. "Washington and the Cities: 1934." *National Municipal Review* 23 (August 1934): 415–19, 423.

"Bill and George." *Time* 48 (July 29, 1946): 18–19.

Blum, John Morton. *V Was for Victory*. New York: Harcourt Brace Jovano-vich, 1976.

———, ed, *The Price of Vision: The Diary of Henry A. Wallace, 1942–1946*. Boston: Houghton Mifflin Co., 1973.

Bollman, H. Gordon. "Cook County's Quadrennial Assessment." *Municipal Finance* 9 (February 1937): 47–50.

Bowly, Devereux, Jr. *The Poorhouse: Subsidized Housing in Chicago, 1895–1976*. Carbondale: Southern Illinois University Press, 1978.

Boxerman, Burton A. "Adolph Joachim Sabath in Congress: The Roosevelt and Truman Years." *Journal of the Illinois State Historical Society* 66 (Winter 1973): 428–43.

Bradley, Donald S., and Zald, Mayer N. "From Commercial Elite to Political Administrator: The Recruitment of the Mayors of Chicago." *American Journal of Sociology* 71 (September 1965): 153–67.

Bright, John. *Hizzoner Big Bill Thompson*. New York: Jonathan Cape and Harrison Smith, 1930.

Bristol, Margaret Cochran. "Changes in Work Relief in Chicago." *Social Service Review* 9 (June 1935): 243–55.

———. "WPA in Chicago: Summer, 1936." *Social Service Review* 11 (September 1937): 372–94.

Brown, Earl. "The Truth about the Detroit Riot." *Harper's* 187 (November 1943): 488–98.

Brown, Josephine C. *Public Relief, 1929–1939*. New York: Henry Holt and Co., 1940.

Brown, V. K. "Chicago Makes Her Preparations for the Recreation Con-gress." *Recreation* 29 (July 1935): 203–5.

Bukowski, Douglas. "Judge Edmund K. Jarecki: A Rather Regular Indepen-dent." *Chicago History* 8 (Winter 1979–80): 206–18.

———. "William Dever and Prohibition: The Mayoral Elections of 1923 and 1927." *Chicago History* 7 (Summer 1978): 109–18.

Burbank, Lyman B. "Chicago Public Schools and the Depression Years of 1928–1937." *Journal of the Illinois State Historical Society* 64 (Winter 1971): 365–81.

Burnham, Daniel H., and Bennett, Edward H. *Plan of Chicago*. Chicago: Commercial Club of Chicago, 1908.

Burns, Arthur E. "Federal Emergency Relief Administration." *Municipal Year Book, 1937*, pp. 382–418.

Burns, James MacGregor. *Roosevelt: The Lion and the Fox*. New York: Harcourt, Brace and World, 1956.

Byrnes, James F. *All in One Lifetime*. New York: Harper and Row, 1958.

Calkins, Fay. *The CIO and the Democratic Party*. Chicago: University of Chicago Press, 1952.

"Call Me Jack." *Time* 48 (July 22, 1946): 19–20.

Campbell, Angus. *Elections and the Political Order*. New York: Harper and Row, 1966.

"A Candidate Is Picked." *Time* 41 (January 4, 1943): 19.

Capeci, Dominic J., Jr. *The Harlem Riot of 1943*. Philadelphia: Temple University Press, 1977.

"The Case of William Heirans." *Life* 21 (July 29, 1946): 30–31.

Casey, Robert J., and Douglas, W. A. S. *The Midwesterner: The Story of Dwight H. Green*. Chicago: Wilcox and Follett, 1948.

Charles, Searle F. *Minister of Relief: Harry Hopkins and the Depression*. Syracuse, N.Y.: Syracuse University Press, 1963.

"Chicago Swaps Bosses." *New Republic* 66 (April 22, 1931): 260–62.

Clive, Alan. *State of War: Michigan in World War Two*. Ann Arbor: University of Michigan Press, 1979.

Colby, Peter W., and Green, Paul Michael. "The Consolidation of Clout." *Illinois Issues* 5 (February 1979): 11–20.

Condit, Carl W. *Chicago, 1930–1970: Building, Planning, and Urban Technology*. Chicago: University of Chicago Press, 1974.

Davenport, Walter. "From Whom All Blessings Flow." *Collier's* 96 (July 20, 1935): 7–8, 34–36.

Dedmon, Emmett. *Fabulous Chicago*. New York: Random House, 1953.

Degler, Carl. "American Political Parties and the Rise of the City: An Interpretation." *Journal of American History* 51 (June 1964): 50–59.

Demaris, Ovid. *Captive City: Chicago in Chains*. New York: Lyle Stuart, 1969.

"Detroit Is Dynamite." *Life* 13 (August 17, 1942): 15–23.

Dillard, Irving. "Chicago as a Sign for 1944." *New Republic* 108 (April 26, 1943): 563–64.

Dobyns, Fletcher. *The Underworld of American Politics*. New York: Kingsport Press, 1932.

Dodds, Harold W. "Federal Aid for the City." *Yale Review* 25 (September 1935): 96–112.

Dorsett, Lyle W. *Franklin D. Roosevelt and the City Bosses*. Port Washington, N.Y.: Kennikat Press, 1977.

———. *The Pendergast Machine*. New York: Oxford University Press, 1968.

Douglas, Paul H. "Chicago's Financial Muddle." *New Republic* 61 (February 12, 1930): 324–26.

———. *In the Fullness of Time*. New York: Harcourt Brace Jovanovich, 1971.

Drake, St. Clare, and Cayton, Horace R. *Black Metropolis: A Study of Negro Life in a Northern City*. New York: Harcourt, Brace and Co., 1945.

Dreiske, John. *Your Government and Mine: Metropolitan Chicago*. New York: Oceana Publications, 1959.

Duncan, Otis D., and Duncan, Beverly. *The Negro Population of Chicago*. Chicago: University of Chicago Press, 1957.

"Ed Kelly Comes Through with an All Time Record Majority; Gets to Work on Patronage." *Newsweek* 5 (April 13, 1935): 7–8.

Eldersveld, Samuel J. "The Influence of Metropolitan Party Pluralities in Presidential Elections since 1920: A Study of Twelve Key Cities." *American Political Science Review* 43 (December 1949): 1189–1206.

"Elected to Fill Former Mayor Cermak's Unexpired Term." *Newsweek* 1 (April 22, 1933): 19.

Fanning, Charles. *Finley Peter Dunne and Mr. Dooley: The Chicago Years*. Lexington: University Press of Kentucky, 1978.

Farley, James A. *Jim Farley's Story: The Roosevelt Years*. New York: McGraw-Hill, 1948.

"The Financial Troubles of Our Cities." *Saturday Evening Post* 206 (June 9, 1934): 26.

Fleming, Thomas J. "I Am the Law." *American Heritage* 20 (June 1969): 32–48.

Flynn, John T. "These Our Rulers." *Collier's* 105 (June 29, 1940): 14–15, 40, 42–43.

———. "These Our Rulers." *Collier's* 106 (July 6, 1940): 24, 56, 58–61.

———. "These Our Rulers." *Collier's* 106 (July 13, 1940): 22, 23, 46–48.

———. "These Our Rulers." *Collier's* 106 (July 20, 1940): 18–19, 52–55.

———. "Too Much Fun." *Collier's* 104 (October 7, 1939): 14–15, 34–36.

Flynn, Edward J. *You're the Boss.* New York: Viking Press, 1947.

Forthal, Sonya. *Cogwheels of Democracy: A Study of the Precinct Captain.* New York: William-Frederick Press, 1946.

Foster, Mark. "Frank Hague of New Jersey: The Boss as Reformer." *New Jersey History* 86 (Summer 1968): 106–17.

Frankel, Stanley, and Alexander, Holmes. "Arvey of Illinois: New Style Political Boss." *Collier's* 123 (July 23, 1949): 9–11, 65–67.

Freeman, Lester. "Behind the Cermak Closet Door." *Real America* 2 (September 1933): 8–17, 60.

———. "The End of 'Boss' Cermak." *Real America* 2 (November 1933): 19–27.

———. "Tony Cermak, the Political Attila—None Ever Wielded Such Power—None Misused Power More." *Real America* 2 (October 1933): 46–49, 59–62.

Friedland, Louis L. "Organized Labor and the City Boss." *Annals of the American Academy of Political and Social Science* 353 (May 1964): 40–51.

"Funeral of a Boss." *Life* 29 (November 6, 1950): 40–41.

Gayer, Arthur D. *Public Works in Prosperity and Depression.* New York: National Bureau of Economic Research, 1935.

Gelfand, Mark I. *A Nation of Cities: The Federal Government and Urban America, 1933–1965.* New York: Oxford University Press, 1975.

Gleason, Bill. *Daley of Chicago.* New York: Simon and Schuster, 1970.

Glick, Frank Z. "Allocating Funds to Local Governments: The System of the Illinois Emergency Relief Commission." *Social Science Review* 11 (December 1937): 634–49.

———. "The Illinois Emergency Relief Commission." *Social Science Review* 7 (March 1933): 23–48.

———. *The Illinois Emergency Relief Commission.* Chicago: University of Chicago Press, 1940.

Gordon, Rita W. "The Change in the Political Alignment of Chicago's Negroes during the New Deal." *Journal of American History* 56 (December 1969) : 584–603.

Gosnell, Harold F. "The Chicago 'Black Belt' as a Political Background." *American Journal of Sociology* 39 (November 1933): 329–41.

———. *Machine Politics: Chicago Model.* Chicago: University of Chicago Press, 1937.

———. *Negro Politicians: The Rise of Negro Politics in Chicago.* Chicago: University of Chicago Press, 1935.

———. "The Negro Vote in Northern Cities." *National Municipal Review* 30 (May 1941): 264–67, 278.

Gosnell, Harold F., and Gill, Norman. "An Analysis of the 1932 Presidential Vote in Chicago." *American Political Science Review* 29 (December 1935): 967–84.

Gottfried, Alex. *Boss Cermak of Chicago: A Study of Political Leadership.* Seattle: University of Washington Press, 1962.

Graebner, Norman A. "Depression and Urban Votes." *Current History* 23 (October 1952): 234–38.

"A Grand Jury Investigation of Chicago Public Schools Asked by a Civic Group." *School and Society* 63 (March 2, 1946): 147.

Hachey, Thomas E., ed. "A Confidential Account of Mayor Kelly's Visit to

London, November 1945." *Journal of the Illinois State Historical Society* 70 (November 1977): 276–82.

Halberstam, David. "Daley of Chicago." *Harper's* 237 (August 1968): 25–36.

Hansen, Alvin H., and Perloff, Harvey S. *State and Local Finance in the National Economy*. New York: W. W. Norton and Co., 1944.

Havard, William C. "From Bossism to Cosmopolitanism: Changes in the Relationship of Urban Leadership to State Politics." *Annals of the American Academy of Political and Social Science* 353 (May 1964): 84–94.

Hayes, Dorsha B. *Chicago: Crossroads of American Enterprise*. New York: Julian Messner, 1944.

Hepner, Arthur. "Call Me Jake." *New Republic* 116 (March 24, 1947): 20–23.

Herrick, Mary J. *The Chicago Schools: A Social and Political History*. Beverly Hills, Calif.: Sage Publications, 1971.

Herring, E. Pendleton. *The Politics of Democracy: American Parties in Action*. New York: Rinehart and Co., 1940.

High, Stanley. "WPA: Politician's Playground." *Current History* 50 (May 1939): 23–25, 62.

Hollander, Sidney. "The Public Holds Its Nose." *Survey Mid-Monthly* 74 (May 1938): 173–76.

Holman, Charles T. "Chicago Elects a New Mayor." *Christian Century* 50 (April 26, 1933): 567–68.

———. "Chicago Heads in Tax Trouble." *Christian Century* 50 (September 6, 1933): 1122.

Hopkins, Harry L. "Food for the Hungry." *Collier's* 96 (December 7, 1935): 10–11, 61–62.

———. "They'd Rather Work." *Collier's* 96 (November 16, 1935): 7–9, 41.

Huzar, Elias. "Federal Unemployment Relief Policies: The First Decade." *Journal of Politics* 2 (August 1940): 321–35.

Ickes, Harold L. *The Autobiography of a Curmudgeon*. Chicago: Quadrangle Books, 1969.

———. *The Secret Diary of Harold L. Ickes: The First Thousand Days, 1933–1936*. New York: Simon and Schuster, 1954.

———. *The Secret Diary of Harold L. Ickes: The Inside Struggle, 1936–1939*. New York: Simon and Schuster, 1954.

———. *The Secret Diary of Harold L. Ickes: The Lowering Clouds, 1939–1941*. New York: Simon and Schuster, 1954.

Isakoff, Jack F. *The Public Works Administration*. Urbana: University of Illinois Press, 1938.

Janeway, Eliot. *The Struggle for Survival*. New Haven: Yale University Press, 1951.

Jones, Gene Delon. "The Origin of the Alliance between the New Deal and the Chicago Machine." *Journal of the Illinois State Historical Society* 67 (June 1974): 253–74.

Kantowicz, Edward R. *Polish-American Politics in Chicago, 1888–1940*. Chicago: University of Chicago Press, 1975.

Kelly, Edward J., with Davenport, Walter. "Politics Is People." *Collier's* 117 (April 13, 1946): 13, 73–75.

"The Kelly-Nash Political Machine." *Fortune* 14 (August 1936): 47–52, 114, 117, 118, 120, 123, 124, 126, 130.

Kennedy, Eugene. *Himself! The Life and Times of Mayor Richard J. Daley*. New York: Viking Press, 1978.

Key, V. O., Jr. *The Administration of Federal Grants to States*. Chicago: Public Administration Service, 1937.

———. "A Theory of Critical Elections." *Journal of Politics* 17 (February 1955): 3–18.

Kilpatrick, Wylie. "Federal Assistance to Municipal Recovery." *National Municipal Review* 6 (July 1937): 337–44, 351.

Knauss, Peter R. *Chicago: A One-Party State*. Champaign, Ill.: Stipes Publishing Co., 1972.

Kohn, Walter S. G. "Illinois Ratifies the Twenty-first Amendment." *Journal of the Illinois State Historical Society* 56 (Winter 1963): 692–712.

Langland, James, ed. *Daily News Almanac and Year Book For 1930*. Chicago: Chicago Daily News, 1929.

Lee, Alfred McClung, and Humphrey, Norman Daymond. *Race Riot*. New York: Dryden Press, 1943.

Leitzell, Ted. "Chicago, City of Corruption." *American Mercury* 49 (February 1940): 143–51.

Lepawsky, Albert. "Chicago, Metropolis in the Making." *National Municipal Review* 30 (April 1941): 211–16.

———. *Home Rule for Metropolitan Chicago*. Chicago: University of Chicago Press, 1935.

Leuchtenburg, William E. *Franklin D. Roosevelt and the New Deal*. New York: Harper and Row, 1963.

Levine, Edward M. *The Irish and Irish Politicians*. Notre Dame, Ind.: University of Notre Dame Press, 1966.

Littlewood, Thomas B. *Horner of Illinois*. Evanston, Ill.: Northwestern University Press, 1969.

Lubell, Samuel. *The Future of American Politics*. New York: Harper and Row, 1952.

Ludwig, C. C. "Cities and the National Government under the New Deal." *American Political Science Review* 29 (August 1935): 640–48.

Lyons, Leo M. "Illinois Investigates the Relief Situation." *National Municipal Review* 27 (January 1938): 24–29.

McKitrick, Eric L. "The Study of Corruption." *Political Science Quarterly* 72 (December 1957): 502–14.

MacMahon, Arthur W.; Millett, John D.; and Ogden, Gladys. *The Administration of Federal Work Relief*. New York: De Capo Press, 1971.

MacRae, Duncan, Jr., and Meldrum, James A. "Critical Elections in Illinois: 1888–1958." *American Political Science Review* 54 (September 1960): 669–83.

Madigan, John. "The Durable Mr. Dawson of Cook County, Illinois." *Reporter* 15 (August 9, 1956): 39–40.

Madison, Ralph. "Letter from Chicago." *New Republic* 112 (April 23, 1945): 549–51.

"The Making of a Maverick." *Time* 55 (January 16, 1950): 18–19.

Mann, Arthur. *LaGuardia: A Fighter against His Times, 1882-1933*. Chicago: University of Chicago Press, 1959.

———. *LaGuardia Comes to Power, 1933*. Chicago: University of Chicago Press, 1965.

Markowitz, Norman D. *The Rise and Fall of the People's Century*. New York: Free Press, 1973.

Martin, John Bartlow. *Adlai Stevenson of Illinois*. Garden City, N.Y.: Doubleday and Co., 1976.

———. "Al Capone's Successors." *American Mercury* 68 (June 1949): 729–34.

———. "Incident at Fernwood." *Harper's* 199 (October 1949): 86–98.

Matthews, William H. "These Past Five Years." *Survey Midmonthly* 84 (March 1938): 70–72.

Maxwell, Joseph A. *The Fiscal Impact of Federalism in the United States.* Cambridge: Harvard University Press, 1946.

Mayer, Harold M., and Wade, Richard C. *Chicago: Growth of a Metropolis.* Chicago: University of Chicago Press, 1969.

Mayer, Milton S. "Chicago Doesn't Care." *Nation* 146 (February 5, 1938): 149–52.

———. "Chicago: Time for Another Fire." *Harper's* 177 (November 1938): 561–71.

———. "It's Hell to Be a Chicago Liberal." *Nation* 148 (February 25, 1939): 223–24.

"Mayor Kelly's Chicago." *Life* 17 (July 17, 1944): 67–77.

"Mayor Kelly's Own Story." *Chicago Herald-American,* May 5, 6, 8, 12, 13, 14, 15, 17, 1947.

Merriam, Charles E. *Chicago: A More Intimate View of Urban Politics.* New York: Macmillan, 1929.

Meyerson, Martin, and Banfield, Edward C. *Politics, Planning, and the Public Interest.* Glencoe, Ill.: Free Press, 1955.

Miles, Arthur F. *Federal Aid and Public Assistance in Illinois.* Chicago: University of Chicago Press, 1941.

"Millennium for Straphangers." *Time* 50 (September 8, 1947): 24–25.

Miller, Neville. "The American City in Relation to the Works Program Administration and Direct Relief." *Social Science Review* 10 (September 1936): 413–23.

Miller, Zane. *Boss Cox's Cincinnati: Urban Politics in the Progressive Era.* New York: Oxford University Press, 1968.

"Mister Farley's Successor." *New Republic* 102 (April 8, 1940): 471.

Mitchell, Broadus. *Depression Decade.* New York: Rinehart and Co., 1947.

Mowry, George E. *The Urban Nation, 1920–1960.* New York: Hill and Wang, 1965.

Mushkat, Jerome. *Tammany: The Evolution of a Political Machine.* Syracuse, N.Y.: Syracuse University Press, 1971.

"The NEA's Investigation of Certain Conditions in the Chicago Public Schools." *School and Society* 61 (June 2, 1945) : 356.

Nelli, Humbert S. *The Business of Crime.* New York: Oxford University Press, 1976.

Nelson, Donald M. *Arsenal of Democracy: The Story of American War Production.* New York: Harcourt, Brace and Co., 1946.

"New Chicago Subway Opens." *Life* 14 (April 19, 1943): 32–33.

Newell, Barbara. *Chicago and the Labor Movement: Metropolitan Unionism in the 1930's.* Urbana: University of Illinois Press, 1961.

Nock, Albert J. "WPA—The Modern Tammany." *American Mercury* 45 (October 1938): 215–19.

"No Dog in the Manager." *Time* 48 (December 30, 1946): 17.

"Obituary." *Time* 56 (October 30, 1950): 89.

O'Brien, David J. *American Catholics and Social Reform: The New Deal Years.* New York: Oxford University Press, 1968.

O'Connor, Edward. *The Last Hurrah.* Boston: Little, Brown and Co., 1956.

O'Connor, Len. *Clout: Mayor Daley and His City.* New York: Avon Books, 1975.

"Old Pat." *Newsweek* 22 (October 18, 1943): 62.

Partin, John W. "Roosevelt, Byrnes, and the 1944 Vice-Presidential Nomination." *Historian* 42 (November 1979): 85–100.

Patterson, James T. *The New Deal and the States: Federalism in Transition.* Princeton, N.J.: Princeton University Press, 1969.

Peterson, Florence. "CWA: A Candid Appraisal." *Atlantic Monthly* 153 (May 1934): 587–90.

Peterson, Virgil W. *Barbarians in Our Midst: A History of Chicago Crime and Politics.* Boston: Little, Brown and Co., 1952.

Pierce, Warren H. "Chicago: Unfinished Anomaly." In *Our Fair City,* edited by Robert S. Allen. New York: Vanguard Press, 1947.

Pike, Claude O., ed. *Daily News Almanac and Year Book for 1933.* Chicago: Chicago Daily News, 1932.

"Political Deal." *Life* 18 (February 19, 1945): 32.

"Politics and Relief." *Social Science Review* 12 (September 1938): 495–99.

"Politics and Social Work." *Compass* 14 (November 1932): 2.

Port, Weimar. *Chicago the Pagan.* Chicago: Judy Publishing Co., 1953.

Preis, Art. *Labor's Giant Step: Twenty Years of the CIO.* New York: Pioneer Press, 1964.

"Protected Gambling in Chicago." *Criminal Justice* 74 (May 1947): 20–23.

Rakove, Milton L. *We Don't Want Nobody Nobody Sent: An Oral History of the Daley Years.* Bloomington: Indiana University Press, 1979.

"The Real Boss of City Hall." *Chicago* (March 1955): 14.

Ridley, Clarence R., and Nolting, Orin F., eds. *What the Depression Has Done to Cities: An Appraisal by Thirteen Authorities of the Effects of the Depression on Municipal Activities.* Chicago: International City Managers' Association, 1935.

Riedel, James A. "Boss and Faction." *Annals of the American Academy of Political and Social Science* 353 (May 1964): 14–26.

Robertson, Harriet M., ed. *Dishonest Elections and Why We Have Them: The Records Tell the Story.* Chicago: Women's Civic Council of the Chicago Area, n.d.

Rosenman, Samuel I. *Working with Roosevelt.* New York: Harper and Row, 1952.

Ross, Irwin. *The Loneliest Campaign: The Truman Victory of 1948.* New York: New American Library, 1968.

Royko, Mike. *Boss: Richard J. Daley of Chicago.* New York: E. P. Dutton and Co., 1971.

Rubin, Victor. "You've Gotta Be a Boss." *Collier's* 116 (September 25, 1945): 20, 32, 33, 36.

Saunders, Doris E. "The Day Dawson Saved America from a Racist President." *Ebony* 27 (July 1972): 42–45, 48–50.

Schaaf, Barbara C. *Mr. Dooley's Chicago.* Garden City, N.Y.: Doubleday and Co., 1977.

Schapsmeier, Edward L., and Schapsmeier, Frederick H. *Prophet in Politics: Henry A. Wallace and the War Years, 1940–1945.* Ames, Iowa: Iowa State University Press, 1970.

Schlesinger, Arthur M., Jr. *The Age of Roosevelt: The Politics of Upheaval.* Boston: Houghton Mifflin Co., 1960.

Shannon, William V. *The American Irish.* New York: Macmillan Co., 1963.

Shogan, Robert, and Craig, Tom. *The Detroit Race Riot: A Study in Violence.* Philadelphia: J. B. Lippincott Co., 1964.

Sitkoff, Harvard. "The Detroit Race Riot of 1943." *Michigan History* 53 (Fall 1969): 183–206.

———. "Racial Militancy and Interracial Violence in the Second World War." *Journal of American History* 58 (December 1971): 661–81.

Sofchalk, Donald G. "The Chicago Memorial Day Incident: An Episode of Mass Action." *Labor History* 6 (Winter 1965): 3-43.

Stave, Bruce M. *The New Deal and the Last Hurrah: Pittsburgh Machine Politics.* Pittsburgh: University of Pittsburgh Press, 1970.

Steinberg, Alfred. *The Bosses.* New York: Macmillan Co., 1972.

Steiner, Gilbert Y., and Gove, Samuel K. *Legislative Politics in Illinois.* Urbana: University of Illinois Press, 1960.

Stevenson, Adlai E. *The Papers of Adlai E. Stevenson.* Edited by Walter Johnson and Carol Evans. 3 vols. Boston: Little, Brown and Co., 1972–73.

Strickland, Arvarh E. "The New Deal Comes to Illinois." *Journal of the Illinois State Historical Society* 63 (Spring 1970): 55–68.

Stuart, William H. *The Twenty Incredible Years.* Chicago: M. A. Donahue and Co., 1935.

Sullivan, Lawrence. "The Negro Vote." *Atlantic Monthly* 166 (October 1940): 477–84.

Sutherland, Douglas. *Fifty Years on the Civic Front.* Chicago: Civic Federation, 1943.

Sutherland, Edwin H., and Locke, Harvey J. *Twenty Thousand Homeless Men: A Study of Unemployed Men in the Chicago Shelters.* Philadelphia: J. B. Lippincott Co., 1936.

Tarr, Joel A. "The Urban Politician as Entrepreneur." *Mid-America* 49 (January 1967): 55–67.

Terkel, Studs. *Hard Times.* New York: Avon Books, 1970.

Townsend, Walter A. *Illinois Democracy.* Springfield, Ill.: Democratic Historical Association, 1935.

"Treasure Hunt." *Time* 57 (May 28, 1951): 26.

Trout, Charles H. *Boston, The Great Depression, and the New Deal.* New York: Oxford University Press, 1977.

Truman, Harry S. *Memoirs: Year of Decisions.* Garden City, N.Y.: Doubleday and Co., 1955.

Tugwell, Rexford G. *The Brains Trust.* New York: Viking Press, 1968.

Tully, Grace. *FDR, My Boss.* New York: Charles Scribner's Sons, 1949.

Tuttle, William M., Jr. *Race Riot: Chicago in the Red Summer of 1919.* New York: Atheneum Publishers, 1978.

VanDevander, Charles W. *The Big Bosses.* New York: Howell-Soskin, 1944.

Walker, Forrest A. "Graft and the CWA." *Southwestern Social Science Quarterly* 46 (September 1965): 164–70.

Watters, Mary. *Illinois in the Second World War.* 2 vols. Springfield: Illinois State Historical Library, 1952.

Weisman, Joel, and Whitehead, Ralph, Jr. "Untangling Black Politics." *Chicagoan* 1 (July 1974): 43–45, 74–75.

Wendt, Lloyd, and Kogan, Herman. *Big Bill of Chicago.* Indianapolis: Bobbs-Merrill Co., 1953.

———. *Bosses in Lusty Chicago: The Story of Bathhouse John and Hinky Dink.* Bloomington: Indiana University Press, 1974.

"What about That Toga?" *Time* 39 (February 9, 1942): 16–17.

White, R. Clyde. *Administration of Public Welfare*. New York: American Book Co., 1950.

Whitehead, Ralph, Jr. "The Ward Boss Who Saved the New Deal." *Chicago* 26 (May 1977): 140–42, 176–86.

"The Widow's Mite." *Newsweek* 45 (May 9, 1955): 30.

Williams, Elmer Lynn. *The Fix-It Boys: The Inside Story of the Kelly-Nash Machine*. Chicago: Elmer Lynn Williams, 1940.

Williams, J. Kerwin. *Grants-in-Aid under the Public Works Administration*. New York: Columbia University Press, 1939.

Wilson, James Q. *Negro Politics: The Search for Leadership*. Glencoe, Ill: Free Press of Glencoe, 1960.

Yoder, Robert M. "Chicago Throws a Party." *Saturday Evening Post* 215 (July 18, 1942): 22–23, 62,63.

Zink, Harold. *City Bosses in the United States*. New York: Macmillan Co., 1939.

Newspapers

Beacon (Chicago).
Chicago American.
Chicago Daily News.
Chicago Daily Times.
Chicago Defender.
Chicago Herald-American.
Chicago Herald and Examiner.
Chicago Sun.
Chicago Sun-Times.
Chicago Tribune.
Lightnin' (Chicago).
New York Times.
Public Service Leader (Chicago).

Public Documents

Bickham, Martin H. *Achievements of WPA Workers in Illinois, July 15, 1935, to June 30th, 1938*. Information Service of WPA, n.d.

Board of Election Commissioners of the City of Chicago. *Canvass*. April 2, 1935; April 4, 1939; April 6, 1943.

Casey, Charles. *Final Report, 1935–1943, of the Works Project Administration of Illinois*. Chicago, April 30, 1943.

Chicago Plan Commission. *Building New Neighborhoods*. June 1943.

———. *Chicago Looks Ahead*. March 1945.

———. *Facing the Future with the Chicago Plan Commission*. December 1941.

———. *Housing Goals for Chicago*. 1946.

———. *S.O.S. Chicago! Ten Radio Broadcasts over Station WJJD*. 1939.

City Council of the City of Chicago. *Journal of the Proceedings of the City Council of the City of Chicago, Illinois*. 1932–33; 1933–34; 1945–46.

City of Chicago. *Chicago's Report to the People, 1933–1946*. March 1947.

Mayor's Commission on Human Relations. *Human Relations in Chicago*. 1946 Annual Report.

———. *Race Relations in Chicago.* 1945.

Mayor's Committee on Race Relations. *Statement of Aims and Purposes.* 1943.

Mayor Kelly's Plan for a Comprehensive Transportation System for the City of Chicago. January 1937.

Mayor Kelly's Plan for a Comprehensive Transportation System for the City of Chicago. October 1937.

Mayor Kelly's Suggested Plan for Settlement of Chicago's Traction Problem. November 22, 1939.

Mayor's Special Committee. *Report on the Administration of Chicago's Public Schools.* June 17, 1946.

Official Opening of Chicago Subway, October 16, 1943.

United States Congress. House of Representatives. Rep. Adolph J. Sabath enters Edward J. Kelly correspondences of April 26, 1946, and April 30, 1946. *Congressional Record: Appendix.* 79th Cong., 2d sess., July 15, 1946. Vol. 92, pt. 12, p. A3935.

———. Rep. Adolph J. Sabath enters Edward J. Kelly statement of February 21, 1946. *Congressional Record: Appendix.* 79th Cong., 2d sess., February 22, 1946. Vol. 92, pt. 9, p. A1016.

———. Rep. Emily Taft Douglas enters Edward J. Kelly Proclamation of June 25, 1945. *Congressional Record: Appendix.* 79th Cong., 1st sess., June 23, 1945. Vol. 91, pt. 12, p. A3023.

———. Rep. Emily Taft Douglas enters Edward J. Kelly speech of April 29, 1945. *Congressional Record: Appendix.* 79th Cong., 1st sess., June 5, 1945. Vol. 91, pt. 11, p. A2683.

———. Rep. Vursell enters letter from Chicago Better Government Association. *Congressional Record.* 78th Cong., 2d sess., February 25, 1944. Vol. 90, pt. 2, pp. 2065–66.

———. Committee on Appropriations. *Emergency Relief Appropriations. Hearings of a Subcommittee of the House Committee on Appropriations.* 74th Cong., 1st sess., 1935.

———. *Emergency Relief Appropriations Act of 1937: Hearings of a Subcommittee of the House Committee on Appropriations.* 75th Cong., 1st sess., 1937.

———. *Emergency Relief Appropriations Act of 1938 and Public Works Administration Act of 1938: Hearings of a Subcommittee of the House Committee on Appropriations.* 75th Cong., 3d sess., 1938.

———. *Federal Emergency Relief and Civil Works Program. Hearings of a Subcommittee of the House Committee on Appropriations.* 73d Cong., 2d sess., 1934.

———. *Investigation and Study of the Works Progress Administration: Hearings before a Subcommittee of the House Committee on Appropriations.* 76th Cong., 1st sess., 1939.

United States Congress. Senate. Sen. Scott Lucas enters an Edward J. Kelly correspondence. *Congressional Record: Appendix.* 78th Cong., 1st sess., September 15, 1943. Vol. 89, pt. 11, pp. A4122–23.

———. Committee on Appropriations. *Emergency Relief Appropriations: Hearings before a Subcommittee of the Senate Committee on Appropriations.* 75th Cong., 1st sess., 1939.

———. Committee on Appropriations. *Emergency Relief Appropriations for 1935: Hearings before a Subcommittee of the Senate Committee on Appropriations.* 74th Cong., 1st sess., 1935.

————. Committee on Appropriations. *Federal Emergency Relief and Civil Works Program: Hearings before a Subcommittee of the Senate Committee on Appropriations*. 73d Cong., 2d sess., 1934.

————. Committee on Appropriations. *Work Relief and Public Works Appropriation Act of 1938: Hearings before a Subcommittee of the Senate Committee on Appropriations*. 75th Cong., 3d sess., 1938.

————. Committee on Appropriations. *Work Relief and Relief, Fiscal Year 1939: Hearings before a Subcommittee of the Senate Committee on Appropriations*. 76th Cong., 1st sess., 1939.

United States Congress. Senate. Committee on Education and Labor. *The Chicago Memorial Day Incident: Hearings before a Subcommittee of the Senate Committee on Education and Labor*. 75th Cong., 1st sess., 1937.

————. Committee to Investigate Senatorial Campaign Expenditures and Use of Governmental Funds in 1938. *Report of the Committee to Investigate Senatorial Campaign Expenditures and Use of Governmental Funds in 1938*. 76th Cong., 1st sess., 1939.

————. Committee on Manufactures. *Federal Aid for Unemployment Relief: Hearings before a Subcommittee of the Senate Committee on Manufactures*. 72d Cong., 2d sess., 1933.

————. Committee on Naval Affairs. *Hearings before the Senate Committee on Naval Affairs*, 76th Cong., 1st sess., 1941.

————. Special Committee to Investigate Organized Crime in Interstate Commerce. *Report of the Senate Special Committee to Investigate Organized Crime in Interstate Commerce*. 82d Cong., 1st sess., 1951.

————. Special Committee to Investigate Unemployment and Relief. *Unemployment and Relief: Hearings before the Senate Special Committee to Investigate Unemployment and Relief*. 75th Cong., 3d Sess., 1938.

Unpublished and Archival Materials

Adamowski, Benjamin. Interview with author. Chicago, Ill., November 1, 1979.

Arvey, Jacob M. Interview with Milton Rakove. Chicago, Ill., August 1976. Transcript in the possession of Rakove, University of Illinois at Chicago.

Barnard, Harry. Interview with author. Wilmette, Ill., January 26, 1980.

Claude A. Barnett Papers. Chicago Historical Society.

Barrett, Paul F. "Mass Transit, The Automobile, and Public Policy in Chicago, 1900–1930." Ph.D. diss., University of Illinois at Chicago Circle, 1976.

Bean, Philip G. "Illinois Politics during the New Deal." Ph.D. diss., University of Illinois, 1976.

Blaisdell, Fred W. "The Republican Party in Chicago." Better Government Association. 1939. Chicago Historical Society.

Bluestein, Milton J. "Voting Tradition and Socio-Economic Factors in the 1936 Presidential Election in Illinois." Master's thesis, University of Chicago, 1950.

John Boettiger Papers. Franklin D. Roosevelt Library, Hyde Park, N.Y.

Branham, Charles. "The Transformation of Black Political Leadership in Chicago, 1865-1942." Ph.D. diss., University of Chicago, 1981.

Burke, Joseph. Interview with author. Chicago, Ill., March 11, 1980.

Burton, Ralph G. "Mass Transportation in the Chicago Region: A Study in Metropolitan Government." Ph.D. diss., University of Chicago, 1939.

Charles, Searle F. "Harry L. Hopkins: New Deal Administrator, 1933–1938." Ph.D. diss., University of Illinois, 1953.

Chicago Chapter of the National Association of Social Workers. Records. Chicago Historical Society.

Chicago City Manager Committee. *The Hocus Pocus of Chicago Government.* 1938. Chicago Historical Society.

Chicago Crime Commission. "A Report on Chicago Crime for 1954." February 2, 1955. Chicago Historical Society.

"Chicago's Record of Accomplishment under Mayor Edward J. Kelly: The Remarkable Regeneration of America's Second City under Its Democratic Mayor." 1940. Chicago Historical Society.

Citizens' Association of Chicago. *Annual Reports of the Citizens' Association of Chicago.* December 1935; January 1937; January 1938. Chicago Historical Society.

Citizens' Association of Chicago Records. Chicago Historical Society.

Citizens' Committee on Public Information. *Out of the Red, Into the Black: The Truth about Chicago's Municipal Government. A Frank Statement Reviewing the Years 1933 to 1938.* 1938. Chicago Historical Society.

Cleveland, Charles. "Biography of Edward J. Kelly." n.d. Typescript in the possession of the author.

Dawson, William L. Interview with James Q. Wilson. Chicago, Ill., September 19, 1958; September 24, 1958; October 3, 1958; October 17, 1958; October 24, 1958; November 14, 1958. Transcript in the possession of the author.

Democratic National Committee Papers. Franklin D. Roosevelt Library, Hyde Park, N.Y.

Dreiske, John. Interview with author. Oak Park, Ill., January 16, 1980.

Duis, Perry R. "Arthur W. Mitchell, New Deal Negro in Congress." Master's thesis, University of Chicago, 1966.

East, John Leonard. Interview with author. Chicago, Ill., November 13, 1979.

"Edward J. Kelly." Anonymous biography. Municipal Reference Library of Chicago.

John Fitzpatrick Papers. Chicago Historical Society.

Irene McCoy Gaines Papers. Chicago Historical Society.

Hart, Walter C. "Relief—As the Clients See It." Master's thesis, University of Chicago, 1936.

Henderson, Elmer W. "A Study of the Basic Factors Involved in the Change in the Party Alignment of Negroes in Chicago, 1932–1938." Master's thesis, University of Chicago, 1939.

Hennessey, James F. "Spike." Interview with author. Chicago, Ill., January 9, 1980.

Lorena Hickok Papers. Franklin D. Roosevelt Library. Hyde Park, N.Y.

Hillman, William A. "Urbanization and the Organization of Welfare in the Metropolitan Community of Chicago." Ph.D. diss., University of Chicago, 1940.

Hirsch, Arnold R. "Making the Second Ghetto: Race and Housing in Chicago, 1940–1960." Ph.D. diss., University of Illinois at Chicago Circle, 1978.

Hoellen, John. Interview with author. Chicago, Ill., October 27, 1979.

Harry Hopkins Papers. Franklin D. Roosevelt Library. Hyde Park, N.Y.

Henry Horner Papers. Illinois State Historical Library, Springfield.

Henry Horner Scrapbooks. Chicago Historical Society.

Harold Ickes Papers. Library of Congress.

Independent Voters of Illinois Papers. Chicago Historical Society.

Edmund K. Jarecki Papers. University of Illinois at Chicago Circle.

Johnson, Gustave E. "The Swedes of Chicago." Ph.D. diss., University of Chicago, 1940.

Johnson, Walter. Letter to author, January 23, 1980.

Walter Johnson Papers. University of Chicago.

Jones, Gene Delon. "The Local Political Significance of New Deal Relief Legislation in Chicago: 1933–1940." Ph.D. diss., Northwestern University, 1970.

Kantowicz, Edward R. "American Politics in Polonia's Capital: 1888–1940." Ph.D. diss., University of Chicago, 1972.

Keenan, Frank. Interview with author. Evanston, Ill., May 6, 1980.

Kennedy, Robert E. Interview with author. Marco Island, Fla., December 1, 1979.

Martin H. Kennelly Papers. University of Illinois at Chicago Circle.

Korshak, Marshall. Interview with author. Chicago, Ill., January 7, 1980.

Labor's Non-Partisan League of Cook County. *Now It Must Be Told! Mayoralty Election. The Truth about Courntney. The Real Facts about the Phony Reformer and New Deal Enemy, Courtney.* 1939. Chicago Historical Society.

Lindell, Arthur G. *City Hall: Chicago's Corporate History.* 1966. Municipal Reference Library of Chicago.

————. *City Hall: Chronology.* 1966. Municipal Reference Library of Chicago.

Love, Edison. Interview with author. Chicago, Ill., November 15, 1979.

Scott Lucas Papers. Illinois State Historical Library. Springfield.

Marovitz, Abraham L. Interview with author. Chicago, Ill., November 14, 1979.

Mazur, Edward H. "Minyans for a Prairie City: The Politics of Chicago Jewry, 1850–1940." Ph.D. diss., University of Chicago, 1974.

Charles E. Merriam Papers. University of Chicago Library.

Arthur W. Mitchell Papers. Chicago Historical Society.

Morris, Harry W. "The Chicago Negro and the Major Political Parties, 1940–1948." Master's thesis, University of Chicago, 1950.

Frank J. Murphy Papers. University of Michigan, Ann Arbor.

National Commission for the Defense of Democracy through Education of the National Education Association of the United States. *Certain Personnel Practices in the Chicago Public Schools.* May 1945. Chicago Historical Society.

O'Malley, Peter J. "Mayor Martin H. Kennelly of Chicago: A Political Biography." Ph.D. diss., University of Illinois at Chicago Circle, 1980.

Peterson, Virgil W. "Gambling: Should It Be Legalized?" Chicago Crime Commission. 1945. Chicago Historical Society.

————. Interview with author. Riverside, Ill., December 5, 1979.

Polish-American Democratic Organization Papers. Chicago Historical Society.

Records of the Civil Works Agency. Record Group 69. National Archives.

Records of the Federal Emergency Relief Administration. Record Group 69. National Archives.

Records of the Secretary of the Interior. Record Group 69. National Archives.

Records of the Works Projects Administration. Record Group 69. National Archives.

Report of Citizens' Joint Commission of Inquiry on South Chicago Memorial Day Incident. August 31, 1937. Municipal Reference Library of Chicago.

Franklin D. Roosevelt Papers. Franklin D. Roosevelt Library, Hyde Park, N.Y.

Smith, Aaron. "The Administration of Mayor Anton J. Cermak, 1931–1933." Masters' thesis, University of Illinois, 1955.

Harry S Truman Papers. Harry S Truman Library, Independence, Mo.

Unitarian Fellowship for Social Justice. *Matters Now of Public Record Concerning the Conduct of William H. Johnson, Superintendent of the Chicago Public Schools.* 1939. Chicago Historical Society.

Frank Walker Papers. University of Notre Dame Library, South Bend, Ind.

Henry A. Wallace Papers. University of Iowa, Iowa City.

Wheeler, Charles N. "Kelly's Life Full of Drama, Peril, Conflict, Fame." n.d. Chicago Historical Society.

White, John P. "Lithuanians and the Democratic Party: A Case Study of Nationality Politics in Chicago and Cook County." Ph.D. diss., University of Chicago, 1953.

Aubrey Williams Papers. Franklin D. Roosevelt Library. Hyde Park, N.Y.

Williams, Elmer Lynn. *The Curious Career of Tom Courtney Unveiled: A Documented Report of the Little Known Political History of a Payroll Patriot.* 1944. Chicago Historical Society.

Wilson, James Q. "Negro Leaders in Chicago." Ph.D. diss., University of Chicago, 1959.

Zolot, Herbert M. "The Issue of Good Government and James Michael Curley: Curley and the Boston Scene from 1897 to 1918." Ph.D. diss., State University of New York at Stony Brook, 1975.

Index